THE POLITICS OF
THE NUCLEAR
FREEZE

THE POLITICS OF THE NUCLEAR FREEZE

Adam M. Garfinkle

Philadelphia Policy Papers

Foreign Policy Research Institute
Philadelphia, Pennsylvania
1984

Library of Congress Cataloging in Publication Data

Garfinkle, Adam M., 1951–
  The politics of the nuclear freeze.

  (Philadelphia policy papers)
  1. Atomic weapons and disarmament.   2. Antinuclear
movement—United States.   I. Title.   II. Series.
JX1974.7.G34   1984   327.1'74   84-6030
ISBN 0-910191-08-5

Foreign Policy Research Institute
3508 Market Street, Suite 350
Philadelphia, PA 19104

The Foreign Policy Research Institute is a publicly supported, nonprofit,
tax-exempt corporation as described in Section 170 (b) (1) (A) (vi) of the
Internal Revenue Code. All contributions to the Institute are tax deductible.

FOREIGN POLICY RESEARCH INSTITUTE

The Foreign Policy Research Institute is a nonprofit organization devoted to scholarly research and analysis of international developments affecting the national security interests of the United States. The Institute's major activities include a highly diverse publications program; seminars, workshops, and conferences for business, government, and academic leaders; and important research projects for a wide range of government agencies.

The Institute's research and publications programs are designed to:
- Identify and explore political, military, and economic trends in the international system;
- Analyze the fundamental issues facing U.S. foreign policy;
- Suggest guidelines for U.S. foreign policy that contribute both to American security and to the development of a stable international order.

To accomplish these purposes, the Institute:
- Maintains a staff of specialists in the field of international relations as well as an extensive library of pertinent periodicals, books, and information files. The Institute's library is open to use by scholars, students, and the general public;
- Draws upon the expertise of leading academicians and persons in public life who are concerned with international affairs;
- Convenes and publishes the results of conferences and symposia of U.S. and foreign experts on contemporary international problems.

The products of the Institute's research program include the following publications:
- **ORBIS:** a quarterly journal of world affairs, widely recognized as a leading forum for research in the field of international and strategic studies;
- **Foreign Policy Issues:** a book series (in cooperation with Praeger Publishers) of important studies written by authorities in the field of international and strategic studies;
- **Philadelphia Policy Papers:** analyses of timely issues and developments having serious implications for U.S. foreign and defense policy;
- **Research Reports:** sponsored by various institutions, including agencies of the U.S. government.

The opinions expressed in publications of the Foreign Policy Research Institute are those of the authors and should not be construed as representing those of the Institute.

*To the memory of my father
Milton Garfinkle (1905–1983),
who was sweet and gentle in life*

CONTENTS

PREFACE

The debate over the proposal to freeze the testing, production, and deployment of nuclear weapons has seized a prominent share of the center stage of American politics over the past three years and seems destined to play a significant role in the presidential politics of 1984 and beyond. On one level this is to be welcomed, for the main issues to which the freeze pertains—the prospects for war and peace, national security, and arms control—are serious indeed. Regrettably, however, the seriousness of these issues exceeds by far the average level of intelligent thought that has been brought to bear on the freeze, either in promoting, opposing, or understanding it. Emotionalism and partisanship have taken a heavy helping from the reservoir of truth, not to speak of a pervasive ignorance of the complex issues at hand.

Political debates in open societies tend to become polarized, simplified, and strident in rough proportion to the emotional pulse of the issue under scrutiny. The debate over the nuclear freeze proposal has exhibited all these characteristics vividly because of the very high stakes presumed to be at issue by the opposing sides. On one extreme, some advocates of the freeze believe that the Reagan Administration's military and strategic views and policies are the gravest threat to world peace, and even to the survival of the human species, to come along in more than two centuries of American politics. Some freeze advocates question not only the judgment, logic, and morality of the administration and its supporters, but also their sanity. On the other extreme, some opponents of a nuclear freeze believe that the freeze movement is the product of a KGB disinformation campaign designed to bring about the unilateral disarmament of the United States. From this perspective, what is really at stake is not the stability of the strategic balance and the surety of deterrence, but the survival of human liberty and freedom in what is, for some, God's most cherished chunk of Creation.

Between these extreme and highly emotional views lie the more equivocal attitudes of most Americans. Because the debate over the freeze is not composed of a simple opposition between two cohesive and coherent camps, but rather of a bewildering spectrum of imperfectly overlapping interests and arguments, the issue is particularly resistant to crisp and clean analysis. The political and institutional heterogeneity of both camps is such that some people can support the freeze proposal for very different, even antithetical, reasons while others may disagree over the freeze and still share most of the same underlying assumptions about the character of the nuclear dilemma.

Somewhere between the extreme views, too, the freeze proposal is being judged and is making an impact within the broader political context. Any analysis of the significance of the nuclear freeze movement in American politics, and particularly its influence on strategic arms and arms control policies, must look beyond the language of the political broadside to the murky estuaries of real, but more ambiguous, political effect. It is clear now, as it has been from the start, that there will not be a quickly negotiated bilateral and verifiable nuclear freeze between the United States and the Soviet Union. There is therefore, no need, to strain oneself imagining the particulars of this paradise lost or of this calamity averted—depending on one's point of view. It is just as clear, however, that the political environment in which strategic and arms control policies are conceived and implemented has been greatly affected.

As the freeze debate has aged, it has been seized by the political process and driven further toward the center from its origin in the institutions of the political Left. Indeed, some of the original architects of the freeze movement have reacted to this development by breaking with the majority pro-freeze view, pronouncing themselves in favor of a unilateral freeze on all U.S. strategic weapons development, testing, and deployment. On the other side, many anti-freeze proponents despair of the respectability—undeserved in their view—provided the freeze by the plethora of politicians seeking to parlay public agitation and angst over nuclear war into personal political gain.

Its increasing domesticity has also turned the freeze into something of a lightning rod, attracting to its aegis many volatile political and moral issues both within and outside government. Included now in the list of political issues that orbit the freeze proposal itself are the size and composition of the defense budget; the future of the MX missile, the B-1 bomber, the cruise and

Pershing II missiles, and the Trident II program; the question of ballistic missile defense and civil defense; the sincerity, coherence, and competence of the Reagan Administration in dealing with arms control issues; and controversial shifts in the conception and technics of nuclear deterrence, strategy, and doctrine epitomized by the Defense Department's most recent five-year defense guidance programs. Debates outside government that have been catalyzed by the freeze movement, organized around it, or redefined by it include: arguments over the responsibility of educators and religious leaders to "do something" about nuclear weapons and, with it, debate over the proper role of moral considerations in military policy and doctrine; the role of religious institutions and professional associations in public policy debates on national security; debate over the proper political agenda—in substance and in scope—of environmental, antinuclear power, women's rights, and other parochially oriented groups; the role of scientists and engineers in national defense efforts, and many others.

It is not possible in this study to examine all of these questions fully. This volume has three limited objectives designed to help the concerned but perplexed citizen transcend the simplifications and emotionalism of the freeze debate in order to gain a more sophisticated understanding of the issues.

The first objective is to identify the range of opinion that exists in American politics on the freeze and to identify the tacit or explicit strategic theory of each "school" as may be identified. Only with reference to a more abstract paradigm of nuclear deterrence, U.S.-Soviet relations, and the nature of contemporary international politics does the freeze proposal find its meaning. Thus, the narrative that follows sometimes leaves off direct discussion of the freeze in order to attend to these prior matters. This is a complex task, for the *dramatis personae* of the nuclear freeze debate vary widely, as do the views and assumptions represented by them. Hewing ideal types out of this rich mixture stands to do at least some violence to the complexity of the arguments and to understate the scope of human idiosyncrasies. But all forms of analysis—scientific and political—survive and prosper by imposing categories onto data otherwise resistant to simple division. To offset the pitfalls of reification risked by such artificial division, the analyst gains an ability to manage abstractions, to see patterns, and as Ernst Mach once put it, to provide "an economy of thought." The use of ideal types is also less dangerous to intelligent thinking when those who employ them recall constantly their humble origins and limitations.

For the purposes of this inquiry, the cast of characters in the nuclear freeze debate may be organized into five categories: (1) the Professional Left, (2) the Far Right, (3) the Left-Liberal Establishment, (4) the Pragmatic Center, and (5) the Conservative Mainstream. This organization, covering first more radical views and then moving from left of center to right of center, does not imply any judgment about the merits of certain perspectives contrasted against others. It is simply a logical and convenient way to weave concept and chronicle, given that the focusing agent for the politics of the nuclear freeze has been, and remains, the Reagan Administration.

In the course of describing these five schools of thought on the freeze, a separate chapter being devoted to each, this volume will tackle a second objective, that of tracing the origins and political evolution of the nuclear freeze proposal over the past three and a half years. It has been an interesting journey, and one whose recounting, it is hoped, will bring the insight of a flesh-and-blood history to what might otherwise be too detached and remote a narrative. A sixth chapter, entitled "The Freeze Comes to Washington," relates what befell the freeze as it was cast into the maelstrom of congressional politics, and the seventh and last chapter distills the political experience of the freeze, analyzes its effects, and charts its most probable future as the United States moves toward and beyond the 1984 elections.

The approach chosen here to analyze the nuclear freeze movement is different deliberately from that which most others have so far elected to take. The strategic and military implications of the freeze have not been neglected in the pages that follow, but I have been more interested in the domestic politics of the movement itself and its opposition. Though strategic analysts frequently ignore it, the truth is that foreign and defense policies are often more a product of internal political considerations than they are of objective strategic requirements or rarified logical analyses. By looking at the political worldviews across the American political spectrum that underlie the varying attitudes toward the freeze, I have tried to get at the ceaseless tension that is caused by the pull of extremist views of foreign and defense policy on the pragmatic tasks of governance. Herein lies the third objective of this study: to help the reader understand how the sometimes ungainly process of creating informal governing consensus on major issues works—or does not work, as the case may be. What follows, therefore, may be read as a case study of the role of domestic politics in the formation of U.S. national security policy. I hope the reader will forgive the occasional diversions in the narrative required by this approach in the interest of the fuller, more edifying context it provides.

Acknowledgments

I am grateful to have had help with this project. First and foremost, thanks are due to those who have reviewed the manuscript either in full or in part. They include: James S. Bell of Bell Associates, Alan Luxenberg, Associate Director for Development of the Foreign Policy Research Institute, John H. Maurer, Research Associate at the Foreign Policy Research Institute, Harvey Sicherman, Special Assistant to the Secretary of State, 1981–82, Marvin Wachman, President of FPRI, and Nils Wessell, Director of FPRI. Priscilla E. Taylor, with whom I am joyously wed, did much more to help than read and critique the manuscript. Words cannot suffice to express my thanks for her support. My son Gabriel helped light the spark within me that produced whatever entertainment there may be in these pages.

My gratitude also extends to the many people and their organizations on all sides of a strangely shaped fence who have talked with me, bared their files, and offered their libraries and services. A selective list includes the American Friends Service Committee, SANE, the Heritage Foundation, the Bureau of Public Affairs of the Arms Control and Disarmament Agency, the National Institute for Public Policy, the reference staff of the Van Pelt Library of the University of Pennsylvania, the Nuclear Freeze Campaign Clearinghouse in St. Louis and its Washington office, and CBS News. I also benefited from talking with Ambassador Robert Strausz-Hupé, General Edward Rowny, and the late Senator Henry M. Jackson. I would like nothing more than to be able to talk with the Senator again.

I was also happy to have had the pleasure of haranguing some of my colleagues at the Foreign Policy Research Institute, using them freely to test out both ideas and their expression. I am not sure that *they* consider this process to have been a pleasure, but I am happy for it just the same. Aaron Gershowitz helped me assemble some of the voluminous literature on the freeze, and though he does not yet know it, he will also be thanked for refiling the piles of material that presently litter my office. Louis Meixler assisted in the preparation of the index. I am also grateful for the steadfast efforts at cryptography and typing supplied by Saundra Ingram Bailey and the copyediting performed by Peggy Hoover. Last but not least, Beth Dunlap and Marcia Maziarz of the Foreign Policy Research Institute staff helped see the manuscript safely through the journey from pen to press.

At this point, authors usually engage in the ritual of staking out a preclusive claim to any and all error that may be contained in what follows. If I do so here, I make myself part of a large crowd, because the freeze debate has been awash with factual and judgmental error—innocent and willful—from nearly every quarter. Any errors here *are* mine, but I claim them only because I must, not because I enjoy censure.

Finally, a note about sources is in order. As the reader will soon discover, this volume is attended by a multitude of notes. There are three reasons for this: so that the more than casual reader may check further into the matter at hand if so desired; so that my own judgments can be assayed in a broader intellectual context by the skeptical or curious reader; and so that interesting anecdotes and insights that might interrupt the flow of the narrative were they included in the text might be made available to the reader. The notes are assembled and placed at the end of each chapter so as not to constitute a distraction. Taken together, they form the raw material for a bibliographical essay on the literature of the nuclear freeze debate.

Adam M. Garfinkle
Philadelphia, Pennsylvania
June 1984

Glossary

Anti-Ballistic Missile (ABM): a reference to a particular BMD technology emphasizing the use of ballistic intercept missiles to destroy incoming enemy ballistic missile warheads.

Area-defense: a reference to the use of ballistic missile defense (BMD) to protect large geographical areas containing urban-industrial centers and large numbers of people.

B-52: a subsonic intercontinental bomber first deployed by the United States in 1955 and subsequently modernized. The B-52 can carry both nuclear and non-nuclear ordnance.

Ballistic Missile Defense (BMD): technological systems of different types, both nuclear and non-nuclear, endo- and exo-atmospheric, designed to intercept and destroy incoming enemy ballistic missiles.

Civil Defense (CD): the protection of civilian population from nuclear attack through passive means, such as shelter construction and urban evacuation programs.

Counterforce: a reference to a weapon or a strategy designed to attack the military forces of an enemy.

Countervalue: a reference to a weapon or a strategy designed to attack the population and industry of an enemy.

Cruise Missile: a pilotless aircraft that flies at subsonic speed within the earth's atmosphere. Cruise missiles can be armed with nuclear and non-nuclear ordnance, and can be launched from a variety of land, sea, and air platforms.

First-Strike: a pre-emptive attack on the military forces of the adversary.

ICBM (Intercontinental Ballistic Missile): any land-based ballistic missile with a range of at least 3,000 nautical miles.

IRBM (Intermediate-range Ballistic Missile): a ballistic missile with a range of roughly 1,000-3,000 nautical miles.

Launch-on-Warning: a defense posture specifying the launch of ballistic missiles and the dispatch of bombers upon confirmed warning of impending attack.

Minimum Deterrence: a variety of mutual assured destruction theory advocating the deployment of the smallest possible credible second-strike countervalue force.

MIRV (Multiple Independently Targetable Re-entry Vehicle): one of a number of re-entry vehicles carried on a single missile, each capable of striking a different pre-selected target.

Mutual Assured Destruction (MAD): a theory of deterrence stressing the mutual threat of credible second-strike counter-value retaliation.

MX (Missile Experimental): a U.S. ICBM, currently under development, designed to carry ten warheads and to be counterforce-capable. Initially, MX was designed to be a semi-mobile system.

Neutron bomb: the popular name for the enhanced radiation warhead (ERW), a fission-fusion warhead with reduced blast effects and enhanced initial neutron production through the use of cobalt.

PD-59 (Presidential Directive 59): a decision made by President Jimmy Carter in 1979 to reorient U.S. nuclear targeting posture further toward counterforce capability and strategy.

Point-defense: a reference to the use of ballistic missile defenses (BMD) to protect limited geographical areas containing military assets, particularly ICBM silos.

Second-Strike: a retaliatory attack on either the military forces of the enemy, the urban-industrial centers of the enemy, or both. A second-strike may be initiated after riding out the enemy's first strike or while under attack.

SLBM (Submarine-Launched Ballistic Missile): ballistic missile launched from an underwater platform.

Throw-weight: the total weight that a ballistic missile booster can carry into orbit, divided into explosive devices, penetration aids, and in the case of MIRV'd missiles, the postboost vehicle (PBV) or "bus."

War-fighting: a theory of deterrence advocating either a second-strike counterforce posture or a strategy of prevailing militarily in a protracted nuclear war.

Warhead: that part of a ballistic missile containing the nuclear explosive charge.

Chapter 1

THE PROFESSIONAL LEFT

Convictions are more dangerous enemies of truth than lies.

—Friedrich Nietzsche

Intellectual Roots of the Freeze

Contemporary American political culture is said by political sociologists to be perhaps the most extensively organized and stratified in history.[1] Among the thousands of "associational" groups that serve as mediators between government and the body politic,[2] a few are devoted to revolutionary political change along Marxist-Leninist lines. On the national level this includes, clearly, the Communist party USA, Youth Against War and Fascism, the Revolutionary Workers party, fronts of these organizations such as the U.S. Peace Council, and many other obscure, tiny, and often short-lived groups.

There are other groups on what we have chosen to call the Professional Left, however, that are always less explicit and usually less doctrinaire about Socialist or Marxist ideology and that while not necessarily pro-Soviet do espouse an eclectic variety of anticapitalist views with respect to national and global economic organization. Concomitant with such views, generally, is a strong positive disposition toward a foreign policy orientation sympathetic to the "Third World" agenda, and an equally strong opposition to U.S. military power of all sorts. Some of these groups are the Institute for Policy Studies, the Women's International League for Peace and Freedom, the War Resister's League, the American Friends Service Committee, the Fellowship of Reconciliation, SANE, Benjamin Spock's Mobilization for Survival, Clergy and Laity Concerned, the Coalition for a New Foreign and Military Policy, Women's Strike for Peace, and many others. Most of these groups have their own publications that outline their views. One can also consult a coterie of more general periodical publications, particularly *The Progressive, Mother Jones, The Nation, In These Times, Nuclear Times, The Village Voice, The*

1

Rolling Stone, The Guardian (New York), and sometimes the op-ed pages of the nation's most influential newspapers.

Some of these groups claim to be pacifist, some do not; some are religiously based, some are not. All claim to be patriotic in the truest sense. Although each group is unique with respect to its origins and guiding personalities, and while each has its own set of ideological eccentricities that can and do spawn heated disagreements, they have nevertheless many inclinations in common. They are also knit together in an "interlocking directorate," sitting on each others' executive boards and committees. Most of the organizations of the Professional Left have sprung from one another over the years in a profusion of splits, mergers, and resplits.

The general worldview of this group of organizations may be summarized like this:

(1) The superpowers have the military capacity to destroy the world, but this is only a latent threat. More important, they both have and use the ability to suppress the freedoms, to exploit the resources, and to wreak violence upon the weaker states of the world and their citizens.

(2) While Soviet totalitarianism and militarism are unpleasant, the mistakes of the Soviet government do not invalidate the fundamental tenets of Marxism, nor do they disprove the superiority of socialist forms of economic organization over capitalist forms. The United States, as leader of the capitalist world, is really the more serious problem, for through the power of "corporate capitalism," using the vehicle of the multinational corporation, Washington seeks to exploit the labor and resources of the entire world, and the Third World in particular.

(3) This impoverishing neocolonialism is aided by greedy and rapacious cliques in exploited countries, who benefit personally from the rape of their own societies. Therefore "liberation" movements that seek to overturn this neocolonialist empire by forcibly removing these cliques from power deserve support.

(4) The same forces of repression that have turned the United States into an international oppressor are also those responsible for inequality, racism, sexism, police brutality, and FBI/CIA harassment at home.

(5) U.S. military and police power, insofar as it serves to support oppression at home and U.S. neocolonialism abroad, is therefore a negative force and should be limited in any way possible.

(6) The real causes of the nuclear arms race, which was started by the United States and continues mainly because of the United States, is that the military-industrial complex—the central pillar of corporate capitalism—would stand to lose billions of dollars should the race cease. This is why the Reagan Administration is not and cannot be seriously interested in halting the arms race through arms control, and it is also why ordinary arms control can never work. Disarmament is the only answer, and if we do not have disarmament, we will have nuclear holocaust.[3] But in order to get disarmament, it follows that the power structure of the United States must first be overturned and corporate capitalism dethroned. Use of the existing political process is one (of many) ways to pursue this end.

The heroes of these organizations include the late Salvador Gossens Allende, E. P. Thompson, Ho Chi Minh, Olof Palme, Fidel Castro, Yasir Arafat, SWAPO, the José Martí Farabundo Front in El Salvador, and the Sandinista government of Nicaragua, among others. The villains include Augusto Pinochet, all U.S.-based multinational corporations, Israel, South Africa, the Pentagon, and the entire Republican party with the (possible) exceptions of Mark Hatfield, because he supports the freeze, and Paul McCloskey and Charles Percy, because they sympathize with the Palestine Liberation Organization and defend its legitimacy.

Today, the most intellectually intricate exposition of this general worldview is the product of the Institute for Policy Studies (IPS), led by Richard J. Barnet and Marcus G. Raskin. Barnet, co-author of *Global Reach*,[4] a book whose main thesis is that U.S.-based multinational corporations are responsible for the poverty of the Third World, is an active supporter of a nuclear freeze. In a recent book, *The Lean Years*, Barnet states what is essentially a modernized version of the Leninist theory of imperialism: "For a generation or more, the U.S. has operated on the fundamental premise that political and military control over foreign societies is essential to obtain access to minerals at favorable prices. Despite

3

their official capitalist ideology, the national security managers have deeply distrusted the free market to provide the resources they needed or thought they needed."[5] Nuclear superiority, writes Barnet, is desired to keep the Soviets from "exercising influence in Third World areas of interest to the United States" so that U.S. dominance can be maintained and extended.[6]

Marcus G. Raskin, co-founder of the IPS in 1963, is known for developing the concept of the "national security state" which he defines as "the actualizing mechanism of ruling elites to implement their imperial schemes and misplaced ideals."[7] Raskin says, "In the modern-day United States, neither a democracy nor a republic exists in operation. The state helps the powerful. The emergence of large-scale armed forces and corporate capitalism colonizes people into huge organizational structures."[8] The United States is really a "modern tyranny," according to Raskin, defined as "the maintenance of organized power in the hands of the state, its military and bureaucratic apparatus, and its corporate system. The corporate forms seek the death of politics, favoring instead hierarchic and administrative processes through which human concerns are transformed into matters of interest, ideological pretension, or quantitative measurement."[9] In such a system, dominated by the corporations, a president, says Raskin in a chapter entitled "The President's Burlesque," cannot act on behalf of the poor and working class without "doing battle with capitalism and imperialism. He would be required, therefore, to fashion a new set of symbols from the American landscape of myths and dreams which would cause direct confrontation with the bloated genocide-preparing military system."[10] Naturally, this "system," concludes Raskin, "menaces the freedom and well-being of its citizenry" and "poses a danger to world civilization."[11]

This view of American society and politics carries with it its own "strategic theory." This theory is made clear in the writings of the *philosophes* of the freeze movement—Jonathan Schell, Richard Falk, Robert Jay Lifton, E. P. Thompson, and Jerome Frank—all of whom believe, with Raskin and Barnet, that arms control and deterrence are as much the enemies as nuclear weapons, "nuclearism," and the "national security state."[12] What

4

we must do, says Schell, is to reinvent international politics by abolishing national sovereignty.[13] Falk, moreover, observes that:

Most current action within the peace movement is dedicated, whether deliberately or not, to *stabilizing* rather than *eliminating* nuclearism. The goal is to shift from certain *adventurist* forms of nuclearism (arms race, counterforce strategy, first-strike options, limited war and war-fighting scenarios) toward some variant of a *defensive* nuclear posture (nuclear weapons are retained but their role is strictly limited to providing protection against nuclear blackmail and surprise attack by one enemy state).[14]

This may be permissible as a tactic, explains Falk, but not as an end, because:

reliance on nuclear weapons inevitably concentrates anti-democratic authority in governmental institutions and builds a strong permanent disposition to engage in ultimate war as to negate the atmosphere and structure of genuine peace. We can never taste real peace again until we find the means to eliminate nuclear weapons altogether.[15]

Intellectually, the "strategic theory" of the Professional Left is difficult to take seriously. It is less a theory than a collection of pecksniffian odes to disarmament utopias and "progressive political change." It is really a half-theory, but as Robert Nisbet has pointed out, a half-theory is like a half-brick in that it can be thrown much farther than a whole one.

A Freeze Is Born

Although it is not widely known, it is from the organizations of the Professional Left that the concept of the nuclear freeze was first born and subsequently organized. As should be clear from the general worldview of the Professional Left described above, the motives clearly transcended a concern for the stability of peace and nuclear deterrence as it is commonly understood.

The nuclear freeze resolution calls for a *mutual* and verifiable freeze on the testing, production, and deployment of nuclear weapons, but this is not how the freeze began. In the summer of 1979, the American Friends Service Committee (AFSC) adopted a plan for a "nuclear moratorium" which called upon the United

5

States to halt *unilaterally* the production and deployment of nuclear weapons for three years.[16] The prime movers of the unilateral moratorium within the AFSC were its disarmament director, Terry Provance, and Stewart Meacham. Provance, however, may also have been one of about forty U.S. members of the World Peace Council (WPC), a post to which he was supposedly elected in Warsaw in 1977, though Provance has denied this, saying that the whole thing was a misunderstanding.[17]

There is no doubt that the WPC is a Soviet front organization dominated by the KGB; its Frederick-Joliot Curie Gold Medal for Peace has gone to, among others, Yasir Arafat and Leonid Brezhnev. But, as the FBI concluded, the WPC is the only such obvious front that has been actively involved on an organizational level in the freeze movement. While the WPC's influence over the freeze movement may have been significant in the beginning, owing perhaps to Provance's prominent role in the AFSC, it was soon greatly and decisively diffused. Provance and the AFSC turned to Randall Forsberg, aptly described by one sympathetic journalist as "a young, radical arms-control specialist," and asked her to work on the matter.[18] Sidney Lens, a member of the Chicago chapter of World Peace Council, USA, confirmed in *The Progressive* that the freeze was indeed "organized on the initiative" of Provance and Forsberg.[19]

Who is Randall Forsberg and what did she do to the AFSC's unilateralist proposal? Forsberg once worked at the Stockholm International Peace Research Institute (SIPRI) editing manuscripts and typing.[20] Inspired by SIPRI's attitude and work, Forsberg returned to the United States to study international relations and strategic affairs at the Massachusetts Institute of Technology. After her studies at M.I.T. (which for years has housed many prominent antistrategic modernization advocates) Forsberg established the Institute for Defense and Disarmament Studies, which quickly made contact with the relevant U.S. "peace" and "pacifist" organizations.

By March 1980, Forsberg had transformed the AFSC moratorium proposal into the founding document of the nuclear freeze movement, originally entitled "Call to Halt the Nuclear Arms Race" (see Appendix A). Unlike the original AFSC initiative, this was *bilateral* in approach, but the AFSC nevertheless lent support to the new approach, as did the Fellowship of Reconciliation, another smaller "pacifist" group.[21] Forsberg went on a speaking tour, talking to peace and antinuclear power groups across the nation. Meanwhile the AFSC, using local Quaker organizations, began petition drives to get Forsberg's freeze resolution on local ballots in preparation for the November 1980 elections.

With the failure of SALT II to pass muster in the Senate and the rise of conservatism in the 1980 election campaign, epitomized by then-candidate Ronald Reagan, the freeze notion attracted grassroots support among many of the liberally oriented who had put their faith in arms control and who were frightened of Reagan. This enabled freeze organizers like Randall Kehler, a peace activist who had once been jailed for draft evasion, to help freeze resolutions pass on some local levels. In Massachusetts, Kehler helped freeze resolutions pass in three state senate districts that had also supported Reagan for president![22]

The growth of the freeze movement, now transformed into a bilateral proposition that insisted, at least rhetorically, in verifiability, was truly a grassroots phenomenon on one level. But the growth of general support for the freeze exacted a cost in organizational unity. The dilution of the AFSC's original unilateralist demands alienated radical purists, especially those of the War Resister's League (WRL). Not only was the freeze not radical enough for the War Resister's League, and its use as a tactic "capitulationist," but the freeze was not adequately linked to the revolutionary ethos writ large in its view. The freeze failed to make the proper connections between antimilitary advocacy on the one hand and "anti-racist, anti-sexist and a whole variety of other oppressed peoples' struggles" on the other hand.[23] Steve Leeds, a WRL member, made the point this way:

People talk about nuclear weapons as an aberration or something horrible that's just sort of happened. And I think the reality is that nuclear weapons are the dominant force in U.S. foreign policy since 1945, and they've been a major part of the United States dominating the world—economically, socially, and politically. And they're very much tied into the military-industrial complex. The corporate structure that controls the country is the same corporate structure that perpetrates the arms race.[24]

What was at issue for the groups of the Professional Left was not whether traditional approaches to arms *control* were adequate, for all agreed that they were not. Not arms *control* but *disarmament* was the aim; the argument was over tactics. Whereas the AFSC, the Fellowship of Reconciliation, the Women's International League for Peace and Freedom, Mobilization for Survival, and others could accept an effort to transform arms control into disarmament through political action, the War Resister's League could not, at least not at first. Most of the groups went along happily, but their motives varied. Most sincerely believed in the cause and were led by their paradigm of U.S. and world politics to fear the absolute worst from Reagan and the conservatives. But on another level it was clear that politicizing the nuclear issue was a method of enhancing the influence of these small elite groups. It was, put colloquially, a power trip—a way to make these tiny, fringe organizations more important to other public advocacy groups that were closer to the center of the political spectrum. It was also the perfect issue to use in order to raise money. Despite their shirt-sleeve, antimaterialist, proletarian veneer, these organizations are no less covetous of money than are other organizations of limited means and less limited ambition. Many of the freeze groups, older established organizations, and newer umbrella coalitions, have generated huge amounts of money through sophisticated mass-mail solicitation campaigns. These solicitations are themselves fascinating documents. The pitch they give exemplifies both the broader motives of their creators and their judgment as to what will persuade skeptical potential sympathizers to fork over their money. Two examples should suffice.

Selling the Freeze

In the spring of 1983, SANE issued a solicitation whose basic theme was that, as the solicitation's first sentences put it, "the economic policies of President Reagan are bankrupting the American people. The President is pouring hundreds of billions of dollars into an already bloated Pentagon budget while robbing funds from human services and domestic employment." After arguing, in effect, that it is wrong to starve little children in order to buy the MX missile and the B-1 bomber, the solicitation, signed by SANE's executive director, David Cortright, tells us that "these

8

insane budget priorities must be stopped" and that "Congress and the President will not be brought to their senses without immediate, widespread citizen pressure."

In the cover letter itself, nothing is said about a nuclear freeze; rather, the alleged ill-conceived and unjust nature of the president's budget priorities is the subject. But in an accompanying pamphlet we are told:

> Despite recent Soviet advances, the United States remains ahead in the total number of nuclear weapons. The United States and its NATO allies also lead the Soviet bloc in military spending. It is time to stop the arms race—before new weapons are added on both sides. A mutual, verifiable nuclear weapons freeze would advance U.S. security by halting the arms buildup and paving the way for reductions.

The same pamphlet also tells us that "military spending is one of the least efficient ways of creating employment." Finally, we are again told that money should not be taken away from social programs to fund the military, implying that there is a zero-sum financial trade-off between the two and that we should convert the current "military economy" into a "civilian economy." With this latter argument comes the assertion, illustrated by a multicolored bar graph, that military spending as a percentage of gross national product is inversely proportional to the annual rate of growth in manufacturing productivity in industrial societies.[25] The convinced can pay SANE in two ways, one directly to SANE, the other to the National SANE Education Fund, in which case the contribution is tax deductible. Contributions of either sort are to be mailed to the "Ben Spock Center for Peace" in Washington, D.C.

SANE's approach to raising money is modestly pitched, and aimed at those whose views rest in the mainstream of liberal opinion. This in part reflects SANE's origins as an offshoot of the American Friends Service Committee back in the days when the AFSC was still what most people think of when they think of a "pacifist" organization. In an attempt to reach out to non-pacifists, Lawrence Scott, an AFSC executive, founded SANE in 1957, and through the years there has been considerable coordination between the two organizations. But SANE's original relative moderation was disturbed periodically by efforts to radi-

9

calize it. In 1960 the organization was forced to protect itself from Communist penetration; one-fourth of its chapters were purged from the organization.[26] Another period of confrontation erupted during the Vietnam War, when even the AFSC underwent a fundamental ideological shift to the left. In this battle, ultimately won by the radicals, SANE's executive director, Donald Keys, resigned his post along with other moderates.

While SANE has been moved leftward by its core leadership, its broader constituency and its style have remained more stable, gray-suited, and moderate. David Cortright, SANE's executive director, got his start in the "peace business" at the Institute for Policy Studies in 1972, where he prepared *Soldiers in Revolt,* a chronicle and, as Cortright put it, "a product of the struggle within the American military against repression and the Indochina intervention."[27] In the book's preface, Cortright noted that his "greatest debt is to my principal advisor over the past two and a half years, Marcus Raskin."[28] Raskin in turn wrote the book's introduction, which praised Cortright for teaching us that the "struggle was not only against the war, but also against an authoritarian military machine oiled for world imperialism."[29] Raskin is a member of SANE's Executive Committee.

The driving intellectual force at SANE, however, is neither Cortright nor Raskin but one of its co-chairmen, Seymour Melman. Like Raskin, Melman believes that the military-industrial complex, in one malignant incarnation or another, explains the unfortunate evolution of American politics and society. In his 1970 book, *Pentagon Capitalism: The Political Economy of War,* Melman wrote: "The Government of the United States now includes a self expanding war machine that uses military power for diverse political operations. . . . To the older pattern of exploitive imperialism abroad, there is now an institutional network that is parasitic at home. This combination is the new imperialism."[30]

Despite the obvious differences between the real beliefs of SANE's founders and leaders and the genteel touch of its solicitations, these solicitations have worked. In 1981 alone, SANE grew by 70 per cent, to 15,000 paying members.[31]

In contrast to the apparent modesty of SANE's solicitations, which mention nothing *explicit* about "Pentagon capitalism," the "national security state," or "the new imperialism," the War Resister's League clearly aims to capture a more radical audience. Actor Martin Sheen fronted a WRL solicitation in early 1983 that, while it had more to do ostensibly with Central America than with a nuclear freeze, is an excellent example of the WRL's approach. The solicitation arrives in a legal-sized envelope emblazoned in half-inch-high bold red lettering reading: "U.S. Out of El Salvador—Now!" In smaller red lettering the envelope announces that this is a message from "Martin Sheen, Star of 'Gandhi'" and in a box in the lower right-hand corner is inscribed: "IMPORTANT: DECLARATION AGAINST WAR ENCLOSED—Please Sign and Mail Immediately!" (Funny: most people thought the star of *Gandhi* was Ben Kingsley.)

Inside the envelope, one finds first a description of a barbarous massacre of innocent peasants, women, and children by Salvadoran soldiers. The story excerpt is said to be from the *New York Times* of February 23, 1983, but when one goes to the source, one finds that these words do not appear in the *New York Times* of that date, the previous date, the next date, or any other date.

Sheen's own text begins by telling the reader that our tax dollars are financing "atrocities" in Central America that are "as horrifying as the ones you and I remember from Vietnam—the napalm, the wanton destruction of whole villages, the incredible loss of life." Next, we find out the basis for Sheen's expertise on such matters: "I learned a lot about the evil of war when I starred in a movie about Vietnam—'Apocalypse Now.'" (Funny: most people thought the star of *Apocalypse Now* was Marlon Brando.) "Recently," Sheen continues, "my role in another movie taught me *an even deeper lesson* about war: that a man, a woman, or a whole nation can reject and resist violence by *choosing* to live in peace. That movie's name: 'Gandhi.'"

This is more than just an attempt to parlay the popularity of the movie *Gandhi* and the cult of reverence that surrounds the man Gandhi into dollars for the War Resister's League. Indeed, the allusion to Gandhi accurately describes the position of the WRL, which is that the United States should unilaterally disarm and practice the "non-violent defense of the country," although this is nowhere stated explicitly in WRL solicitations.

The solicitation is geared to bring the supposed analogy between Vietnam and El Salvador into high relief. Beyond the mention of Vietnam, noted above, Sheen delivers the following, optimistic alarum: "I believe it is not too late to prevent this nation from committing another Vietnam—*or worse*." Thus it is suggested, semantically, that Vietnam was not a strategic miscalculation, a lapse of sanity, or even a deed of shame, but a *crime*. Sheen's reference to some still "worse" crime is clarified on the back side of the letter. He explains that as the violence escalates in Central America,

the Reagan Administration is increasing U.S. war readiness with a five-year *$2.2 trillion* military-nuclear build-up—*the largest in the history of the world*—including a new generation of warheads and missiles especially designed to fight 'limited' nuclear war. I am deeply concerned that President Reagan—totally committed to a "Holy Crusade" against an "Evil Empire," but unwilling to risk another Vietnam-style defeat of American troops in a foreign jungle—might be prepared to launch a 'limited' nuclear war rather than lose in Central America.[32]

With this, Sheen's letter switches to capital letters: "THAT IS WHY IT IS URGENTLY IMPORTANT . . . TO STOP THE U.S. WAR IN EL SALVADOR, BEFORE *SOMETHING EVEN MORE UNTHINKABLE THAN ANOTHER VIETNAM* TURNS OUR WORLD INTO A SMOKING RUIN." Now we know: what is at stake in U.S. policies in Central America today is nothing less than the future of life on earth.[33]

With this we are informed that "the War Resister's League is at the forefront of the international non-violent movement for peace and nuclear disarmament" in the spirit of "Gandhi and Dr. Martin Luther King, Jr."—yet another holy spirit called into use.[34] The WRL has also named as its "honorary chairman" none other than Albert Einstein. With company such as this, it would be easy for the unsuspecting to get the impression that the WRL really believes very deeply in nonviolence and nonintervention "whether by this country or by the Soviet Union," as Sheen forthrightly states. But as with SANE's solicitation, one can contribute directly to the WRL or to the tax-deductible "A. J. Muste Memorial Institute." Once one understands who A. J. Muste was and what he believed, one gets a better appreciation of what the WRL means by "non-violence" and how it views U.S., as opposed to Soviet, society and foreign policy.

12

Pacifism and the Freeze Movement

Real pacifism, as most of us understand it today and as was universally understood twenty years ago, dictates that one cannot separate ends from means. Violent means cannot be used to support nonviolent ends any more than one can "grow a rose from a cactus seed."[35] A. J. Muste changed all that. Muste was a member of the Fellowship of Reconciliation (FOR) during a time of great ferment in the pacifist movement after World War I and the Bolshevik Revolution. While traditional pacifists hewed to the means-ends unity, others, like Muste, entertained the notion that to prevent international warfare, one had to wage class warfare. Muste became general secretary of the Communist League of America in the 1930s, a member of the Fourth International (Trotskyite). Although he left communism and rejoined the FOR in 1937—after a "religious experience"—he did so with a radically changed idea of pacifism. Muste believed that "the economic, social, political order in which we live was built up largely by violence, is now being extended by violence, and is maintained only by violence."[36] Since 90 per cent of the world's violence was caused by the forces of the status quo, it was "ludicrous" to focus so intently on the 10 per cent perpetrated by revolutionary forces. Muste argued that it was wrong to try to persuade other people to be nonviolent as long as pacifists took succor from the existing, violent order. And moreover, he reasoned that since the violence of the status quo was a *prior* violence, violence directed against it was not quite as bad since its aim was justice rather than exploitation and oppression

From such a view the anticapitalist attitudes of the AFSC and the Fellowship of Reconciliation arise. Simply put, these neopacifist groups are not anticapitalist because they are pro-Marxist but because they believe that a society based on a capitalist economy necessarily engenders coercive relationships. The pacifist groups, and the WRL, which was a nonreligiously-based offshoot of the FOR in 1923, accept the view that while *they* are dedicated to "political, economic and social revolution by nonviolent means,"[37] the right of others to employ violence for just ends cannot be criticized. Indeed, they often *support* such violence, sometimes with alacrity.

Since Muste's time, the WRL, the FOR, and the AFSC have

13

done further intellectual surgery on the concepts of pacifism and nonviolence. David Dellinger, an original member of the Chicago Seven of 1968 and now a member of the WRL, has advocated "strikes, sabotage and seizure of public property now being held by private owners."[38] According to Dellinger, "public property" includes all food, housing, and clothing. More vividly, David McReynolds, a WRL leader, believes that the worst violence occurs when the "state kills people" with poor housing, sexism, racism, and so forth. He argues that the violence of being unemployed is the same "as napalm falling on Vietnam." Similarly, when a woman is denied equal pay for equal work, this is violence. According to WRL president, Norma Becker, there must be a revolution in the United States overturning all institutions, "because unless these institutions are eradicated" it will not be possible "to really practice non-violence."[39]

Most astonishing is the list of people willing to grace the letterhead of the WRL and be counted as backers of solicitations like those of Martin Sheen. On Sheen's letter are listed Bella Abzug, Herman Badillo, Joan Baez, Harry Belafonte, Leonard Bernstein, the Berrigan brothers, Helen Caldicott, Congressmen Ronald Dellums and Ted Weiss, Professors George Wald and Linus Pauling, Benjamin Spock, Nat Hentoff, Pete Seeger, Susan Sarandon, and others. Can it be that all of these people really adhere fully to the views of Muste, McReynolds, and Becker noted above? Or are some celebrities so determined to do something "worthwhile," or so guilty about their wealth, that the degree of their radicalism has somehow become proportional to the psychological catharsis it provides?

Not all the prominent freeze groups claim to be pacifist or try to infuse their efforts with religious tonalities. Besides SANE, there is Benjamin Spock's Mobilization for Survival (MFS), a group that advocates massive civil disobedience, nonpayment of the "military tax," and noncompliance with draft registration laws.[40] Mobilization for Survival is an unusual organization in that it was founded as an umbrella organization to plan and coordinate fund raising, marches, demonstrations, and so forth. Early movers in the MFS, founded in 1977, were Peggy Duff, a British activist associated with the World Peace Council; Sidney Lens, editor of *The Progressive* and a member of the U.S. Peace Council;

14

and Sidney Peck, a sociology professor at the University of Wisconsin who is a member of the Communist party USA. Upon its founding, MFS was joined by SANE, Clergy and Laity Concerned, the U.S. Communist party, and later, in 1979, the U.S. Peace Council. The MFS also took some of its key staff from these organizations: the ubiquitous Terry Provance became MFS's International Task Force director, and Gil Green, a member of the Communist party USA, became its Labor Task Force director.[41]

As interest in the freeze grew, curiosity about its institutional origins grew as well. Revelations about the early sponsors of the freeze, their at least tangential association with Soviet fronts like the World Peace Council, and their general worldview began to appear. Some investigations of the freeze movement were honest and balanced, others were deliberate smears fostered by those on the Far Right. This diversity enabled freeze supporters on the Professional Left, in a kind of reversal of red-baiting, to discredit all allegations against the freeze by lumping all criticism together and branding it McCarthyism. Frank Donner's defense of the freeze in *The Nation* is a premier example of this. Donner caught the Far Right detractors of the freeze in a few minor errors and tried by association to discredit all anti-freeze findings. He asserted that "opponents of the freeze" are "the paladins of unlimited weaponry . . . committed to the modern secular religion of a long, twilight struggle with the Soviet Union in which our ultimate victory is assured by our moral superiority."[42]

Donner also engaged in a spirited, if indirect, defense of the integrity of the World Peace Council. After detailing accusations against the WPC, Donner wrote: "The fact that the W.P.C. is recognized by the United Nations as a non-governmental organization and has been invited to participate in official discussions on disarmament and colonialism does not seem to diminish its sinister character" for the denizens of the Right.[43] But then again, why should it? Donner did not deny the links between the WPC and the KGB; he merely tried to resuscitate the WPC's image by relating its favorable status at the United Nations. But this proves only that the United Nations is not a serious place; it is subject to Soviet manipulation to a greater degree than either the European peace movement or U.S. peace movement. If the Right did

15

indeed sin by failing to distinguish between the motivations of various freeze supporters, Donner reciprocated by lumping all freeze opponents into as far right a corner as he could construct. Quite likely, most of the errors of the Far Right were honest ones, reflecting deep confusion and myopia but not willful distortion. Donner, on the other hand, seems too clever not to know quite well what he was doing.

An Anarchist's Aside

Not all groups or individuals commonly supposed to be on the Left see merit in a nuclear freeze, not only because it is insufficiently "radical" but also because in some quarters it is deemed to be irrelevant. Among the loosely knit networks of American anarchists—who reject Marxism and Capitalism alike as Tweedledum and Tweedledee varieties of political statism and hierarchical elitism—strategic theory exists as an extension of a general theory of society.[44] That theory holds that the artificial structures of society, imposed by a variety of interlocking hierarchical relationships, have alienated people from their own interests and implanted false and pernicious measures of success and value that invariably lead to the perversion of society and politics.

The answer to this perverse state is "human liberation," the process of putting oneself back in touch with putatively "natural" feelings, needs, and insights. From the regeneration of individuals—from the bottom up, that is—society will be redeemed. All institutions and all "experts" are open to criticism and attack in this scheme. For example, while natural foods cleanse the body, the corporate packaging of ersatz nutrition and chemical additives reflects the sickness and alienation of society. Natural, herbal, "holistic medicine" heals the body; the rapacious automatons produced by the American Medical Association, for-profit hospital corporations, and the megadollar pharmaceutical industry make their money from people being sick, not from people being healthy. Anarchists oppose militarism, statism, bureaucracy, and bigness of all kinds—whether in business or government—as infringements on the liberty and creative potential of the individual. As opposed to the common caricature of anarchists in the popular media and lexicon, most anarchists are not wedded to terrorism

16

or violence. Most tend toward idealism, even utopianism, by inclination. Most believe that nationalism tends to breed chauvinism and racism and that the world would be far better off without it. Many are syndicalists, believing that the workplace is the natural focus of democratic governance; most are deeply suspicious of the profit motive and its—to their mind—inevitable excesses and distortions of human relationships. Its heroes include Mikail Bakunin, Peter Kropotkin, Emma Goldman, Joe Hill, the IWW (Industrial Workers of the World), and the Spanish syndicalists of 1936-39.

Over the past dozen or so years, the ranks of American anarchists have been swelled by the emergence of a radicalized shard of the environmental movement of the 1970s, whose basic worldview is almost wholly compatible with anarchist beliefs. Radical environmentalism extends to far more than physical nature; it encompasses a full-blown political, social, and economic theory that is at bottom anticapitalist *and* antistatist. Its goal is the perfect human social relationship with the ecosphere. A number of the newer ecological organizations house advocates of the new environmentalism—Friends of the Earth, Environmental Action, and Greenpeace, the vigilante of the group. Older groups, especially the Sierra Club, have yet to be overcome by the new wave, but they have been influenced by it. Many if not most environmentalists, old and new, support the freeze and speak of nuclear war as the ultimate "ecotastrophe." But those who have drifted farthest toward the old labor-anarchists do not.

The "natural is holy" and "small is beautiful"[45] critique of society has a moderate amount in common with the Marxist critiques of American society put forward by the Professional Left, but its preferred solutions are utterly at odds with those of the Marxist Left. As to the "nuclear problem," anarchist critics do not swallow the leftist proposition that the Soviet Union somehow poses less of a problem for world survival than the United States. Indeed, many anarchists believe that since Soviet society is, if anything, more statist and more intrusive a force in the life of the individual than is American society, it must be a *more* pernicious force.

Anarchists divide into optimists and pessimists over the dangers of nuclear war and the prospects for escaping it. Optimists tend to be those who have kept their distance from the more abstractive religious dimension of the "movement for a new society," as one anarchist network refers to itself. They believe in changing first the individual, then the community, and then the fuller society by building alternative lifestyles that "work" in pragmatic ways. They believe in nonviolence, "non-coercive relationships," and stark honesty. They have had nothing to do with the mainstream freeze organizations of the Professional Left—they do not trust them or their motives. Most American anarchists cannot understand how middle-class leftists with their personal bourgeois habits—from love of fancy cars, underarm deodorants, and Wonder Bread to condominiums, money-market accounts, and subscriptions to *High Times*—can possibly do anyone any good.

The pessimists on the nuclear question are the real dropouts, who have found refuge in a constantly shifting amalgam of "Eastern transcendental philosophy," macrobiotics, reincarnation, and heaven knows what else. Like pessimists of all faiths, they believe that this world has a predetermined, inevitable fate. Karen Hale writes:

The TV movie, "The Day After," was accurate, compelling and effective, but it changes nothing. We must have a nuclear holocaust.

We must have a nuclear holocaust because having one is more important to us than our lives, just as having an excess of food for dinner is more important than our own bodies, and being acceptable to everyone is more important than our self-respect.

The possibility of having a nuclear war arises not out of the meeting rooms of politicians, or the greed of opposing nations. It comes out of the loss of what we are as human beings.[46]

Hale continues:

I merely propose a new nuclear movement: human liberation. It is the simplest answer of all.

Human liberation will explode the myth that one has to look a particular way to be acceptable to one's fellow humans. Thousands will rise up against the glassy ads and smooth commercial jingles which harmlessly (we thought) promised us happiness through conformity. Or perfection.

18

[A] person who lives his or her life by these superficial measures, and who rejects or accepts others by such measures, is removed from the comparative imperfection of genuine human living. It is a sort of living death, and to this person, genuine death will not be any different.[47]

In other words, there will be a nuclear holocaust because self-alienation has reached such a point that we, as a society, are no longer genuinely motivated to prevent it. Employing holistic metaphors, Hale goes on:

These unfeeling people have cut themselves off from half of human experience, and they now wish to cut everyone off from the other half. Nature works within a wholeness, and when the whole is invaded, or part of it removed, it works to restore balance. We will be united—in life, or in death.[48]

The best one can do is cleanse oneself for the inevitable. Using both "small is beautiful" and "slower is better" themes, we are advised:

Human liberation will start small—at the human level. And we will find that it is the small arena which contains the large one, in a strange paradox of belief. If we can say "no" to the little chinks put in us by people who deny human feeling and human needs, we can say no to denial of body rhythms by this fast-paced society hurtling out of control.[49]

One reason for describing the anarchist school of thought on social ills and the nuclear danger is to demonstrate that critics of the "establishment" who are often lumped together as "the Left" compose a diverse lot. Neither the freeze proposal nor the freeze groups are universally revered instruments in this niche of the political world. But there is another, more important purpose. It is easy to scoff at such unconventional views, particularly when expressed in bizarre, stylized language. But many people navigate the social mainstream harboring private convictions not far different from these but afraid to tell anyone in expectation of ridicule. If we set aside the "new world" jargon, those who believe that the pace of modern life is unhealthy, that Wall Street and Madison Avenue are slowly sucking the soul out of America, and that things *are* too big and too complicated for many people to feel secure in their own basic human competence, are quite numerous. Most do not care to admit it, but there is a latent technophobe in each of us. After all, the infamous Ned Ludd was only *half* mad; Charlie Chaplin's *Modern Times* is still as engrossing today as it was fifty years ago.

When the frustrations of modern life coalesce—as they did in Paris in May 1968—the very definition of rational politics can be called into question. A reservoir of mostly inchoate discontent in the United States—a potential source of convulsive, arational politics—has benefited the freeze movement, even though the few who have tried explicitly to come to grips with this discontent have tended to reject the freeze itself and the agenda of its originators. The popularity of the freeze is in no small way a function of social frustration and a kind of cultural fatigue. The established order is not providing the emotional security thought by many to be its purpose. The freeze movement has provided a way for people to vent these frustrations, to strike back at the imputed source of their disappointment. In this sense, the freeze is doing what many popular movements before it have done, and that is less to focus on a particular issue or to advance a specific program for amelioration, and more to capture an undercurrent at work below the surface of public life.

The Religious Left

One important aspect of the religious dimension of the U.S. freeze movement concerns the institutional politics of the main religious establishment. Though their most profound concerns may be celestial, their most pressing concerns are always terrestrial. Any major religious denomination that failed to understand the strength of public agitation over nuclear war and demurred from riding its crest risked alienating a withering constituency. Church leaders could hardly afford to ignore the largest pulsation in the body politic since the movement against the Vietnam War, whatever their personal convictions.

The professional politicians of the Left thus found important allies within the bastions of America's traditional religious establishments in the United States, particularly the Catholic bishops through the agency of Pax Christi and the World Council of

Churches. There is no question that the early and stror
of the American Friends Service Committee in the f:
ment gave the entire enterprise a moral or religious a
start. But the nature of the Friends' religiosity and that ∪.
Roman Catholic Church, for example, is not the same and some
distinctions must be drawn between them.

In the first place, the AFSC itself is not a religious organization per se, nor is it linked institutionally to the Quaker
"church." Indeed, there is no such thing as a Quaker church; there
are individual Quaker meetings which can and do vary considerably in both theology and political disposition. (Neither is the
AFSC a kind of intra-Quaker organizational apparatus. There *is*
such an organization, but it is not the AFSC; it is a separate,
apolitical group called the Friends World Committee.) The AFSC,
rather, represents the apogee of the notion of the social gospel at
its most advanced stage of secularization. Of all Christian denominations, Quakerism is the most decentralized and least theistic in
the sense that many Quakers do not adhere to the classical Christian doctrine of the literal divinity of Jesus. This is certainly true
for the Philadelphia-centered Quakers of the AFSC, for whom
the politics of the social gospel and theology have become virtually indistinguishable. The AFSC is a *political* organization based
on religious principles and while the AFSC lent a moral aura to
the freeze, its motives were from the start political. Obviously,
the same cannot be said for the Catholic bishops as a group. Nor
can it be said of the World Council of Churches—at least not to
the same degree.

What can be said, however, is that in both the Roman Catholic Church and Protestant denominations in the United States, a
politicization process has been growing, especially among
younger clergy.[50] It is a politicization that undoubtedly has prior
religious motivations in most cases, and consequent political implications, rather than the other way around. In the Roman Catholic Church in the United States, the advancing politicization of
the clergy has had a number of important effects. First, the general
balance of the American church has moved further away from the
traditionalists who still dominate the Vatican. Pope John Paul II
is aware of this and of far more radical shifts elsewhere, particu-

larly the "liberation theology" of the Church in Latin America.[51] Thus, he has carefully mixed elements of the social gospel and support for disarmament with conservative positions on canonical matters and an unrelenting anti-Soviet perspective inherent in the Church's support for Solidarity in Poland. Second, politicized Catholics in the United States have increasingly found common ground with similarly politicized Protestants—and even Jews—and Catholic groups have been more willing to join politically minded coalitions than before. Third, the intensity of conviction of politically minded clergy has given rise to an aggressive intra-bishop pacifist organization—Pax Christi USA—which has overturned the balance of political power within the American Catholic hierarchy. Pax Christi is a society of bishops, about forty in all, who are known to one another, but who will not divulge their names publicly. They have lobbied hard and successfully for support in major archdioceses and parishes around the country.

Some of Pax Christi's members are radical unilateralists on nuclear issues. Archbishop Raymond Hunthausan of Seattle told his congregation that he had had a vision of thousands of citizens refusing to pay part of their federal income taxes to protest President Reagan's military build-up. He also declared that if a bilateral freeze could not be arranged quickly, "we as a country have a responsibility to undertake unilateral disarmament."[52] This sort of behavior prompted the Vatican to undertake unprecedented measures. It ordered Archbishop James A. Hickey of Washington, D.C. to go to Seattle to look into criticism regarding Hunthausan's pastoral ministry.[53] Hickey went to Seattle as ordered, but this did not stop Hunthausan. A few months later, he and a dozen other colleagues organized "direct action" and civil disobedience to stop trains carrying nuclear weapons from Amarillo, Texas to Bangor, Washington and from Amarillo to Charleston, South Carolina. Hunthausan likened these trains to those carrying victims to Nazi death camps.[54]

Pax Christi was undoubtedly the source of the famous pastoral letter and the political machine inside the Church that sold it to the bishops as a group. This was not an easy thing to do, but it was accomplished through modest compromise and hard bargaining. It may well be, for example, that the explicit linking of the dangers of nuclear war with the abomination of abortion was something other than a theological observation about the sanctity of human life on every level.[55] More likely, it was a concession made by Pax Christi and its supporters to the Church's old guard, for whom abortion was, and remains, the most vexing and pressing issue of the day. And it was clear too that had it not been for the freeze movement there would have been no Pax Christi effort to create and publicize a pastoral letter. The letter was Pax Christi's way of mobilizing the Roman Catholic Church in support of the freeze, which was from the early months of 1981 focused first and foremost on opposition to the Reagan Administration. Critics within the Church charged that Pax Christi sought to use the shield of God to give cover to a partisan political activity. Pax Christi and its supporters have denied this charge.

The pope's concern, the president's pleading, and the impassioned warnings of prominent Catholics in the Reagan Administration failed utterly to dissuade the bishops.[56] This bit of jousting was inevitable, however, and its outcome predictable. Despite pleas by some commentators that the president stay away from religious metaphors about evil empires and that religious leaders stay away from nuclear politics,[57] the U.S.-Soviet struggle cannot be waged as if it were simply a cold-blooded geopolitical contest bereft of philosophic import and ideological energy. Nor can the churches ignore an issue with such profound religious implications. On the other hand, as Isaiah Berlin pointed out in his brilliant essay on the originality of Machiavelli, it is in vain that temporal authorities wait for the church to approach politics according to the logic of "reasons of state."[58] Thus, the administration's entry into the bishops' debate in hope of softening the proposed wording of the pastoral letter was predictably ill-fated and probably ill-advised. Pax Christi continued its work. In September 1983, at the height of the MX debate, fourteen of its members assailed the MX program as a "threat to the future of the world."[59]

The World Council of Churches (WCC) was an early supporter of the nuclear freeze. Its situation falls somewhere between the AFSC and the Roman Catholic Church. The WCC represents many Protestant movements and denominations and clearly lacks

23

the hierarchy and organization of the Catholic Church. But while the WCC's political inclinations as a whole are quite radical,[60] many of its members are motivated primarily by a religious orientation and are not seeking to exploit the church for political ends, at least not consciously. Certainly, most members of the local congregations represented in the WCC do not share their representatives' proclivity to see the Christian message dressed in Marxist or liberation theology garb. Unlike the AFSC, most of those affiliated with the WCC have not yet effaced all distinctions between politics and theology. Outside the WCC, as well, there have arisen a number of anti-establishment Protestant-based groups espousing radical politics justified on religious grounds. Sojourners is a good case in point. Books and magazines have tumbled forth from these organizations by the score.[61]

The American Jewish community has also been split by the freeze. Many major Jewish religious organizations have supported the freeze, but not all.[62] Some Jewish-based peace organizations have picked up the freeze as well, notably Arthur Waskow's Rainbow Sign and the New Jewish Agenda. As a rule, these anti-establishment Jewish organizations tend to fall in line with the Israeli Left when it comes to their views on the Palestinians, the PLO, and the like. Thus, they are not troubled by the inconsistency of supporting strong U.S. aid and protection for Israel on the one hand, and arguing against a stronger U.S. military posture on the other hand. More mainstream Jewish groups do have a problem here and Jewish opponents of the freeze have pointed it out, to their discomfort.[63]

Priest vs. Priest

The most interesting aspects of the moral dimension of the nuclear freeze movement lie not in the institutional politics of the religious establishments, but in intellectual domains that go well beyond such institutional strictures. There is, for example, the claim by the coryphaei of the freeze movement that nuclear theorists and "conventional" arms control "experts" have functioned as a "nuclear priesthood," exercising a pernicious anti-democratic influence over public policy.[64] This fits in both with the Raskinesque notion of the "national security state" and the psychologisms of Jerome Frank, Robert Lifton, and others, who claim that "nuclearism" is a kind of social disease arising from the very existence of nuclear weapons which has inherently anti-democratic implications. Clearly, the use of religious metaphors to wield accusations of antidemocratic conspiracies is heady stuff.

There is no end to claims that an antidemocratic nuclear priesthood has befuddled the issues before "the people." Accusations about the supposed existence of a nuclear priesthood is really the bailiwick of the Professional Left, at least in origin, but it has a much wider following. When Falk, Lifton, Schell, and others describe this priesthood, it is depicted as a part of the anti-democratic conspiracy of the "national security state." Those closer to the political mainstream are much less truculent; there may be no conspiracy, but there *is* a secretive group of "experts" who have been allowed to dominate policy for too long to the detriment of national security.

In the first freeze debate in the House of Representatives, Fortney Stark (Dem., California) put it very simply, employing Stanley Kubrick's famous cinema character as an adjective: "[Our people] do not want to be incinerated so some Dr. Strangelove theorist can test his belief that nuclear war is winnable."[65] To this, Tom Harkin (Dem., Indiana) added that, with a freeze, "no longer will the people of the United States allow their lives to be held in constant peril by the decisions of an elite group of generals, politicians and scientists."[66] Toby Moffett, who left the House to run (unsuccessfully) for a Senate seat in 1982, also railed against the "experts": "And the people are sick and tired of leaving their fate totally in the hands of the experts, including us, because we have failed. The experts have failed. There are more weapons. There is more tension. There is more likelihood of war, not less, and the people are telling us that."[67]

The mass mail solicitations of Common Cause have picked up the same theme. "The issue of nuclear war and nuclear arms control belongs to the people," says Fred Wertheimer. "But, sadly, the discussion of these issues has been left to the experts, who speak only to other experts. These experts talk beyond the comprehension of the average citizen of this country, and that's just plain wrong. The only way to address these issues in a de-

mocracy is to get the information before the people." Further-
more, the "democratization" of the issue, says Freeze Fact Sheet
Number 1 "gives hope to the people," breaking through "the
fatalism and sense of helplessness that has kept many people from
responding to the threat of nuclear war, which is the greatest
threat to human existence the world has ever faced." In a final
offering to the mystical efficacy of democracy, the fact sheet continues: "The Freeze has helped people see that there *is* a way to
stop the nuclear arms race before it's too late. The American
people have become more concerned about this problem than ever
before. The fact alone means that there's more hope of solving it
than in the past." Frankly, it is difficult to see how. Democracy
describes a political *process,* not an act of puerile thaumaturgical
magic.

Robert Karl Manoff, then-managing editor of *Harper's*
applies the coercive notion of nuclearism to the media and, indeed,
to the freedom of inquiry writ large. His sermon includes the
following peroration:

As it has developed over the last four decades, the actual epistemological
structure of the nuclear regime is both rigid and restrictive. Since it is
this structure that sets the parameters of knowledge in journalism, science and politics, I think we must conclude that the cognitive history of
the nuclear era is the history of the relative restriction of socially available
knowledge even as the possibilities for its expansion have in fact increased.

Thirty-eight years after Hiroshima, it is time to come to grips with the
central political fact of modern American life: The epistemological structure of the nuclear regime is incompatible with the epistemological structure of democracy itself. Nuclearism and democracy embody antago-
nistic ideals of knowledge. They foresee different patterns for its dissem-
ination. They contemplate entirely different consequences for social action
and political participation.

This suggests a disturbing but unmistakable conclusion: The United
States cannot long endure as both nuclear and democratic. This country
cannot be nuclear and democratic at the same time, for one system is
closed and the other is open; one system requires secrecy, the other, in
the finest sense of the word, publicity; one system must concentrate
control, the other exists in order to diffuse it.[68]

The conclusion that follows from this inane thesis—that the existence of nuclear weapons presupposes cultural malignancy and constitutional deformity—flows as naturally as day follows night and is just as predictable. Since an overwhelming majority of the American people want real arms control, and given that the U.S. government has "failed to produce it," it is only fair to conclude, writes Manoff, that the government is no longer representative of the will of the people. "Not until this conflict has been resolved," he warns, "not until democratic values reassert their primacy over nuclear ones, will elite and governmental priorities shift, and, along with them, the cognitive possibilities of science, politics and the press."[69]

Nuclear freeze advocates have gone out of their way to champion the "right" of everyone to a confident opinion about national security issues, no matter how complex. Implicit in this claim is that the issues are not nearly so complicated as the "nuclear priesthood" makes them out to be. The freeze's assault on institutionally privileged expertise is part of a much broader attack on "experts," some of which is undoubtedly justified.[70] It may be true, too, that the community of strategic analysts has tended to be excessively narrow in its perspective, overly arcane in its writing, and utterly insensitive to public education.[71] But for all the sins of the "experts," the issues *are* complicated and some important truths about the nuclear age are confusingly counterintuitive.

Freeze activists argue that the "nuclear priesthood" is Big Brotheresque, and that they are the real democrats. The intellectuals of the American freeze movement suggest that the strategic "experts" are the obfuscating priests and that they are the liberating prophets. But it makes at least as much sense to look upon these purveyors of the apocalypse as a new priesthood, wielding the dogma of the final calamity of nuclear war in much the same way that priests of old fanned the fear of eternal damnation to enforce the discipline and shape the thinking of their flock. It is interesting to speculate on the extent to which the moral dimension of the nuclear freeze movement represents the secularization of classical Christian eschatology in a society that has steeled itself against traditional faith and that, in its most private honesty, thinks of God as a quaint literary anachronism.

Freeze intellectuals are also fond of claiming that the "expert's priesthood" is engaged in the "denial of death" and the dehumanizing and moral anesthetizing of the nuclear dilemma. But many of those who oppose the freeze say that it is the priesthood of nuclear purity that rather denies reality and by doing so invites the very disaster it wishes to avoid. How else can one explain the view of Schell, Falk, Lifton, and others that the only way to avoid nuclear holocaust is to remake world politics, "to reinvent the world," as Schell put it? The danger of nuclear war, says the new priesthood, is really only a symptom of a deep-seated disease of human society and only the coming of the secular messiah can save us from destruction, defined by Schell as "global disarmament, both nuclear and conventional, and the invention of political means by which the world can peacefully settle the issues that throughout human history it has settled by war."[72] In other words, what we need is the most fundamental transformation of human society since the dawn of history, we need it in a single generation, and nothing else will do.

There is another curious phenomenon at work here. While the gray-suited technocrats and "strategic priests" stand accused of being moral automatons, there are some true believers in the freeze movement who seem to have what can only be described as a macabre fascination with the holocaust to come. The Physicians for Social Responsibility, in particular, seem obsessed with the gruesome statistics of Armageddon. Reading their literature and viewing their films gives the sensation of riding a mammoth psychological roller coaster. For reasons psychologists have yet to explain fully, some people like to terrify themselves. That is perhaps unfortunate, but worse still, some people like to terrify others, as well. Whatever the reasons for this, the freeze movement in its more fervent moralistic manifestations gives the impression of being a semi-secularized premillenarian movement.[73]

Yet another hint of the religious passion of the freeze movement is the unmistakable tendency for its arguments and assumptions to become unambiguous and unassailable—in short, to become dogma. It is beyond question, for example, that one of the underlying sources of public concern in the contemporary nuclear debate touches on the apocalyptical aura of war and peace in the nuclear age. Most freeze advocates appear to believe that if a nuclear war actually began, either willfully or by mistake, it would inexorably escalate to total war, bringing with it the end of life on this planet, or certainly the end of civilization. Nuclear freeze activists have done their utmost to reinforce this popular view, even though it is probably not true. The death and destruction that *any* nuclear exchange would cause is hardly trivial, but it is not the same as the end of the world.[74] Besides, it is not true that any nuclear exchange would automatically escalate into total war; other possibilities exist that are at least as likely.

Freeze activists, however, seem to need very much the belief in the apocalypse for reasons of personal commitment; that is why they insist upon it as though it were part of a new nuclear catechism. After all, the future of life and death on this planet—the fate of all future generations, as Schell puts it—is worthy of one's very best effort, is it not? The more portentous and dramatic the stake, the more praiseworthy one's dedication becomes and the more unequivocal one's commitment must be. Few will put their heart and soul into an issue that has more gray area than black or white, with real political complications and genuine intellectual open-endedness. Simple Manichean metaphors that offer the clarity of moral certainty work much better. Indeed, a kind of internal escalation of commitment seems to take place, wherein uncertainties and ambiguities are assuaged by increased psychological investment. This is what Nisbet may have had in mind when he observed that "zeal and passion feed on themselves in political-moral causes, as in revolutions."[75]

There is also a social aspect to this. Many freeze advocates appear to have a strong personal impulse to be politically organized and active around some anti-establishment cause, and a need to express moral sentiments with others through politics. This is a powerful magnet, as is any sincere form of communal worship. Social bonds reinforce personal faith and commitment, commitment re-forges social bonds with new strength. In any case, the emotional backdrop of the nuclear freeze movement, the personal catharsis it provides many of its adherents, and the peer support it can provide go far toward explaining why some freeze advocates are utterly impervious to logic and rational argument. It is not only that many are ignorant of the facts, but rather that facts are subordinate to feelings. When people have a strong need to believe something, mere facts are powerless to stop them.[76]

Not only have religion and religious imagery been used to promote the freeze, but so have other symbols of reverence in American culture—especially science.[77] The freeze movement has been promoted vigorously by some scientists who have sought to use their professional expertise in service of the cause. The manipulation of science for the sake of politics is nothing new; indeed, Thomas Hobbes pointed out over three hundred years ago that were it not in the interest of the sovereign that two plus two be four, then it would not. Yet this is still a potent instrument of advocacy, no matter how common a practice and no matter if the practitioner is a sincere true believer who knows not what he is doing to his profession, or a self-aware manipulator who knows quite well what he is doing. It is a little like a clever advertising agency using the actor Robert Young to sell Sanka while dressed as Marcus Welby, M.D. Many people simply cannot be bothered with distinguishing between reality and role-playing.

We have heard, for example, physicists and even astronomers tell us that a nuclear war would irrevocably change the earth's climate, though the evidence is ambiguous.[78] When a physicist like William Shockley wanders from his field of expertise to promote controversial genetic theories that are at once questionable and bear plainly unpopular social implications, the guardians of the academic world descend like angry bees to purge the hive of impurity.[79] But when Carl Sagan ventures into a field just as distant from his area of expertise to offer questionable but *popular* conclusions about the effects of a nuclear war, we hear nothing more than an occasional grumble easily passed off as jealousy or excessive professional zeal.

Aside from the politicization of climatology and meteorology, there have been less dramatic politicizations of virtually every natural and social scientific field in existence, or at least attempts at it.[80] This has been less notable in research than in teaching, and here the various attempts to teach about nuclear war in the classroom have been vigorously promoted by the National Education Association (NEA), which in tandem with the Union of Concerned Scientists produced a pamphlet for use in schools across the nation entitled *Choices*.[81] Thus, even the sanctity of education has been used to foster a particular view of the nuclear balance and the arms competition that is decidedly pro-freeze. The NEA's role in the freeze, led by its director, Terry Herndon, who is also president of Citizens Against Nuclear War, aroused angry opposition from throughout the political spectrum, from those on the right who disagree with the conclusions and slant of *Choices* to people like Albert Shanker, president of the American Federation of Teachers, who may sympathize with the freeze movement but who nevertheless oppose the prostitution of education for partisan causes.[82]

The medical profession has played its part as well. Dr. Helen Caldicott's Physicians for Social Responsibility (PSR) is the most notable example, but there is also a group called International Physicians for the Prevention of Nuclear War (IPPNW). Even the Soviet government has seen the utility of using medicine as a shill to promote pacifism and disarmament in the West. In front of Western media and in the company of visiting pro-freeze Western physicians, Soviet physicians have been led on parade espousing the morbid health effects of nuclear war at IPPNW meetings.[83] As for Physicians for Social Responsibility, it has counseled medical groups and hospitals not to participate in any civil defense planning or medical contingency planning—not even stocking extra hospital beds—lest such preparedness make nuclear war a more "thinkable and therefore a more likely" prospect.[84]

Caldicott's utilization of medical imagery was clear in her introduction to PSR's book and film *The Final Epidemic*. There she tells us, "The world is moving rapidly toward the final medical epidemic, thermonuclear war." According to Caldicott, the patient—the earth—is near death and extreme measures must be taken to save it. When "warnings are heeded and patients begin to look realistically at the threats they face, they may find the prospect terrifying, but this experience is essential to the emotional adaptation necessary for effective political action." Facing terrifying prospects is therapeutic, then, says Caldicott, given the gravity of the situation, and physicians have not only a right but a duty to administer such terror as a means of political awakening.

"Nothing less will save this Earth," asserts Caldicott. "Let us join together, doctors and patients, to preserve what may be the only life in the universe. We are at the crossroads of time. Only emotional maturity, evoked by extreme danger combined with personal responsibility and total commitment, will save our planet for our descendants."[85]

Beyond religion, the professions, and the natural sciences, even children have been pressed into the service of the nuclear freeze movement. Dr. John E. Mack at Harvard and a group called Educators for Social Responsibility are the main perpetrators, using the recent romanticization of children in popular culture to bolster the claim that while most adults do not understand the nuclear question in its essence, children do. There is evidence that children *are* more worried about nuclear war today then they were three or four years ago, but the reason is not "the Reagan nuclear buildup" as freeze advocates claim—as if eight-year-olds regularly read national and international news—but the nuclear freeze movement itself. As Morton Kondracke observed, the freeze movement itself is "the real culprit in traumatizing children." Freeze advocates have "not been satisfied merely to conduct an adult debate on nuclear policy with the Reagan Administration, but have used fear of a nuclear holocaust as a basic organizing tool."[86] Between the National Education Association and the Physicians for Social Responsibility, a parent could not be faulted for wondering whether a public school is still a safe place to send a child.

Caldicott and her associates have spared no effort to provide threats that terrify young people—even grade schoolers—both in print and on the movie screen.[87] If the diagnosis is wrong, however, who will accept the responsibility for the psychological damage done by such fear-mongering? Besides, terrorizing people does not necessarily lead them to rational activism. As the late Raymond Aron once said: "The habit of prophesying doom is testimony less to lucidity than to resignation."[88]

The nuclear freeze movement has declared not just war against the "nuclear establishment," but holy war. It is a holy war whose use of religious imagery and moral vigor has gone far beyond the involvement of the institutional apparatus of the religious establishment. All symbols of reverence and respect have been pressed into service. For those who believe in the possibility of a truly rational politics, such a development is cause for despair. For those who see politics as the organized expression of an unresolvable, but unavoidable, collision of mutually exclusive systems of value, it is an inevitable feature of debate over any broadly consequential issue.

But it is more than inevitable. It is, on balance, benign. As unrealistic, counterproductive, and irritating as the archdeacons of the freeze movement can be, their absence would be even more frightening, just as total absence of their would-be counterparts from Soviet society is frightening. Those who cherish living in a free society have no desire that the state monopolize the definition of good and evil, or that it still even woefully wrongheaded discussion about it. In the end, we should be happy to admit that putting up with a periodic pulse of foolishness is a price we gladly pay for our liberty.

NOTES

1. One can find this assertion in almost any American government and politics textbook. For discussions, see Thomas R. Dye and L. Harmon Zeigler, *The Irony of Democracy* (North Scituate, Mass.: Duxbury Press, 1975), pp. 258-62; and Gabriel Almond and Sidney Verba, *The Civic Culture* (Boston: Little, Brown, 1965). For a theory of politico-economic inertia based on the proliferation of such groups, see Mancur Olson, *The Rise and Decline of Nations* (New Haven: Yale University Press, 1982).

2. An associational group is defined as a voluntary social collective based on shared interests. Other groups in society, according to one typology, include non-associational groups, anomic groups, and institutional groups. Non-associational groups are communities of people tied together by kinship, language, race, or some other characteristic that people are generally "born into." Institutional groups are voluntary associations which are formed for non-political purposes, but which occasionally play political roles. Professional associations are examples of institutional groups. Anomic groups are more or less spontaneous agglomerations of people, the best example being the political mob. See Gabriel A. Almond and James S. Coleman, eds., *The Politics of the Developing Areas* (Princeton: Princeton University Press, 1960), pp. 33-34.

3. This sort of proto-Marxist "theory" to explain the arms race is expounded by Seymour Melman, co-chairman of SANE, and many others. See his *Pentagon Capitalism: The Political Economy of War* (New York: McGraw-Hill, 1979). For statements disparaging arms control in favor of disarmament, see Marcus G. Raskin, "Now Reconsider Disarming," which appeared in the *New York Times* on April 1, 1983. See also Raskin's "Time for an Arms Rollback," *New York Times,* November 1, 1983; and Sidney Lens, "Deterrence Hardly Deters," *New York Times,* December 27, 1983.

4. Richard J. Barnet and Ronald E. Muller, *Global Reach: The Power of the Multinational Corporations* (New York: Simon and Schuster, 1974).

5. Richard J. Barnet, *The Lean Years: Politics in an Age of Scarcity* (New York: Simon and Schuster, 1980), p. 226.

6. Ibid. For more of Barnet's theories, see his *Real Security: Restoring American Power in a Dangerous Decade* (New York: Simon and Schuster, 1981) and Barnet's three contributions to Jim Wallis, ed., *Waging Peace: A Handbook for the Struggle to Abolish Nuclear Weapons* (San Francisco: Harper and Row, 1982). In reviewing Barnet's latest book, *The Alliance* (New York: Simon and Schuster, 1983), Daniel Yergin asserts that Barnet's "outlook has decidedly shifted, from that of a radical critic of United States foreign policy to one of measured respect and judicious admiration for the alliance at a time when this view is hardly fashionable." See "Unequal Partners," *New York Times Book Review,* December 18, 1983, pp. 6, 17. But see Barnet's "The Sources of Insecurity," *The Progressive,* July 1984, pp. 30-33. For background on the IPS, see Rael Jean Isaac, "The Institute for Policy Studies: Empire on the Left," *Midstream,* June/July 1982, pp. 1-12.

7. Marcus G. Raskin, *The Politics of National Security* (New Brunswick, N.J.: Transaction Books, 1979), p. 31. For more examples and a useful discussion, see Arch Puddington and Marco Carynnyk, "Soviet Apologists: Then and Now," *Commentary,* November 1983, pp. 25-31.

8. Marcus G. Raskin, *Notes on the Old System* (New York: David McKay Co., 1974), p. 4.

9. Ibid, p. 5.

10. Ibid., pp. 21-22.

11. Raskin, *The Politics of National Security,* p. 31.

12. The relevant works here include Jonathan Schell, *The Fate of the Earth* (New York: Knopf Books, 1982); Robert Jay Lifton and Richard Falk, *Indefensible*

Weapons: The Political and Psychological Case Against Nuclearism (New York: Basic Books, 1982); Helen Caldicott, *Nuclear Madness: What Can We Do?* (Brookline, Mass.: Autumn Press, 1979); E. P. Thompson, "Notes on Exterminism, the Last Stage of Civilization," in *Exterminism and Cold War* (London: Verso, 1982); and Jerome D. Frank, *Sanity and Survival in the Nuclear Age: Psychological Aspects of War and Peace* (New York: Random House, 1967, 1982). For a trenchant critique of Schell, see Theodore Draper, "How Not to Think About Nuclear War," *New York Review of Books*, November 4, 1982, reprinted in Draper's *Present History: On Nuclear War, Détente, and Other Controversies* (New York: Random House, 1983). See also Patrick Glynn, "Anti-Nuclear Fantasies," *Commentary*, January 1983.

13. Schell, *The Fate of the Earth*, p. 226.

14. Lifton and Falk, *Indefensible Weapons*, p. 248. (Emphasis in original.)

15. Ibid, p. 246.

16. See Peter Pringle, "Putting World War III on Ice," *Inquiry*, July 1982, pp. 15-16. Pringle is quite sympathetic to the freeze. See also, as commentary on this article, the letter by this writer entitled "Junk-Think Journalism," *Inquiry*, September 1982. Pringle is co-author (with William M. Arkin of the IPS) of a book whose title reveals its nature, *SIOP: The Secret U.S. Plan for Nuclear War* (New York: W. W. Norton, 1983). The AFSC's support for unilateral U.S. disarmament is not new; it has been a part of their agenda for decades. See here Mulford Q. Sibley, *Unilateral Initiatives and Disarmament* (Philadelphia: American Friends Service Committee, 1962).

17. See Rael Jean Isaac and Erich Isaac, "The Counterfeit Peacemakers: Atomic Freeze," *American Spectator*, June 1982, p. 14. See also Ronald Radosh, "The 'Peace Council' and Peace," *The New Republic*, January 31, 1983, pp. 14-18. In defense of Provance, see Frank Donner, "But Will They Come? The Campaign to Smear the Nuclear Freeze Movement," *The Nation*, November 6, 1982, p. 461.

18. Pringle, "Putting World War III on Ice," p. 15.

19. Sidney Lens, "How Deep A Freeze?" *The Progressive*, May 1982, p. 16.

20. Forsberg moved to Sweden in 1967 when she married a Swedish student. SIPRI had been established only a year earlier and was in search of an international staff. See Fox Butterfield, "Anatomy of the Nuclear Protest," *New York Times Magazine*, July 11, 1982.

21. See Isaac and Isaac, "The Counterfeit Peacemakers," p. 8. Both the AFSC and the Fellowship of Reconciliation originated as pacifist movements

during World War I. The unilateralist tone of the freeze did not disappear all at once. There were at least three variations of "Call to Halt the Nuclear Arms Race," the "international" version, the first AFSC version, and the second AFSC version. The "international" version included a call for a halt on "research and development" as well as "testing, manufacture and deployment of nuclear bombs and missiles." The first AFSC version, available in 1981, suggested two *unilateral* actions that the United States could, and by implication, should take to demonstrate good faith: (1) undertake a three-month moratorium on nuclear test explosions, to be extended if reciprocated; (2) stop further deployment, for a specified period, of one new strategic weapon, or improvement of an existing weapon. In the second and final AFSC version, these two sentences were omitted.

22. Pringle, "Putting World War III on Ice," p. 15.

23. Isaac and Isaac, "The Counterfeit Peacemakers," p. 15.

24. Quoted in Carol Polsgrove, "The Freeze Heats Up," *Inquiry,* July 1982, p. 17.

25. This argument is a mainstay of Melman's thesis that Pentagon capitalism is destroying the United States. See *Pentagon Capitalism,* esp. chap. 8, "The Cost of the Para-State to American Society." Recently, however, a gadfly has fallen into Melman's soup. Lynn Turgeon, an economics professor at Hofstra University, has been arguing the more classically Marxist theory that U.S. military spending has propped up an otherwise "rotten system." Most scholars are reluctant to assume a one-to-one relationship between these two factors, reasoning instead that many factors, working differently in different societies, stand between military expenditures and manufacturing productivity.

26. See Isaac and Isaac, "The Counterfeit Peacemakers," p. 16. For details about the origins and evolution of SANE—in a sympathetic context—see Charles DeBenedetti, *The Peace Reform in American History* (Bloomington: Indiana University Press, 1980), chap. 7.

27. David Cortright, *Soldiers in Revolt* (New York: Anchor Press/Doubleday, 1975), p. vii.

28. Ibid., p. ix.

29. Ibid., p. xi.

30. Melman, *Pentagon Capitalism,* p. 34.

36

31. Gerald F. Seib, "Antinuclear Voices Grow Louder in U.S. Despite Defense Mood," *Wall Street Journal,* December 9, 1981.

32. There *are* no jungles in El Salvador.

33. The same theme was struck by the November 12 Coalition in the aftermath of the U.S. intervention in Grenada in October 1983. The Coalition, which was virtually coterminous with freeze support groups and organizers, called for "decisive action which will halt such *ad hoc* military adventurism. If we do not act *now*, the clock of nuclear conflict might soon approach midnight. What is next? An invasion of Nicaragua? An invasion of Cuba? A slaughter of the insurgent forces in El Salvador and Guatemala? We cannot expect that many such steps can be taken before we reach the dreadful end of the road to world war." See the ad taken out by the AFSC in the *New York Times,* November 6, 1983.

34. King was a member of the Fellowship of Reconciliation which was associated with A. J. Muste, the intellectual hero of the WRL. See Nat Hentoff, *Peace Agitator: The Story of A. J. Muste* (New York: Macmillan, 1963), pp. 17-18. See also Jo Ann Ooiman Robinson, *Abraham Went Out: A Biography of A. J. Muste* (Philadelphia: Temple University Press, 1981).

35. From an article in the journal of the Fellowship of Reconciliation, cited in Isaac and Isaac, "The Counterfeit Peacemakers," p. 9.

36. "Pacifism and Class War," *The World Tomorrow,* September 1928, reprinted in Nat Hentoff, ed., *The Essays of A. J. Muste* (New York: Simon and Schuster, 1970), p. 180.

37. Cited in Isaac and Isaac, "The Counterfeit Peacemakers," p. 10.

38. Cited in ibid. See also Dellinger's *Revolutionary Nonviolence* (New York: War Resister's League, 1971).

39. See Isaac and Isaac, "The Counterfeit Peacemakers," p. 10. Also see David McReynolds, *We Have Been Invaded by the Twenty-first Century* (New York: War Resister's League, 1970).

40. For example see the reportage in Robert Linsey, "Hundreds Arrested Protesting Nuclear Weapons," *New York Times,* June 21, 1983. MFS and other like-minded groups have been forced to reassess their tactics after enduring stiff penalties in their late June 1983 actions. See Leon Lindsay, "Stiff Penalties Force Review of Antinuclear Strategy," *Christian Science Monitor,* July 1, 1983.

41. This discussion follows Isaac and Isaac, "The Counterfeit Peacemakers," p. 14.

42. Donner, "But Will They Come?" p. 457.

43. Ibid., pp. 458-59.

44. For expressions of this thesis, see the works of Murray Bookchin, who is a guru to many. See his *Post-Scarcity Anarchism* (New York: Ramparts, 1980) and *The Ecology of Freedom: The Emergence and Dissolution of Hierarchy*, (Palo Alto, Calif.: Cheshire Books, 1982). For a historical treatment of anarchism in the United States, see David DeLeon, *The American as Anarchist* (Baltimore: Johns Hopkins University Press, 1978); and Laurence Veysey, *The Communal Experience: Anarchism, Mystical Countercultures in America* (New York: Harper and Row, 1973). For the theory and history of anarchism, see James Joll, *The Anarchists* (Cambridge, Mass.: Harvard University Press, 1980).

45. "Small is beautiful" refers to the late E. F. Schumacher's *Small is Beautiful: Economics As If People Mattered* (New York: Harper and Row, 1976). Both Schumacher's memory and his book are revered by many.

46. Karen B. Hale, "Human Liberation, or, Why We Must Have a Holocaust," *Welcomat* (Philadelphia), December 14, 1983, p. 5.

47. Ibid.

48. Ibid., p. 47.

49. Ibid. The dangers of a life that is too fast-paced were given prominent play in Alvin Toffler's pop-social commentary *Future Shock* (New York: Random House, 1970). For a very unorthodox book that combines anarchism, encounter-group jargon, and Buddhist mysticism, see Joanna Rogers Macy, *Despair and Personal Power in the Nuclear Age* (Philadelphia: Movement for a New Society Press, 1983).

50. The magazine *Christianity Today* has devoted considerable space to this issue over the past two years. See also Donald L. Davidson, *Nuclear Weapons and the American Churches* (Boulder: Westview, 1983).

51. For a discussion of liberation theology see James V. Schall, ed., *Liberation Theology, Latin America* (New York: Paulist Press, 1982).

52. Hunthausan's remarks are quoted in Gerald F. Seib, "Atomic Angst," *Wall Street Journal*, December 9, 1981. See also Charlotte Hays's feature on J.

Bryan Hehir, "The Voice in the Bishops' Ear," *Washington Post Magazine,* April 3, 1983, pp. 6, 11-12. Hehir wrote the pastoral letter, or most of it; he works for Cardinal Joseph Bernardin of Chicago. See his "The Use of Force in the International System Today," in J. A. Derereux, S.J., ed., *The Moral Dimensions of International Conduct* (Washington: Georgetown University Press, 1982), pp. 85-110. Hunthausen's formal remarks on this subject can be found in full in his "Address to the Pacific Northwest Synod of the Lutheran Church in America, July 12, 1981," in Robert Heyer, *Nuclear Disarmament* (New York: Paulist Press, 1982), pp. 134-135; and in part in David Hollenbach, *Nuclear Ethics: A Christian Moral Argument* (New York: Paulist Press, 1983), pp. 66-67.

53. See a report of the Vatican's action in "Pope Tells U.S. Archbishop to Check on Seattle Leader," *New York Times,* October 28, 1983.

54. See Robert Lindsey, "Bishops Protest Train Carrying Atom Weapons," *New York Times,* February 24, 1984.

55. For the text and a sympathetic analysis of the pastoral letter, see Jim Castelli, *The Bishops and the Bomb: Waging Peace in a Nuclear Age* (Garden City, N.Y.: Image Books, 1983). See also the observations of Albert Wohlstetter, "Bishops, Statesmen, and Other Strategists on the Bombing of Innocents," *Commentary,* June 1983; Keith B. Payne, "The Bishops and Nuclear Weapons," *Orbis,* Fall 1983, pp. 535-43, who took exception to the Bishops; and those of McGeorge Bundy, "The Bishops and the Bomb," *New York Review of Books,* June 16, 1983, who liked what they wrote. Naturally, not all Catholic *theologians* agreed with the pastoral letter. See Michael Novak, "Moral Clarity in the Nuclear Age," *National Review,* April 1, 1983. See also the analysis of Bruce L. von Voorst, "The Churches and Deterrence," *Foreign Affairs,* September 1983. For an analysis of the media's coverage of the pastoral letter and some details about Pax Christi, see Phyllis Zagano, "Media Morality: The American Catholic Bishops and Deterrence," *Center Journal,* Winter 1983, pp. 177-92. Also, the journal *Thought,* published by Fordham University Press, devoted its entire March 1984 issue to nuclear ethics. Bruce Russett, a political scientist from Yale University, was a key adviser to the bishops in their drafting of the pastoral letter. See his text, *The Prisoners of Insecurity: Nuclear Deterrence, the Arms Race and Arms Control* (San Francisco: W. H. Freeman, 1983). The link between the freeze and abortion is made most directly in paragraph 286: "We are well aware of the differences involved in the taking of human life in warfare and the taking of human life through abortion. As we have discussed throughout this document, even justifiable defense against aggression may result in the indirect or unintended loss of innocent human lives. This is tragic, but may conceivably be proportionate to the values defended. Nothing, however, can justify direct attack on innocent human life, in or out of warfare. Abortion is precisely such an attack."

56. See Steven R. Weisman, "Reagan Calls on Catholics in U.S. to Reject Nuclear Freeze Proposal," *New York Times,* August 4, 1982; and especially John F. Lehman, Jr., "The U.S. Catholic Bishops and Nuclear Arms," *Wall Street Journal,* November 15, 1982.

57. One such commentator was William Safire. See his column, "Bullies in the Pulpit," *New York Times,* March 14, 1983.

58. See Isaiah Berlin, "The Originality of Machiavelli," *Against the Current* (New York: Viking Press, 1980).

59. "14 Catholic Bishops Say MX Threatens World," *New York Times,* September 20, 1983; and Richard Halloran, "Bishops Challenge MX in Testimony," *New York Times,* June 27, 1984.

60. The television show "60 Minutes" presented a scathing, controversial, and basically accurate protrayal of the WCC in early 1983. "The Gospel According to Whom?" was aired January 23, 1983. See also Charles Krauthammer, "Holy Fools," *The New Republic,* September 9, 1981, pp. 10-13.

61. See Ched Meyers, "Nuclear Holocaust and the Nonviolent Movement," *Sojourners,* June/July 1983, pp. 30-31; Ronald J. Sider and Richard K. Taylor, *Nuclear Holocaust and Christian Hope: A Book for Christian Peacemakers* (New York: Paulist Press, 1982); and Jim Wallis, ed., *Waging Peace: A Handbook for the Struggle to Abolish Nuclear Weapons* (San Francisco: Harper and Row, 1982). Wallis also authored *Agenda for Biblical People* and *The Call to Conversion.*

62. See, for example, Charles Austin, "Synagogue Council Endorses Nuclear Freeze," *New York Times,* February 25, 1983. The Synagogue Council of America is an umbrella organization representing six major organizations of Conservative, Reform, and Orthodox Judaism.

63. Shoshana Bryen, "Is the Nuclear Freeze a 'Jewish Issue'?" *Jewish Institute for National Security Affairs Newsletter,* July/August 1983, pp. 1, 7. See also Norman Podhoretz's remarks in "Appeasement by Any Other Name," *Commentary,* July 1983, pp. 32-33. See, too, Stephen S. Rosenfield, "Which Freeze?" *Present Tense,* Summer 1983, pp. 19-20, for a good summary of the arguments. Incidentally, Arthur Waskow is no latecomer to the debate over deterrence. See his essay "The Theory and Practice of Deterrence," in Henry A. Kissinger, ed., *Problems of National Strategy* (New York: Praeger, 1965), pp. 59-84.

64. See for example James Fallows, *National Defense* (New York: Random

House, 1981), chap. 6, entitled "High Priests" and Daniel Ford's similar usage in *The Cult of the Atom* (New York: Simon and Schuster, 1982).

65. U. S. House, *Congressional Record,* August 5, 1982, p. H5311.

66. Ibid., p. H5348.

67. Ibid., p. H5234.

68. Robert Karl Manoff, "The Media: Nuclear Secrecy vs. Democracy," *Bulletin of the Atomic Scientists,* January 1984, p. 29.

69. Ibid. See also Michael Walzer, "Deterrence and Democracy," *The New Republic,* July 2, 1984, pp. 16-21.

70. See Christopher Lasch, *The Culture of Narcissism* (New York: W. W. Norton, 1979).

71. For a discussion, see Colin S. Gray, *Strategic Studies: A Critical Assessment* (Westport, Conn.: Greenwood Press, 1982).

72. Schell, *The Fate of the Earth,* p. 226.

73. See here Leon Festinger, et al., *When Prophecy Fails: A Social-Psychological Study of a Modern Group That Predicted the End of the World* (New York: Harper and Row, 1969).

74. See Kevin Lewis, "The Prompt and Delayed Effects of Nuclear War," *Scientific American,* July 1981. This article, and its aftermath, has an amusing history. *Scientific American* has a reputation for publishing dovish articles on military-related subjects. The title of Lewis's article and the fact that it appeared in *Scientific American* led some freeze groups to assume that the article would conclude that a nuclear war would destroy the planet and everything on it. Evidently, most groups could not spare an individual to actually *read* the article because Lewis, who does not support a nuclear freeze, who works for the Rand Corporation, and whose article says nothing of the sort, has been asked repeatedly to speak and write on behalf of the freeze. (Personal communication with Lewis.)

75. Robert Nisbet, *Prejudices: A Philosophical Dictionary* (Cambridge, Mass.: Harvard University Press, 1982), p. 6. Such phenomena are well known to psychologists under the heading of cognitive dissonance. See Leon Festinger, *Cognitive Dissonance* (Evanston, Ill.: Row, Peterson, 1957). For a briefer discussion specifically attuned to politics, see Robert Jervis, *Perception and*

Misperception in International Relations (Princeton: Princeton University Press, 1976), pp. 382-408.

76. See Festinger et al., *When Prophecy Fails.* For a more general discussion, consult the chapter on "Myth and Religion" in Ernst Cassirer, *An Essay on Man* (New Haven: Yale University Press, 1944), pp. 72-108.

77. Religion and science have more in common psychologically than many people realize. See Peter Berger, *The Sacred Canopy: Elements of a Sociological Theory of Religion* (Garden City, N.Y.: Anchor Press/Doubleday, 1967).

78. See for example, Walter Sullivan, "Specialists Detail 'Nuclear Winter'," *New York Times,* December 26, 1983; "Scientists Describe 'Nuclear Winter'," *Science,* November 18, 1983, pp. 80-83; Ernest J. Sternglass and William T. Lind, "A Nuclear War's Devastating Effect on Climate," *New York Times,* May 28, 1982; and Carl Sagan, "Nuclear War and Climatic Catastrophe: Some Policy Implications," *Foreign Affairs,* Winter 1983-84.

79. On the Shockley controversy, see M. Rogers, "Brave New Shockley," *Esquire,* January 1973.

80. See, for example, the special issue of *Journal of College Science Teaching* devoted to "Nuclear Education," March/April 1983. I am indebted to Priscilla E. Taylor for bringing this to my attention.

81. *Choices: A Unit on Conflict and Nuclear War,* a project of the Union of Concerned Scientists, the Massachusetts Teachers Association, and the National Education Association (Washington: National Education Association, 1983).

82. See "Teaching About Nuclear War," *Newsweek,* July 18, 1983, p. 78; Barry Goldwater, "NEA's Nuclear 'Choices'," *Washington Post,* June 18, 1983; "26 Groups Join Against Arms," *New York Times,* October 17, 1982; and Patrick Buchanan, "Is NEA Politicizing Our Schoolchildren?" *Washington Times,* October 17, 1983, p. 2C. The NEA has had plenty of help in the preparation of "educational materials" for students and itself sponsors a group called Student-Teacher Organization to Prevent Nuclear War (S.T.O.P. Nuclear War). There is also Children's Creative Response to Conflict, located in New York City; the Consortium on Peace Research Education and Development, also in New York; Educators for Social Responsibility, an offshoot of Physicians for Social Responsibility located at the same address in Cambridge, Massachusetts; the Institute for World Order; Ground Zero; Jobs with Peace, another Boston-area group; Network to Educate for World Security; and the World Council for Curriculum and Instruction, located at Columbia University.

83. Anthony Lewis of the *New York Times* accepted the whole show at face

value. See his "The Neglected Question," *New York Times,* July 30, 1981. The Soviets also seized the climatology affair. See Tom Wicker, "A Grim Agreement," *New York Times,* December 12, 1983; and Leon Goure, "Soviet Scientists as Shills for a Freeze," *Washington Times,* December 19, 1983. See also Peter Kerr, "Physicians Urge End to Arms Race," *New York Times,* June 10, 1984.

84. See the IPPNW book by Eric Chivian, Susanna Chivian, Robert Jay Lifton, and John E. Mack, *Last Aid* (San Francisco: W. H. Freeman, 1982), and the PSR book edited by Jennifer Leaning and Langley Keyes, *The Counterfeit Ark: Crisis Relocation for Nuclear War* (Cambridge, Mass.: Ballinger, 1984).

85. Ruth Adams and Susan Cullen, *The Final Epidemic* (Chicago: Educational Foundation for Nuclear Science, 1981), pp. 1, 3. On Caldicott, see Tom Ricks, "Dr. Caldicott Goes to War," *Washington Journalism Review,* October 1982.

86. Morton Kondracke, "The Children Against Nukes," *Washington Times,* April 5, 1984, p. 2C. See also Charles Krauthammer, "Kids' Stuff," *The New Republic,* February 13, 1984, pp. 10-11; and Nisbet, *Prejudices,* pp. 3-4.

87. Among other audiovisual efforts are *The Atomic Cafe,* an Archives Project; *The Bomb Will Make the Rainbow Break,* by Zahm-Hurwitz Productions; *Eight Minutes to Midnight,* a hagiography in cinema about Helen Caldicott produced by Direct Cinema; *John, Mary, MIRV and MARV,* produced by the Institute for World Order; *The Last Slide Show,* produced by the Packard Manse Media Project; *War Without Winners,* produced by the Michigan International Council; *No Frames, No Boundaries,* a product of Creative Initiatives, and dozens more. Not all films on this topic *have* to be bad. See John Corry, "TV: 'Nova' Examines 40 Years' Nuclear Policy," *New York Times,* December 13, 1983.

88. Raymond Aron, *The Century of Total War* (Boston: Beacon Press, 1954), p. 67.

Chapter 2

THE FAR RIGHT

You might as well fall flat on your face as lean over too far backwards.

—James Thurber

Right-Viewing the World

In American politics the attitude of the Far Right toward the notion of a nuclear freeze has been unambiguously negative. The various groups of the Far Right see the freeze as unabashed unilateral disarmament either masterminded or actively exploited by the Soviet secret police—the KGB. The arrival of the freeze in the House of Representatives indicated to the groups of the Far Right that "Communist penetration" of the U.S. Congress was frighteningly well advanced. Indeed, the images and language of Senator Joseph McCarthy returned to Capitol Hill through the few representatives of the Far Right that have earned places of public responsibility from the electorate.

As with the Professional Left, the groups that make up the Far Right have been stereotyped into distortion—mainly by the media—and lumped together in such a way as to efface important distinctions among them. Some of these groups are religiously oriented, some are not. Some find their major source of support in the South, others do not. Many groups display views on domestic issues that are very conservative, some do not. Some groups, like the American Nazi party, the Minutemen, and the Ku Klux Klan, can barely hide racist and anti-Semitic inclinations; most others have no such inclinations. Despite such differences, the Far Right, like the Professional Left, does have a worldview that can be summarized without doing excessive violence to the truth.

Groups on the Far Right in American politics are *not* status quo conservatives, as is sometimes thought. They do not oppose what can only be described as radical social change; it is only the direction and nature of that change that is at issue. What confuses some casual observers is that rightist ideology in the United States

45

idealizes and mythologizes the past and so becomes identified with traditional virtues. But the Right wishes to return the nation not to some prior historical epoch but to a highly figurative, adumbrated view of what that past was like. While the Golden Age of the Left lies before us in the Enlightenment concept of ceaseless forward progress, the Golden Age of the Far Right lies behind us in a pristine paradise lost.[1]

In a sense, the radical critics of American society on the Right and the Left are engaged in the continuing great debate over modernity itself. Does the salvation of humankind lie in shedding the institutions of the past and forging new ones in accordance with the modern oracles of science and secularism? Or does it lie instead in perfecting the institutional structures of the past, partly by purifying them from the political pathologies of the twentieth century? Taking sides in this debate often turns on the direction of one's fears. Everyone acknowledges human frailties, and few observers of social and political life can ignore the barbarities into which we have fallen as a result of those frailties. But while those on the Left put their faith in the hope that the future cannot be worse than the past, those on the Right have no such confidence.

There is a fascinating similarity between the politics of the Marxist Left and the politics of the religious Right that often escapes attention because the *content* of an ideology usually garners more attention than its *structure*. Classical Marxist and Christian ideologies share their having raised their respective versions of utopia to a "natural" and inevitable last stage of human history. For Marxists, the culmination of the class struggle through the law of dialectical materialism will bring about an earthly paradise of peace, prosperity, and the withering away of the state. The evolution to communist society is ordained by the master science—Marxism—and according to this scientific oracle, the outcome is a logical necessity. Some major schools of Christian theology have also advanced a definite philosophy of history, a joining of the Jewish idea of the sanctity of history wrought by divine intervention and concern, with the Greek metaphysical emphasis on the teleology of nature itself.[2] This philosophy of history was articulated specifically and completely in Augustine's *City of God,* where he wrote that mankind had passed through five historical stages or epochs, all of them sequential and necessary, since

46

the Creation. The then-current sixth stage would pass into a glorious seventh, a period of peace, prosperity, and righteousness on earth, and from there into the eighth and final stage, that of eternity, perfection, and a full reconciliation of the God with his Creation. Thus, Augustine, like Marx more than a thousand years later, took Heaven out of the realm of hope and put it into the realm of historical necessity. Wielders of both ideologies have benefited from this construction. It is much easier to sacrifice, and to demand sacrifice, in the name of the inevitable than in the name of the desirable.

What is the idealized past to which the Far Right would restore us? It has three basic components—all intertwined, as any grand synoptic scheme must be: (1) a fusion of patriotic nationalism and religious faith; (2) a return to a laissez-faire market system, buttressed by an attitude toward social ills and personal adversity that can only be described—somewhat ironically—as Social Darwinism; (3) an equally Social Darwinist view of international politics, in which the only safeguard of American freedoms is U.S. military might and the fortitude to use it.

America: The New Jerusalem

Patriotism is an old-fashioned value that retains many practical and important uses. It is an agent of social cohesiveness, a description of a will to identify with others. It is, as well, an affirmation of social values that may be good in and of themselves, symbolized and brought into unity and harmony by the Nation or the State. Patriotism is not synonymous with national chauvinism, bellicosity toward other peoples, nor a blindness to the shortcomings of one's own society. But in practice the definition of chauvinism, bellicosity, and blindness is a many-splintered thing.

Rightists bemoan the lack of "true patriotism" in the United States and the labeling of true patriotism by the "ultraliberal" national media precisely as chauvinist, bellicose, and blind. Since the Vietnam War, in particular, the Far Right claims, patriotism has become a dirty word, perhaps irremediably so, to a whole generation of Americans. Reverence for national symbols, the flag, national hymns, and the institutions of government has been depicted as reactionary and generally outdated. The sense that expressing pride in one's nation should be reason for embarrassment, according to the Right, symbolizes the erosion of American values, unity, and national determination. The lack of patriotism, aided and abetted by the Professional Left, the Left-Liberal Establishment, and America's enemies abroad have uprooted trust in government and made governing the country more difficult. It has also made a strong and vigilant foreign policy difficult if not impossible, for with the degradation of patriotism came the disdain for all things military.

According to the Right, healthy values—patriotism, family, work—have been eroded by the decay of morality, abetted primarily by the false images and the atheistic philosophies of liberalism. Morality is defined as that designated by Protestant Christianity in its supposedly most pure, most traditional form. There is no question that identification of certain groups within Protestant Christianity with the politics of the Far Right has given the Right its special moralistic flavor, and this relationship goes back a long way.

Throughout American history, the belief that the birth and expansion of the United States was the will of God has been strong. It was America's "manifest destiny" to conquer the North American continent, bring the American Indian to Christianity, and defeat the Papist Spanish and French empires of the decayed Old World. Scores of evangelists predicted that the Second Coming of Christ would take place in America, the "New Jerusalem." Premillenarian groups predicted the Great Apocalypse in accordance with the pulse of American history, and many believed strongly that the United States was born to prepare the world for the messianic age. This required the ingathering of the Jews in Palestine, giving rise to a sort of Christian Zionism. In 1814, John McDonald, a Presbyterian minister in Albany, New York, wrote: "Jehovah . . . dispatched swift American messengers to the relief of his prodigal children. Rise, American ambassadors, and prepare to carry the tidings of joy and salvation to your Savior's kinsmen in disgrace!"[3] Some writers, like Hal Lindsey in *The Late Great Planet Earth,* continue this tradition today to the acclaim of millions of readers. Indeed, the entire raison d'être of the Mormon church—the most American of the American churches—rests on notions of the new promised land and the transfer of God's grace to America. The popularity in the nineteenth century of the myth that the North American Indian tribes were the ten lost tribes of Israel is testimony to how seriously people sought to live in the present and prepare for the future according to (their version of) biblical prophecy.[4]

It would be absurd to suggest that what engaged the imagination of nineteenth-century America still does so with equal force today. But it would be equally absurd to claim that such a historically well-rooted fusion of the American experience with Christian eschatology has lost all its power in contemporary American culture. It has not. The Moral Majority is one manifestation of this basic cosmology, and Jerry Falwell and his followers clearly fall into the category of the New Right, if not the Far Right. Falwell himself has put it directly: "The godless minority of treacherous individuals who have been permitted to formulate national policy must now realize they do not represent the majority. They must be made to see that moral Americans are a powerful group who will no longer permit them to destroy our country with their godless, liberal philosophies."[5]

Political Roots of the New Right

All this would matter very little if Christians such as these rendered unto Caesar what was Caesar's, staying aloof from the cares of the temporal world in anticipation of Heavenly salvation, but they have not. Sometimes rightist ideology has taken an anti-Catholic tilt, as the phenomenon of the Know-Nothing party of the 1850s attests. There is no question, too, that this basic religious cosmology first rationalized and then justified slavery in the United States *on religious grounds.* There were those in the Free Silver movement of the 1880s who believed that the government in Washington had been seized by "Jesuit thugs" who were siphoning off the wealth of the United States to finance their international plots. Around the turn of the century, partly as a backlash against Reconstruction and partly through the diffuse introduction of European political ideas into the United States, a significant stream of rightist politics adopted an avowedly racist attitude. The Ku Klux Klan (KKK), founded in its second incarnation in 1915, rose to national political prominence; at both the Democratic and Republican national conventions of 1924, the

KKK controlled or influenced more than 30 per cent of the electors on both sides.[6] In the controversy over U.S. emigration policy that erupted in the 1920s, many preachers and politicians blended varieties of Joseph Arthur de Gobineau's theories of racial purity into religiously garbed arguments against the "pollution of America's bloodline" with Jews, Slavs, southern Europeans, and Asians.[7] This nexus of racism, evangelical Christianity, and ultra-conservative populist politics was the source of anti-miscegenation laws in dozens of states. This same combination propelled politicians like Louisiana's Huey Long to national stature, and enabled the Reverend Charles Coughlin to bend a significant stream of American populism into an ultra-nationalist, proto-fascist movement in the mid-1930s buttressed by religious justification.[8]

The politics of the Far Right in American history has never been far detached from populism and can be said to have been one of its many currents throughout the years.[9] Both populism and the politics of the Far Right have been primarily rural phenomena, and as long as the nation remained predominantly agricultural, lacking a large urban middle class or an industrial proletariat, these social forces served as the backdrop for all national politics. But as the nation's economy and demography changed dramatically between the 1880s and the first two decades of the twentieth century, what had been a major force receded increasingly into an opposition role on the national, but not always the local, level. As a consequence, the politics of the Right, like populist politics in general, acquired a provincial image. Also as a consequence it has always harbored suspicion and antipathy toward the great corporations and wealthy industrialists whose energies overturned the balance of American politics and delivered the nation to the control of its cities. Contemporary rightists blame the large corporations and their cozy relations with big government for a parade of sins: distorting the laissez-faire, free market system with huge monopolistic concentrations of wealth; encouraging government subsidization of unworthy enterprises; encouraging federal "regulation" that further skews the workings of the market and bloats a self-serving public bureaucracy rivaling that of the corporations; promoting inflationary monetary policies that benefit big business and speculators but that hurt the little

50

guy; deceiving the people with high-powered, tax-deductible advertising and placing the burden of taxation on the little guy as a result; financing Soviet imperialism; and dozens of other lesser iniquities.[10]

To most people, large businesses seem to be in the forefront of defending the capitalist way of life in various ways, but here the critique of the Far Right merges with that of Libertarians and even anarchists in pointing out that "corporate capitalism" and "free-market capitalism" are in practice two different things. To the ideologues of the Far Right, corporate capitalism verges on being a planned economy. The fact that a few dozen major corporations and banks do the planning, aided and abetted by the Federal Reserve Board and the government, rather than the State itself, is of little practical consequence.

Here it is difficult to resist making an intriguing observation: the populist, antibig-business orientation of the Far Right, and the equally populist, antibig-anything orientation of the *anarchist* Left are often virtually indistinguishable. They both agree, for example, that the socialist or Marxist Left is wrongly unperturbed about the scale or nature of economic enterprise, caring only about who owns the mammoth means of production and how to divide the benefits. In this respect, anyway, both see more pernicious similarities between corporate capitalism and socialist statism than significant differences.

Another area of at least marginal agreement concerns welfare. Some on the Far Right believe in a version of Social Darwinism which postulates that poor people earn their poverty and deserve it. Some evangelical Christians believe that upsetting the social balance with welfare pollutes God's purpose on earth; others feel that a socially mandated, impersonal system of taking care of the poor and needy obviates tithing, which some fundamentalist Christians take very seriously. Besides, many members of the old Far Right believe that welfare disproportionately aids blacks and Hispanics, which to them is like rewarding indolence and encouraging it. The New Right, however, makes more practical arguments. Says Richard A. Viguerie:

In practice, welfare in America has served to create dependency among blacks. Worse yet, it has made many black women directly dependent on government, while making their men either economically useless or actually turning them into obstacles to acquiring welfare. Could there be a worse formula for the black family?

According to the New Right, liberal programs like welfare, affirmative action, busing, the minimum wage, and inflationary monetary policies are either counterproductive, immoral, or both. Viguerie predicts that blacks will come to support the New Right in the future for the following reasons:

- Because conservatives (not liberals) strongly disapprove of drugs and will fight to get them out of black schools and neighborhoods.
- Because conservatives (not liberals) are determined to put those who are terrorizing black neighborhoods with muggings, robbery, rape, and murder in jail for long terms.
- Because conservatives (not liberals) realize the danger of making welfare a way of life rather than just a safety net for the truly needy.
- Because conservatives (not liberals) understand that making black neighborhoods safe from crime and drugs will help bring back business and industry. And jobs.
- Because conservatives (not liberals) insist that our public schools must start teaching black children to read, write and add.
- Because conservatives (not liberals) realize the destructiveness of many well-meaning (liberal) economic and social policies.[11]

The anarchist critique parts company here in many respects, but it does believe that the only real kind of help is self-help and help that arises from within the community of peers. Paternalistic help from outside merely perpetuates the superior-inferior relationship and mentality that are the sources of the problem in the first place. If the economy were not distorted by the corporate system and the profit motive that stimulates it, there would be no unemployment and thus no need for welfare on that level. The anarchist critique holds that capital/labor ratios that maximize business profits necessarily create unemployment, and that capital/labor ratios that would best conserve the land and provide reasonable and healthy work for everyone would preclude profits. In the rightist critique, welfare violates natural law, is counterproductive and chafes at religious obligation. In the anarchist critique, welfare is merely a band-aid for a symptom that would disappear only with a social revolution that starts from the ground up.

Another area of common concern is that both the Far Right and the anarchist Left would like to reduce the scale of economic agglomeration in the United States, and for both, the ideal reality is an idyllic reality. Thus, the Far Right has occasionally found common ground with the anarchist Left in supporting the environmental movement of the 1970s, though for different reasons. Each in its own way abhors the erosion of reverence for the land, and each is a declared enemy of agribusiness. The anarchist Left sees in its ideal future an egalitarian society without racism, sexism, the need for police, or overarching governmental structures, and *with* "appropriate technologies," free-form communal living, and religious eclecticism.[12] But in its ideal vision, the Far Right sees the resuscitation of the traditional nuclear family, the return to Christ, church, the Constitution, "law and order," and, for a small minority, the return of racial segregation.[13] So there are big differences. Nevertheless, contrary to the dominant metaphor of a political spectrum that postulates a straight line stretching from Left to Right, it is more useful to think of a spectrum in the shape of a broad bending arc, where even hints of rounding the circle occasionally come into view.[14]

International Politics and the Right

When it comes to the third element in the rightist scheme of things, the irreplaceable need for military power, the Far Right stands alone in the spectrum of U.S. strategic theories. As the Far Right sees the world, the United States is the brightest beacon of hope and freedom for the world, and opposed to the United States irrevocably is the Communist world, led by the Soviet Union. The harshest, most Manichean Cold War imagery positing the monolithic character of the Communist world and Moscow's carefully constructed master plan for world domination is alive and well on the Far Right. On the Far Right it often passes as common knowledge that we "lost" China because of Communists in the State Department, that the Trilateral Commission is a leftist conspiracy, that Henry Kissinger was and remains a hireling of the Kremlin,[15] that the United Nations is a Communist front, and that all the mainstream media and half the Congress have been penetrated by the KGB.

The image of U.S.-Soviet relations as an unalterably zero-sum struggle to the finish sits very well with evangelical notions of the end-of-days. Work-symbols such as Armaggedon and Apocalypse have double religious-political meanings, the religious concepts serving as a template for organizing the international power struggle. Jerry Falwell is a contemporary case in point. In his newest book, *Nuclear War and the Second Coming of Christ,* Falwell plays down the significance of nuclear arms control. His argument, based on his interpretation of Scripture, is that the world will continue for at least another thousand years regardless of the acts of man and that therefore there is no reason to be alarmed about nuclear war or the arms race. It is all foreordained. Falwell has also claimed that Ronald Reagan is the equivalent of a biblical king of America, and he has told radio audiences that they must obey and support the powers-that-be "because they are ordained by God." In other words, anyone who opposes the administration is violating biblical injunctions.

On the other hand, some born-again Christians and fundamentalists are certain that a nuclear war *must* occur. In this and other cases, arcane arguments over the meaning of biblical prophecy have set some radio evangelists against each other. For example, some believe—as Reverend McDonald did—that the ingathering of the Jewish people in Israel (so they can all be converted together in due course) is a harbinger of the Second Coming and so are very pro-Israeli. But others still identify the Jew with the Antichrist and believe, as did the late King Faisal of Saudi Arabia, that either Zionism and Communism are in league with each other or that one is a front for the other. They therefore oppose Israel. Either way, many religiously oriented far rightists are sure that the apocalyptical battle of Gog and Magog will begin over the Middle East.

On balance, the Far Right is isolationist no less than the populism of the 1930s was isolationist. NATO is an entanglement the United States should avoid; the Japanese generally earn much harsher comment that that. The basic strategic wisdom is that the United States should limit its active defense to its hemisphere only. For this reason Latin America is the hottest foreign policy issue among right-wing congressmen today; however naive, many of their constituents are convinced that only geographically contiguous areas are important to U.S. security. This is what made the debate over the Panama Canal treaties what it was. Besides, U.S. allies in Europe are, for the Right, often indistinguishable from unreconstructed Leninists. It is difficult indeed for some on the right to distinguish between a Social Democrat and a Marxist-Leninist, just as it seems difficult for a radical leftist to see any differences between a Burkean conservative like Barry Goldwater and a "moral imperialist," as Goldwater once called him, like Jesse Helms.

Far Right, New Right

In the three main elements of rightist philosophy noted above, the New Right differs from the Far Right of old not at all. What *is* different is that the leaders of the New Right are young and vigorous, are skilled in modern communications techniques, and have come on the political scene at a time when the appeal of liberal political philosophies has diminished, fatigued by Vietnam, social ills that have defied solution, an economy out of control, and an aggressive Soviet foreign policy.

The leaders of today's New Right were stung, but not vanquished, by Barry Goldwater's decimation in 1964, and they have learned slowly but well the art of agenda- and coalition-binding. They have also learned the craft of raising large sums of money. And they have profited from and helped bring together a series of traditionalist single-issue social movements that have been catalyzed by opposition to the political initiatives, or failings, of the dominant establishment over the past dozen years.[16] In opposition to the radical swing of the women's movement, anti-Equal Rights Amendment, pro-family, and anti-abortion groups sprang up. In opposition to the banning of prayer in public school, and for other more deeply rooted social causes, American society has experienced in the last ten years another in a series of evangelical revivals which, each time they arise, leave their mark on national politics.[17] This is perhaps the single most important factor in the rise of the New Right. As Viguerie explained:

The New Right has also had its own ready-made network: the thousands

55

of conservative Christian ministers whose daily broadcasts on local and national radio and TV reach an audience of 27 million. Every week, approximately 20 million people view just three such ministers—Jerry Falwell, Pat Robertson, and James Robison.

Until now this whole culture has been a dark continent to the Northeast, coastal-based national media. But these ministers are attacking issues the national media hardly mention: issues like worldwide Communist aggression, school prayer, sex on TV, the failures of the public schools. The conservative ministers are in touch with the people, and now they are in touch with each other.[18]

In opposition to the antimilitary tone of the Vietnam War opposition, lobbies arose in favor of a strong, well-financed defense establishment. In opposition to gun-control initiatives, "right to bear arms" groups coalesced around the National Rifle Association. In response to the environmental and consumer movements of the 1970s, pro-free enterprise societies sprang up. In opposition to the tax bracket creep associated with inflation, the tax revolt movement emerged, first with California's famous Proposition Thirteen and later in other parts of the country.

Conservative politics have been on the rise for some time; even Richard Nixon attempted to tap its potential in 1968. Indeed, Patrick Buchanan, then a Nixon supporter, was not far wrong to speak of *A New Majority,* as his campaign book was titled. But it was the genius of the leaders of the New Right—Richard A. Viguerie, Paul Weyrich, Patrick Buchanan, Terry Dolan, Howard Phillips, Alan Gottlieb, Phyllis Schlafly—to produce a *unified* conservative platform embracing all these traditionalist causes and to articulate a new language for justifying their mutual relations. This is the essence of politics: from many, it makes one. Ideology is most effective when it is most synoptic.[19] Just as Hobbes's Leviathan metaphor captured and expressed the inchoate pieces of a new view of the world in the sixteenth century, so in a way is the New Right attack on "godless liberalism" a unifying metaphor. It links together those who favor unions, the right to abortion, entitlements, the Equal Rights Amendment, arms control, gun control, and the elimination of prayer in school as being of one mind. This is not true, of course, but there is great power to be derived from a polarized depiction of political reality.

56

What is the agenda of the New Right, and how is it woven together? Viguerie provides us with a list and a language of accusation against "the Left" that is hard to improve on for frankness:

- It's the Left that has re-introduced guild privileges based on compulsory unionism, government-imposed racial and sexual discrimination, and oppressive taxes.
- It's the Left that favors a society based on state regulation, supervision, and coercion.
- It's the Left that has defended and even promoted pornography and abortion. (The clock has stopped forever for eight million unborn American children.)
- It's the Left that focuses its compassion on the criminal rather than his victims.
- It's the Left that attacks our allies rather than our enemies.
- It's the Left that favors the nonproducers over the people who work.
- It's the Left that encourages American women to feel that they are failures if they want to be wives and mothers.
- It's the Left that tears apart families and neighbors by the forced busing of children.
- It's the Left that has failed to protest Communist slavery and religious persecution—evils afflicting 1.8 billion human beings.
- It's the Left that's fought to keep prayer out of the schools.
- It's the Left that allowed ruthless Communist takeovers in Vietnam, Laos, Cambodia, and Afghanistan.
- It's the Left that allowed the takeover of Iran, one of America's strongest allies, by a group of terrorists and extremists.
- It's the Left who crippled the CIA and FBI.
- It's the Left who sold the Russians computers and other sophisticated equipment used to oppress their people.[20]

Viguerie then proceeds to make some more general, connecting points:

Liberalism has pitted itself against the best instincts of the American people. . . . Put simply, most Americans no longer look up to liberals. They look down on them.

Liberals have long sensed this. They have tried to make their mistakes irreversible and election-proof. As far as possible, they have sought to turn the powers of government over to the courts and administrative agencies—that is, to unelected and unaccountable public officials.

They have found other ways to impose their will. One of the most

sophisticated has been deficit spending—producing an inflation that reduces blue-collar workers' real pay by pushing them into what used to
be executive tax brackets. By such means liberals have increased government's grip on our wealth without openly raising tax rates.

Somebody had to call a halt to this devious elitism. What used to be
liberalism has turned into socialism on the installment plan.[21]

Viguerie has not quite proffered a conspiracy theory here but
he is close to one. There are indeed times when the New Right's
portrayal of "liberalism" seems indistinguishable from Father
Coughlin's venomous portrayal of Franklin D. Roosevelt's New
Deal. But what he *has* done is to link moral or morally toned
issues together consistently and to hypostatize a singular enemy—
the Left, however defined—against which the New Right must
stand united: "The conservatism was always there. It took the
New Right to give it leadership, organization, and direction. The
key word is *leadership*. Conservatives have had no lack of brilliant
thinkers, brilliant writers, brilliant debaters, brilliant spokesmen.
But none of these is the same thing as a leader."[22] While there
may be some truth in this, it nevertheless effaces an important
distinction. Conservatism and the politics of the Far Right or New
Right in the United States are not synonymous. There has always
been a branch of conservative thought that was morally activist
and not hesitant to dictate communal morality through public
offices when it saw fit. But there is another kind of conservatism
too, more the heritage of Edmund Burke, that rises in revulsion
against such "moral imperialism." Conservatism arose against the
encroachments of the centralized, intrusive State in the second half
of the eighteenth century, and its descendants retain a strong suspicion of all centralized political authority. As time passed, this
tradition grew fond of big business as a counterweight to the State
and became used to the wealth of the elite. The New Right is not
the child of *this* conservative tradition, which is still strong within
the Republican party and well represented, too, within the Reagan
Administration.

These two expressions of conservatism agree about many
things, and this conjunction is the still fluid base of political support undergirding the Reagan Administration. As for the president's own deepest predilections, this remains a grand enigma.

The New Right "claimed" Ronald Reagan in 1980 and expected an administration devoted unflaggingly to its causes. The enemies within—Nixon, Ford, Kissinger, and Rockefeller—had been vanquished. Before long, however, the appointments and policies of the Reagan Administration were cause for great consternation in the New Right; its relative "moderates," like William Rusher, spent much time and ink in *Human Events* trying to convince zealots not to undermine President Reagan lest they bring down the entire movement. Jesse Helms, the "conscience of the New Right," as Viguerie has called him, quipped in mid-1981 that the Right had won the 1980 elections in a big way, "but not yet the White House." The point is that just as the New Right's somewhat mythologized "Left" is in fact not a unity, neither is conservatism in the United States. And just as the Professional Left gave birth to the freeze but could not hold it, so the New Right propelled Ronald Reagan into the White House but could not hold him either.

It is not a foregone conclusion that the main institutions of the New Right—Falwell's Moral Majority, Gregg Hilton's Conservative Victory Fund, Lee Edwards's and Viguerie's *Conservative Digest,* Reed Larson's National Right to Work Committee, Judie Brown's American Life Lobby, Phyllis Schlafly's Stop ERA, Rhonda Stahlman's Conservatives Against Liberal Legislation, Paul Weyrich's Committee for the Survival of a Free Congress, and dozens of other organizations and publications—will all support Ronald Regan's re-election with any real enthusiasm. But whether they do or do not support Reagan in 1984, their influence will persist because the fight for Reagan's legacy has already begun—even before the 1984 election—and the support of the organizations and networks of the New Right remains critical to any would-be king.[23] The New Right is no more a passing fad in American politics than the rise of liberalism in the first half of the twentieth century was a fad. Moreover, it has strong views on military and foreign policy.

Rightist Ideologues, the Strategic Balance, and the Freeze

Those on the Far Right tend toward a Fortress America attitude on national security: isolationism buttressed by unassailable military might. But since the reigning logic of nuclear deterrence posits the indefensibility of the country to nuclear attack, *the Far Right, like the Professional Left, rejects the notion of deterrence as it is most commonly understood.* In other words, the notion that *parity* between the United States and the Soviet Union in nuclear systems is a satisfactory or desirable condition is rejected in favor of other attitudes.

One of these attitudes is that while *parity* may not be stabilizing in the nuclear age, nuclear *superiority* is the next best solution, even if not a perfect or eternal one. Another attitude is that since defense is impossible, war inevitable, and surrender or appeasement unthinkable, survival can be guaranteed only by massive civil defense measures supplemented by survival training of as large a percentage of the population as is feasible.[24] A third, newer point of view is one that denies the impossibility of defense. Buttressed by Daniel Graham's impassioned espousals of the High Frontier—a full-speed-ahead national effort to build an impermeable shield of endo- and exo-atmospheric ballistic missile defense—some members of the Far Right are convinced that total defense is now possible and might lead as well to a renewed U.S. superiority through technological dynamism.[25] For many, space is the new frontier and U.S. military policy in that new high ground should be dictated by a concern for military supremacy, not arms control possibilities.[26] Some people find a way to combine harmoniously the desire for superiority, survival training, and ballistic missile defense.

Beyond their rejection of the desirability and stability of strategic equity, all these attitudes rest on a particular view of the Soviet Union. That view posits that no stable *modus vivendi* with the Soviet Union is possible and that all policies purporting otherwise—like détente—play into the Kremlin's hands. Some believe that the implacable character of Soviet imperialism flows from the Russian character and Russian history. Others believe that the engine within the Soviet juggernaut is Marxist-Leninist ideology and nothing less. Still others see a malign mixture. But it hardly matters whether ideology is the drive chain or merely the lubricating oil—the result is the same. On the Far Left such an image of the Soviet Union is ridiculed as naive and simpleminded. But the dominant leftist image of the Soviet Union as "protector" of progressive change throughout the Third World is hardly less so.[27] A third image—that of the Left-Liberal Establishment, to which we turn in Chapter 3—is that of the Soviet Union as a geriatrically directed status quo power whose revolutionary veneer is simply that—a veneer. This is the image that the Far Right believes it needs to fight the hardest, for it is thought to be the most popular. Clearly, a status quo power concerned for its own security sphere, but not seeking world domination or the overthrow of the U.S. government, can be dealt with; arms control agreements with such a power can be to mutual benefit. But a power whose imperial appetite has no limit is an unsuitable partner for serious arms control and engages in arms control talks only to lull the opposition to sleep and to destroy U.S. alliances with other free nations.

One expression of this view which pays some rhetorical homage to détente and negotiations warns that hope for what a nuclear freeze could achieve is based on

an old Western conceit—the belief that most other people in the world, if treated as though they were like us, in turn will behave like us. . . . No less than six détentes have been engineered between the United States and the Soviet Union based on that kind of optimism. All have come to an end, only to spring up afresh at some later date. Meanwhile, Soviet hegemony over various regions of the globe has expanded dramatically, and so has Soviet repression.[28]

Others do not even bother to throw a bone at "détente" and "arms control." For example, John Lofton of the *Washington Times* wrote that the "Soviets walking out of arms talks with the United States is a cause for rejoicing. These talks have been a dangerous farce, a damaging charade."[29] Lofton spent a few paragraphs asserting that the Soviet Union has violated every arms control agreement it ever signed and concluded with a Socratic flair: "Will the Russians come back to the arms control talks? My answer: I hope not because the agreements we sign with them are not worth the paper they are printed on."[30]

The foolishness of trusting the Soviet Union to keep its word and the ease with which the United States has let the Soviets violate past treaties are popular themes in the New Right press.[31] For example, the New Right, like freeze advocates, opposes the build-down concept, but for different reasons. The Right insists that the build-down is a Magna Carta for Soviet cheating. Whereas in the past Moscow had to "do something" and say nothing to cheat, the build-down would allow Moscow to do nothing and say something to cheat.[32] The perfidy of "leftist organizations" of various kinds is also a popular topic. In 1982 and 1983, the most frequent pilloried of these organizations have included the Institute for Policy Studies, the National Education Association, the Catholic bishops and their pastoral letter, and the World Council of Churches.[33]

But by far the most popular theme of all is the role of Soviet "active measures" in manipulating the "peace movement" and the McCarthyite game of trying to link each and every major pro-freeze supporter with the World Peace Council, the KGB, and the Politburo—in that order.[34] This is an on-going project. It is common knowledge to readers of *Human Events* and *Conservative Digest* that Lee Harvey Oswald was directed by the Soviet and Cuban regimes, that Martin Luther King, Jr. had Communist affiliations, and that one of Jesse Jackson's aides is a former (and perhaps present) member of the Communist party USA. The New Right press has also sought to prove that the leaders of the Black Caucus—Jackson's "Rainbow Coalition" supporters—acted treasonously with respect to Grenada. Congressmen Ronald Dellums and John Conyers have been most directly accused.

Concern with Soviet "active measures" is not limited to the Right. The State Department is concerned, too, and some of the Right's charges have a basis in reality.[35] Within the Right there is a wide array of approaches to the problem. The more careful, moderate groups do not accuse Moscow of masterminding the freeze through the World Peace Council (WPC), only of trying, with mixed success, to exploit it.[36] Others, however, led by a man named John Rees, believe that the whole movement, from its inception, was a KGB plot. Rees has published a periodical called *Information Digest* since 1968 and is the Washington correspondent for the newspaper of the John Birch Society, *The Review of the News*. Through Rees's associate, the late Congressman Larry McDonald, Reed Irvine's *Accuracy in Media (AIM) Report,* and Senator Jeremiah Denton's hearings in his Subcommittee on Security and Terrorism of the Senate Judiciary Committee, Rees's views have been widely disseminated on the Right, and he has even been praised in more mainstream conservative publications like *National Review*.[37] Rees's views are described well by freeze defender Frank Donner: "The Rees line is simple. A political voyeur, he eyes his victims through subversion-colored spyglasses, working on the fixed assumption that peace activists are *prima facie* Communists whose Soviet parentage he then proceeds to establish through intricate and frequently invented lines of consanguinity."[38]

The structure of Rees's logic of guilt by association works by a primacy-of-contamination rule. In other words, since the WPC is involved in the freeze, and the War Register's League and Mobilization for Survival are in contact with the WPC, and since Mobilization for Survival has ties down the line to SANE and the Council for a Livable World, which in turn has relations with the Institute for Policy Studies, which in turn is consulted by some Democratic congressmen, who in turn support the AFL-CIO on some issues, then *all* these groups must be part of a KGB disinformation campaign.[39] Instead of assuming that KGB influence is diluted as it passes downward, Rees assumes that it Sovietizes everything it touches, even indirectly. Even the FBI report on the freeze was selectively interpreted by Rees to fit his own theories and arguments.[40] Rees himself has written: "Our point is that the Soviet Union is running the current worldwide disarmament campaign through the KGB and front organizations led by the World Peace Council. Leaders of the U.S. disarmament groups are up to their necks in this effort."[41]

Rees's "information" about the freeze and the Soviets has popped up in dozens of New Right publications and forums, much of it based on a pilfered, supposedly secret internal memorandum on the freeze to Stewart Mott, a prime financier of the freeze movement from the beginning, from his aide Anne Zill. Rees claimed that the memo was top secret; the freeze movement's defenders say it was not and had been widely circulated in the movement.[42] This is almost amusing. The conspiratorial mentality of the Rees school of freeze-fighting is such that they believe it to be inconceivable that the Left would not try to keep such a treasonous document secret. The naiveté of the freeze Left, on the other hand, is so advanced that they see nothing wrong or unusual about consorting with groups known to be KGB-penetrated or directed fronts if it serves the "cause of peace." In a classical sense, then, Rees and Donner suffer from a failure to communicate; they see the same events, but they relate them to mutually exclusive paradigms of meaning.

Using innuendo and a dubious logic of intergroup causality, and altogether blind to the heterogeneity of the freeze movement, the Rees school of freeze-fighting actually detracts from the efforts of more mainstream critics of the freeze. Rees and his associates serve as a convenient foil for the Left, allowing them to typify all those who oppose the freeze as "paladins of unlimited weaponry" who are "committed to the modern secular religion of a long, twilight struggle with the Soviet Union."[43] Using Rees as his example, Donner claims that "the anti-freeze campaign relies in large part on the use of fear, the most efficient weapon in the American political arsenal."[44] The truth is that the freeze movement itself is no stranger to the use of fear for political purposes; nor are leftist politics less like a secular religion than the politics of the Right. But the activities of Rees and his associates allow the Professional Left to make assertions like these and have them appear much more plausible to those who oppose the freeze than would otherwise be the case.

On the issue of the freeze, the *intellectual* rebuttal of the New Right, as opposed to the guilt-by-association argument, has been weak. The freeze is guilty by association because it is a product of the Left. It is a paragon of deceit, a shield for a hidden radical agenda, and obviously not a serious proposition. Attempts at logical rebuttal in the New Right press—those that do not gainsay the verifiability of *any* arms control agreement with Moscow— are written very generally and couched in moral euphemisms that bear no resemblance to analysis.[45] There are only a few exceptions—the publications and monographs of the few New Right organizations specifically dedicated to military analyses. It is to these analyses that we now turn.

Chimeras of Nuclear Superiority and Unilateralism

The most cogent intellectual arguments made against the freeze on the New Right are no more cogent than arguments made on behalf of a freeze by the Professional Left. Many of the individuals associated with these groups are retired military officers, often from traditionally conservative regions of the nation.[46] Some of the groups have been around for a while and were very active during the 1979 SALT debate. These include John M. Fisher's American Security Council and its umbrella group, the Coalition for Peace Through Strength, and the Institute of American Relations.[47] Newer, smaller, and even less restrained groups include the Committee to Prevent Nuclear War, the Washington Legal Foundation, and others.

Most of the staff members of these organizations would agree with Viguerie that "the basic problem is that most liberals refuse to believe that communists are really working to conquer the world."[48] Most would also agree with Viguerie's summary of major conservative proposals on foreign policy and national defense:

- Regain strategic military superiority without delay.
- Stop any technology, capital investments, or loans which could advance, directly or indirectly, the war-making power of the Soviet Union.
- Expose and condemn Soviet violations of international agreements and laws.
- Develop the conventional military power necessary to respond to the various kinds of Soviet-supported aggression.
- Use diplomatic devices like recalling our ambassador and severing diplomatic relations when the Soviets use force against their satellites or other nations as they did to Czechoslovakia in 1968 and Afghanistan in 1979.
- Free America from arms control restraints which perpetuate U.S. military inferiority and force us to fight the Third World War by Soviet rules.[49]

What unites all these groups is the basic image of the Soviet Union (or, interchangeably, International Communism) as an implacable, devious, and ruthless adversary with whom no stable *modus vivendi* that is both permanent and just is possible. Their positions on the nuclear freeze, though sometimes different in emphasis and rhetorical temperament, are also united around three basic propositions:

(1) Since the Soviet Union seeks world domination and sees military superiority as a major means to this end, it is not logical

to suppose that the Soviet Union would ever accept or adhere to any arms control agreement with the United States that is fair and equitable; therefore, arms control agreements between the Soviet Union and the United States which could serve minimum U.S. interests are impossible, and this includes *any* version of a nuclear freeze.

(2) The Soviet government, it must be admitted, has a more sensible view of strategic nuclear weapons than does the U.S. government, for it knows that outright superiority is the only real means of deterring an enemy. The Soviet Union today enjoys military superiority; we must engage in a national effort to draw even, and then gain back military superiority in as large a measure as possible, including the use of space defenses. A freeze runs in the opposite direction to such a enterprise.

(3) To attain military superiority and ensure the safety of the United States, the United States must disengage from commitments—especially nuclear ones—that increase its risk of being dragged into war and that dissipate its defense effort. A freeze may hurt NATO's theater nuclear prospects, or it may not, but this is irrelevant. If Europe and Japan wish to defend themselves against the Soviet Union, let them develop their own independent nuclear deterrents. If they do not, and succumb, the United States can survive and prosper just the same.

The main institutional advocate of this point of view is John M. Fisher's American Security Council (although the ASC's anti-NATO inclinations are not strong). Gilbert S. Stubbs wrote a pamphlet for the American Security Council in 1982 entitled *How Realistic Is the Nuclear Freeze Proposal?* which sheds much light on the New Right's attitude.[50]

As to the first proposition, Stubbs was careful not to rule out arms control altogether. But the conditions he demands for them to proceed are politically impossible. Stubbs asks that twelve conditions be met, and considers these a rightful "challenge" to the Soviet Union "to demonstrate its professed dedication to disarmament."[51] Some of the conditions are:

(1) Remove all Soviet obstacles to national technical verifi-

cation of arms agreements, including camouflage, concealment, deception, and other means currently employed by the Soviets;

(2) Agree to the principle of unimpeded on-site verification of all aspects of arms development, testing, production, and deployment that cannot be verified by national technical means.

(3) Investigate all disputed Soviet violations of existing arms agreements, using whatever means necessary, including the exchange of data and the physical inspection of test facilities, military hardware, and geographical areas involved in the alleged violations.

(4) In cases where an established violation, a still-disputed violation, or an agreement ambiguity has resulted in a military advantage, make such adjustments as are necessary to nullify that advantage.

(5) Create the procedural means and physical facilities for continual monitoring and inspection operations that are required to guarantee that past violations or suspected violations do not occur in the future.

(6) Agree to U.S.-Soviet equality in total, aggregate throw-weight of ground-launched and submarine-launched ballistic missiles.

(10) Agree to the inclusion in strategic arms agreements of all weapons systems which are capable of being used in a strategic role or capable of being modified without detection to achieve a strategic capability.

(11) Agree to continual, unrestricted on-site inspection of Cuba, where short-range ballistic and cruise missiles could be launched from concealment in strategic first-strike attacks against the United States (with an accompanying agreement of the United States and its allies to similar inspection of areas bordering the Soviet Union).[52]

Stubbs knows that the Soviet Union will not agree to all, or any, of these conditions, thus "proving" their "disinterest" in arms reduction.[53] Such a rejection demonstrates the "utter hopelessness" of seeking fair, meaningful agreements with the Soviet Union.

As to the second proposition, Stubbs said: "The Soviets have already achieved the first strike capability that nuclear freeze advocates say their project would prevent!"[54] Worse, a freeze, "far from producing any semblance of world security . . . would only destroy all hopes for peace by granting a permanent position of military superiority to an aggressor power that presumes to have both the moral justification and 'sacred' duty to extend its domination to all free nations."[55]

As to the third element of the New Right trinity—an unabashed preference for military-strategic unilateralism—the American Security Council demurs. It still supports NATO, though this more mainstream position may erode in the future. The American Security Council has also been active fighting the freeze in other ways. In response to the new cinema of the Professional Left and the freeze movement—films like *If You Love This Planet* and *The Final Epidemic*[56]—the ASC has answered with *Countdown for America.* Moreover, to provide a counter-resolution to freeze ballot resolutions, the ASC has devised a "Model Peace Through Strength Resolution for State Legislatures, County Commissions, Town Councils, and Organizations." (See Appendix B for text.)

The American Security Council is not alone. Laurence W. Beilenson has written the most coherent argument for the Far Right position in a book entitled *Security and Peace in the Nuclear Age.*[57] Along with Samuel T. Cohen, father of the neutron bomb, Beilenson has argued that "nuclear war is extremely likely" unless we have the strongest nuclear "deterrent that money can buy and brains can supply."[58] The argument is put starkly: "Either we restore our nuclear armed might so as to deter nuclear war, or we keep playing catch-up in conventional arms with no hope of reaching parity."[59] Beilenson goes on to argue, with Daniel O. Graham and Edward Teller, for civil defense and space defense.[60] As to NATO, he said:

If the Alliance is to continue there should be four strong nuclear arsenals facing the Soviet Union: France, England, Germany, and the United States. We should make the deterrent far more credible and if those nations won't, *the remedy is to come home.* Until they pull their fair share of the load, we are going to be faced with an impossible situation, where we spend so much defending *their* lives that somehow we don't have the money to protect *our* own.[61]

Proceeding to turn what is commonly taken to be curse into a blessing, Beilenson writes: "To prevent nuclear war, we should bring our forces back home." He explains:

This will be called isolationism by some. What is wrong with isolationism? We did very well with it in the past. . . . Our far-flung military presence is a complete aberration in our history.

History does not support the theory that deploying troops all over the world prevents war. On the contrary, the Roman Empire fought every year of its existence. During the so-called Pax Britannica, England fought on some continent every year. In our case, the wars are likely to become much more serious. The American people do not want to fight wars all over the world and it is wrong to assume a strategy that forces us to do just that.[62]

Birds of Different Feathers Sometimes Flock Together

Here again we see a curious convergence of political views, for the isolationism, or better, the "unilateralism" of the New Right overlaps to a limited degree both with the Far Left and with the Libertarian party and its sponsor, the Cato Institute. The Left is isolationist because it believes that a prominent U.S. role "as world policeman" is not only dangerous[63] but also likely to stifle "progressive" social change in the Third World. Libertarians, on the other hand, are isolationist for reasons not unlike those voiced above by Beilenson. Beilenson's comments on NATO could be those of Earl Ravenal, the Libertarian Party voice on foreign policy and diplomacy and nearly its 1984 presidential candidate, and could have appeared in the Libertarian journal *Inquiry*. (Ravenal is also a fellow of the Institute for Policy Studies!) Many Libertarians favor space-based, High Frontier types of defense, for example, seeing such a development as a way to break free of U.S. entanglements abroad.[64] New Rightists and Libertarians also dislike big business and, in different ways, pay homage to the free market and laissez-faire economics. For this reason alone, Libertarian party politics tend to get a fairer shake in *Human Events* than Democratic party politics.

But there are major differences too. While the New Right is

isolationist, it is not pacifist or passive; it reserves the right to intervene forcibly and decisively wherever it chooses to do so. It is pro-military. But the isolationism of the Libertarians is anti-interventionist, antimilitary and pro-freeze. That is why *Inquiry* can feature articles in the same issue that are *very* conservative when it comes to domestic affairs, along with anti-Pentagon tracts by Institute for Policy Studies staffer Michael Klare and *Village Voice* mainstays Alexander Cockburn and Nat Hentoff.[65] *Inquiry* and *Human Events* can join their voices in shrill complaint that the Reagan Administration has not done enough to reduce the burden of big government on the American people. *Inquiry* and *Human Events* both also berate the president over U.S. national security policy, the latter for not being tough enough on the Russians, the former for allowing the Pentagon to bring the world willy-nilly to the brink of nuclear destruction! With such odd political centaurs buzzing about, it is a wonder that political disputation is ever as orderly as it sometimes seems.

NOTES

1. For a discussion of the political importance of the idea of progress, see J. B. Bury, *Idea of Progress* (New York: Dover, 1932).

2. See Robert Nisbet, *Prejudices: A Philosophical Dictionary* (Cambridge, Mass.: Harvard University Press, 1982), pp. 44-45.

3. This quotation comes from David S. Landes's review, "Old Zion, New Zion," *The New Republic*, December 31, 1983, p. 27. See also Perry Miller, "From the Covenant to the Revival," in *The Shaping of American Religion* (Princeton: Princeton University Press, 1961), pp. 322-68.

4. See Lynn Glaser, *Indians or Jews?* (Gilroy, Calif.: Roy V. Boswell, 1973).

5. Jerry Falwell's introduction to Richard A. Viguerie, *The New Right: We're Ready to Lead* (Falls Church, Va.: Viguerie, 1981), p. v. By the way, Falwell looks like a moderate compared to certain others. John R. Harrell's Christian Conservative Churches of America (CCCA), centered in Flora, Illinois, is a case in point. Harrell's CCCA also sponsors the Christian-Patriots Defense

League, the Citizens Emergency Defense System, the Save America Gun Club, the Women's Survival Corps, and the Paul Revere Club.

6. For a discussion of the Klan in the 1920s, see Preston William Slosson, *The Great Crusade and After, 1914-1928* (New York: Macmillan, 1930), pp. 304-16.

7. For a brief synopsis of Gobineau's views, see the article on Joseph Arthur de Gobineau in *International Encyclopedia of the Social Sciences,* ed., David L. Sills (New York: Macmillan and The Free Press, 1968), vol. 6, pp. 193-94. On the immigration laws controversy, see Lothrop Stoddard, *The Rising Tide of Color* (New York: 1920) for a then-contemporary view, as well as R. DeC. Ward, "Our New Immigration Policy," *Foreign Affairs,* vol. 3, 1928, p. 104. See also Oscar Handlin, *Race and Nationality in American Life* (Garden City, N.Y.: Anchor Press/Doubleday, 1957), chaps. 1, 2, 4, and 5.

8. Huey Long has been immortalized by Robert Penn Warren in his novel *All the King's Men* (New York: Random House, 1950). For Coughlin's views, for example, see the *New York Times,* August 3, 1936, quoted in Charles J. Tull, *Father Coughlin and the New Deal* (Syracuse, N.Y.: Syracuse University Press, 1965). Of course, America's "progressive" politics have not been devoid of religious inspiration. See William Lee Miller, "The Seminarian Strain," *The New Republic,* July 9, 1984, pp. 18-19.

9. This notion was advanced by Victor Ferkiss, among others. See his "Populist Influence on American Fascism," *Western Political Quarterly,* June 1957, pp. 350-57.

10. For a serious right-leaning critique of corporate America, see Antony C. Sutton, *Wall Street and the Bolshevik Revolution* (New Rochelle, N.Y.: Arlington House, 1974). It is worth noting Sutton's dedication, which puts him in that curious limbo between Right and Left: "To those unknown Russian libertarians, also known as Greens, who in 1919 fought both the Reds and the Whites in their attempt to gain a free and voluntary Russia." See also Viguerie, *The New Right,* pp. 107-8, where he says, "Not only is big business often heedless of moral principles, it is often willing to contribute to the Soviet war machine's threat to America and the free world, selling the Soviets the means to destroy us."

11. Viguerie, *The New Right,* pp. 165, 168.

12. For a sophisticated "new world" critique of agribusiness, see Wendell Berry, *The Unsettling of America: Culture and Agriculture* (San Francisco: Sierra, 1977); and Hazel Henderson's *Creating Alternative Futures: The End of Economics* (New York: Berkley, 1978).

13. See John A. Stormer, *The Death of a Nation* (Florissant, Miss.: Liberty Bell Press, 1968), and his *None Dare Call It Treason* (Florissant, Miss.: Liberty Bell Press, 1964).

14. The career of one man, Karl Hess, illustrates something of the logical connections between the Right and the anarchist Left. Hess worked as a speechwriter and aide to Senator Barry Goldwater back in the 1960s but ended up an admirer and colleague of Murray Bookchin, one of the best-known anarchist publicists in the United States.

15. Kissinger is attacked regularly by M. Stanton Evans in *Human Events* and by many in *Conservative Digest.*

16. This phenomenon has been analyzed by Burton Pines, *Back to Basics: The Traditionalist Movement That Is Sweeping Grass-Roots America* (New York: William Morrow, 1982); and Kevin P. Phillips, *Post-Conservative America: People, Politics, and Ideology in a Time of Crisis* (New York: Random House, 1982). See also James L. Sundquist, "Whither the American Party System?—Revisited," *Political Science Quarterly,* Winter 1983-84, pp. 573-93.

17. See William Lee Miller, *Piety Along the Potomac* (Boston: Houghton Mifflin Co., 1964).

18. Viguerie, *The New Right,* p. 6.

19. See Michael Walzer, "On the Role of Symbolism in Political Thought," *Political Science Quarterly,* June 1967; and Clifford Geertz, "Ideology as a Cultural System," in his *The Interpretation of Cultures* (New York: Basic Books, 1973).

20. Viguerie, *The New Right,* pp. 4-5.

21. Ibid., pp. 5-6.

22. Ibid., p. 6.

23. See Sidney Blumenthal, "Let Lehrman Be Reagan," *The New Republic,* December 5, 1983, pp. 15-19.

24. See Robert C. Smith, *How to Survive a Nuclear Disaster* (New York: Zebra Books, 1982).

25. See Robert Poole, Jr., "Countering the MADmen," *Reason,* June 1983, p. 6; Daniel O. Graham, *High Frontier: A New National Strategy* (Washington: Heritage Foundation, 1982); M. Stanton Evans, "Reagan's Welcome Move Away from 'Madness'," *Human Events,* April 23, 1983, p. 7; and William Rusher, "The Liberals' MAD Nuclear Strategy," *Washington Times,* De-

cember 21, 1983. Also pushing this line is the cultish organization of Lyndon LaRouche, Jr. See Fusion Energy Foundation, *Beam Defense: An Alternative to Nuclear Destruction* (Fallbrook, Calif.: Aero Publishers, 1983). On La-Rouche, see Peter Spiro, "Paranoid Politics," *The New Republic*, February 6, 1984, pp. 10-12; and Peter Kerr, "CBS Sells Time to Fringe Candidate for Talk," *New York Times*, January 22, 1984. LaRouche's current ideology contains strong elements of the Far Right and residual elements of the Far Left. Mainly, however, it is just far out.

26. The best-known proponent of this view is Colin S. Gray. See his "U.S. Military Space Policy," in Adam M. Garfinkle, ed., *Global Perspectives on Arms Control* (New York: Praeger, 1984), pp. 133-44.

27. See the examples cited in Arch Puddington and Marco Carynnyk, "Soviet Apologists Then and Now," *Commentary*, November 1983, pp. 25-31.

28. Gerald L. Steibel, "Preface," in Joyce E. Larson and William C. Bodie, *The Intelligent Layperson's Guide to the Nuclear Freeze and Peace Debate* (New York: National Strategy Information Center, 1983), p. 5. See also Albert L. Weeks and William C. Bodie, *War and Peace: Soviet Russia Speaks* (New York: National Strategy Information Center, 1983).

29. John Lofton, "Work Is One Thing and Reality Another," *Washington Times*, December 19, 1983, p. 3.

30. Ibid.

31. See ibid.; M. Stanton Evans, "U.S. Cuts Back—While Moscow Builds," *Human Events*, March 26, 1983, p. 7; and Stephen Roberts, "Will a Nuclear Freeze Be 'Failsafe'?" *Washington Inquirer*, July 22, 1983, p. 6.

32. M. Stanton Evans, "Magna Carta for Soviet Cheating," *Human Events*, October 19, 1983, p. 7.

33. Some titles in *Human Events* in 1983 included "National Council of Churches: Advocate for the World's Militant Left," "Pastoral Letter: Blueprint for Unilateral Disarmament," "The IPS and the Media: Unholy Alliance," "NEA's 'Choices': Pacifist Propaganda for Pupils," and "NEA Head Libels U.S., Ignores Soviet Arms Buildup."

34. There are literally hundreds of examples, the least hysterical of which include John Barron, *KGB Today: The Hidden Hand* (New York: Reader's Digest Press, 1983), chap. 6; John Barron, "The KGB's Magical War for Peace," *Reader's Digest*, October 1982; and Count Hans Huyn, "The Soviet 'Peace' Offensive," *The Heritage Lectures*, no. 17, 1982. Arnaud de Borchgrave has also become popular in conservative circles since his novel *The Spike* made

news. De Borchgrave is a former *Time* correspondent. Martin Cruz Smith, author of *Gorky Park,* is not as well known on the Right, but he has suffered the wrath of his liberal friends for depicting the KGB and Soviet society as they really are. See the feature on Smith by Julia M. Klein, "Will 'Gorky Park' Spoil Its Author?" *Pennsylvania Gazette,* October 1981.

35. See Department of State, "Soviet Active Measures: An Update," July 1981. See also the analysis by Nils H. Wessell, "Arms Control and 'Active Measures'," *Orbis,* Spring 1983, pp. 5-11.

36. In addition to the articles in note 33, above, see M. Stanton Evans, "Moscow's Phony 'Peace' Campaign," *Human Events,* December 31, 1983, p. 7; "How Soviet 'Active Measures' Influence," *Human Events,* March 19, 1973; and "How the Far Left Is Manipulating the U.S. Nuclear Freeze Movement," *Human Events,* April 17, 1982, pp. 1, 8.

37. See "The New Nuke Hysteria," *AIM Report,* May 1, 1982; and Thomas B. Smith, "Soviet Involvement in the Freeze," *Washington Report,* June 1983, pp. 1-7. *Washington Report* is published by the American Security Council, located in Boston, Virginia.

38. Frank Donner, "But Will They Come? The Campaign to Smear the Nuclear Freeze Movement," *The Nation,* November 6, 1982, p. 460.

39. According to Rees's associate Julia Ferguson, anyone who "met with KGB and other Soviet agents in Minneapolis during May 24-29, 1983" could wittingly or unwittingly be part of the KGB campaign. Ferguson listed the entire U.S. delegation, which included Donald McHenry, Harland Cleveland, Patricia Derian, George Rathjens, Paul Warnke, and others who can hardly be accused of such agentry.

40. See Smith, "Soviet Involvement," pp. 1-2; and Les Maitland, "F.B.I. Rules Out Russian Control of Freeze Drive," *New York Times,* March 26, 1983.

41. Rees, quoted in Donner, "But Will They Come?" p. 460, see also John Rees, "Freezers Meet with Soviets to Make Plans," *Review of the News,* June 15, 1983, pp. 31-33.

42. Donner, "But Will They Come?" p. 460, says that 150 people had seen the Zill memo before Rees got wind of it.

43. Ibid., p. 457. The same point is made by James Nuechterlein, "The Republican Future," *Commentary,* January 1983, p. 19.

44. Donner, "But Will They Come?" p. 457.

45. Phyllis Schlafly is guilty of superficiality in writing about the freeze. See her "A True-False Quiz About Freezenik Claims," *Human Events,* September 17, 1983, p. 20; and her "Six Fatal Fallacies of the Nuclear Freeze," *Human Events,* June 25, 1983, p. 17. See also Greg Fossedal's quiz-like "Fifteen Questions for Your Nuclear-Freeze Friends," *Reader's Digest,* May 1983, pp. 31-32, much of which is a logical non sequitur.

46. For some data on the regional stratification of the U.S. officer corps, see R. A. Gabriel and P. L. Savage, *Crisis in Command: Management in the Army* (New York: Hill and Wang, 1978). Even those retired officers who do not belong to organizations per se have overwhelmingly opposed the freeze, as shown by the various periodicals of the retired military associations, such as *Officer Review* and *Air Force Review.* For two examples, see Robert F. Clark, "The Great Disarmament Hoax," *Officer Review,* March 1982, pp. 3-6; and Thomas Moorer, "Assessing the Odds: Nuclear War with the Soviet Union or Regional Conflict," *Wings of Gold,* Winter 1983, pp. 6-7.

47. See, for example, *SALT I Reconsidered* (Washington: Institute of American Relations, 1979). The Institute of American Relations also publishes a news-letter called *West Watch.*

48. Viguerie, *The New Right,* p. 111.

49. Ibid., p. 119.

50. *How Realistic Is the Nuclear Freeze Proposal?* was written by Gilbert S. Stubbs, a staff member of the Charles Stark Draper Laboratories in Cambridge, Massachusetts, and carries a copyright date of 1982. Draper Laboratories was at the center of an unsuccessful attempt by pro-freeze groups in Cambridge to have the town declared a "nuclear free zone." See "Antinuclear Measure Is Aimed at Missile Designer," *New York Times,* October 9, 1983.

51. Stubbs, *How Realistic Is the Nuclear Freeze Proposal?* p. 25.

52. Ibid., pp. 25-27.

53. Ibid., p. 23.

54. Ibid., p. 7.

55. Ibid., p. 21.

56. The former is the brainchild of Helen Caldicott herself. For some fascinating commentary on the popularity of this film, see Richard Grenier, "The Politicized Oscar," *Commentary,* June 1983, pp. 70-74. The latter is the product

of Caldicott's Physicians for Social Responsibility. There is a book by the same title, edited by Ruth Adams and Susan Cullen (Chicago: Educational Foundation for Nuclear Science, 1981). See also "U.S. Orders Disclaimers on Three Canadian Films," *New York Times,* February 25, 1983.

57. Published by Regnery-Gateway, Chicago, 1980.

58. Laurence W. Beilenson, "A Different Perspective," *Defense Science 2000+* May/June 1982, pp. 13-14.

59. Laurence W. Beilenson and Samuel T. Cohen, "A New Nuclear Strategy," *New York Times Magazine,* January 24, 1979, pp. 34, 38-39.

60. See Edward Teller, "Reagan's Courage," *New York Times,* March 30, 1983; and "Civil Defense Is Crucial," *New York Times,* January 3, 1984. For a variety of views on civil defense, see the eight articles in *Society,* September/October 1983, pp. 7-29.

61. Emphasis in the original. Beilenson, "A Different Perspective," pp. 69-70.

62. Ibid., pp. 68-70. See here also the isolationist, anti-NATO views of Roger Speed, a Hoover Institution analyst, in *Strategic Deterrence in the 1980s* (Stanford, Calif.: Hoover Institution, 1983). This book features a foreword by Edward Teller.

63. Gene LaRocque's Center for Defense Information (CDI) seems to fit squarely into this category. The CDI was very much opposed, for example, to the U.S. Marine presence in Lebanon for fear it would drag the United States into war with the Soviet Union.

64. See Robert W. Poole, Jr., ed., *Defending a Free Society: A Reason Foundation Book* (Lexington, Mass.: D. C. Heath and Co., 1984). See also Daniel O. Graham and Gregory A. Fossedal, *A Defense That Defends: Blocking Nuclear Attack* (Old Greenwich, Conn.: Devin-Adair, 1983).

65. See the June 1983 issue in particular. See also Ravenal's articles, "Counterforce and Alliance: The Ultimate Connection," *International Security,* Spring 1982; "Doing Nothing," *Foreign Policy,* Summer 1980; and "Toward Nuclear Stability," *The Atlantic Monthly,* September 1977.

Chapter 3

THE LEFT-LIBERAL ESTABLISHMENT

People believe all they can, and would believe everything if only they could.

—William James

Help from Unexpected Quarters

In one sense, the Professional Left was too successful for its own good with the nuclear freeze movement. A confluence of factors led to the broadening and moderating of the freeze movement and, as a consequence, divested the Professional Left of its early proprietary interest in it.

One factor necessary to the broadening of the movement was the intrinsic appeal of any effort that can present itself in an uncomplicated manner as being against nuclear war. The simplicity of the freeze has been its greatest advantage within the political arena;[1] nobody in their right mind can really be *for* nuclear war. So, to the extent that the freeze movement could make it seem that opposition to nuclear war and support for a freeze are two ways of saying the same thing, the potential constituency for the freeze was virtually unlimited. (The logo on the stationery of the Nuclear Freeze Campaign reads: "The Freeze: Because Nobody Wants A Nuclear War.") Even so, the American Friends Service Committee (AFSC), the Fellowship of Reconciliation (FOR), and the other early promoters of the freeze were themselves surprised at how rapidly the notion spread.

Given the intrinsic appeal of simple propositions like the freeze, it did not take a sophisticated communications network to spread it. But the national AFSC network *is* fairly sophisticated, and its members are well placed in other kinds of organizations to effect a rapid horizontal diffusion in support of the freeze. From the yearly meeting in Philadelphia and the AFSC headquarters there, pro-freeze activity was directed to AFSC chapters and meetings across the country. In turn, members of these meetings were often active in local politics, professional societies, chambers of commerce, environmental groups, outing clubs, clean air councils, and the like, and thus propagated the freeze horizontally through them. From these new branches, awareness of the freeze passed to local politicians, the media, schoolteachers, universities, other religious institutions, and so on. The freeze developed rapidly into a true grassroots movement, in large part through the pre-existing organizational infrastructure of the AFSC and the abutting strata of "associational group" ties.

Beyond the intrinsic appeal of the proposition and the organizational infrastructure that stood ready to promote it, another factor played heavily in the quick expansion of the freeze movement: the contribution of the Reagan Administration. This contribution was of three parts, the first unavoidable, the other two needlessly self-inflicted wounds.

The new administration was committed unalterably to a sizable increase in U.S. defense spending across the board, including the modernization of each leg of the strategic triad. The strategic modernization program flew directly in the face of a nuclear freeze, but there was no avoiding the conflict. The Reagan Administration believed that the Soviet advantage in prompt counterforce capabilities, residing in Moscow's huge and numerous land-based forces, constituted a "window of vulnerability" that had to be closed. But it was not only the Reagan Administration that favored an increase in defense spending and strategic modernization. The Carter Administration, which had presided over modest increases in the defense budget in fiscal years 1978 and 1979, had planned even larger increases in the aftermath of the Iranian revolution and the Soviet invasion of Afghanistan.[2] Moreover, public opinion at the start of 1981 firmly supported the view that the United States needed to take action to redress a perceived drift toward general Soviet military advantage.[3] While there was broad support for increased defense efforts, there was also broad support for arms control. The administration could have bolstered the former urge by actively molding the debate over the latter one, but it failed to do so.

The Reagan Administration did itself unnecessary damage in two ways. First, it never properly explained to the American people how its programs for strategic modernization, its arms control aspirations for "deep cuts" in nuclear weapons, and its negative attitude toward the SALT II treaty all fit together in a strategy for maintaining the peace. Instead of launching an effort at public education, the administration's public diplomacy on these matters was allowed to evolve ad hoc, guided by questions and errant answers at press conferences and bureaucratic cross-talking about protracted nuclear war strategies and the like.[4] In-decision, delay, and incoherence marked the administration's per-formance in some areas, even those initially designated as being of extreme importance—such as the basing of the MX missile. In short, while the administration was asking for record increases in the defense budget, it seemed ill-prepared to handle strategic doctrinal issues, arms control matters, or even to decide on how to close those windows of vulnerability over which it had ago-nized during the campaign. Public support for increased defense preparedness eroded steadily as the state of the economy deteri-orated, and as confidence in the administration's approach to na-tional security issues plummeted amid alarming talk of "limited nuclear war" and "nuclear warning shots across the bow."[5]

The second self-inflicted wound was that, on the specific issue of arms control proposals, the administration seemed to feel no sense of urgency whatsoever.[6] The protracted delay in coming up with proposals of any sort gave the Soviet Union a series of propaganda victories in Europe. This in turn prompted the West German government of Helmut Schmidt to urge on the Reagan Administration the quick resumption of arms talks, lest a delay make it more difficult for Bonn to deflect antinuclear sentiment directed against deployment of cruise and Pershing II missiles there. Moreover, the delay also gave those at home who thought the worst of Reagan and his associates the chance to pursuade others to assume the worst as well.[7] One reason for the delay was argument in the bureaucracy. One school, centered in the De-partment of Defense, held that arms control should await the rebuilding of U.S. military strength. Otherwise, the United States would come to the table without sufficient negotiating assets to fashion an agreement in the U.S. interest, but be forced to trade concessions just the same. The result would be another agreement like SALT II, which was sham arms control and would not serve U.S. interests.[8] Another school, centered in the Department of

State, argued that the United States should prepare bargaining proposals in part to protect the president's political position and strategic programs at home and in Europe, and in part hoping that the Soviets might see an economic incentive for bargaining in good faith. Throughout most of 1981, the Defense Department's view held sway.

There is nothing unusual or even detrimental about bureaucratic contention; on the contrary, it can be and usually is a healthy advocacy process. But what was injurious was that the mixed signals and irresolution were allowed to persist so openly and for so long. It is the job of the president to intervene in such squabbles, settle them, and give direction, and it is the job of the White House staff to ensure that the president finds out quickly about which issues are percolating his way. At least for the first eighteen months of the Reagan Administration, if not beyond, neither the president nor his staff deserved high marks in this regard.

As the Reagan Administration lost credibility on defense and national security issues, the nuclear freeze emerged into a broader spectrum of American political life—it was the simplest alternative to a policy that seemed to combine an unquenchable thirst for defense dollars, a proclivity to fight rather than deter a nuclear war, a decided antipathy toward arms control, and a bellicosity toward the Soviet Union unrivaled in recent memory. It was not necessary to be a member of the War Resister's League, the American Friends Service Committee, or SANE to be concerned about these developments. It was not obvious to the average citizen that there might be a big difference between the image that the administration was trying to project in Moscow through the diplomatic tactic of talking tough, and the operational policy of government. When public concern searched for a vehicle of expression, there stood the nuclear freeze proposal in its naked simplicity and ostensible even-temper.

Together, the simplicity of the freeze concept, the pre-existing organizational network that stood ready to spread it, and the woeful public diplomacy of the Reagan Administration galvanized anti-administration movements on many levels. On the grassroots level, freeze organizers made great headway; by the fall of 1981, there were perhaps as many 45,000 local organizers spread across the nation, outnumbering by far the professional activists of the AFSC, the FOR, the WRL, SANE, the Women's International League for Peace and Freedom (WILPF), and so forth. Organizational links between freeze support groups and religious, ethnic rights, environmental, and antinuclear power groups were forged rapidly. By early 1982 the freeze had arrived as a national movement consisting of nearly 1,400 peace-oriented groups—local, regional, and national—of various sorts.[9]

Despite its success at the grassroots level, the freeze drew relatively little national media attention, partly because, as one journalist suggested, Randall Forsberg, Randall Kehler, and the rest deliberately kept a low profile, preferring to keep the movement growing at the local level rather than expose the freeze idea to serious policy-relevant examination.[10] How did a freeze tie in to SALT II ratification and SALT III? How could the production of nuclear weapons, as opposed to deployment and testing, really be verified? If a freeze took years rather than weeks to negotiate, would it still be worth doing, or would it be counterproductive? If, after an effort to get Soviet agreement, the freeze failed as a bilateral proposition, should the United States freeze unilaterally? Did a freeze apply to the numbers of launchers, as had SALT, or the number of warheads? Would modernization and replacement be permissible as long as agreed numerical ceilings were not violated? After a freeze, what would happen next, and how? Forsberg and Kehler may have feared that if these specifics of the still ambiguous and simple freeze were debated openly and seriously, so many contentious and difficult issues would arise that there would be no hope of keeping together the ungainly coalition of organizing "freeze" institutions. They considered organizational unity on the Left more important than discussions of the freeze's practical application, at least at this stage. The movement would grow, the cash contributions would flow, and the administration would be forced to go public with arms control epistles before it was ready and before it wished to do so.[11]

The Freeze Meets the Establishment

It was not only the nuclear freeze movement that used the Reagan Administration's policies and images as a springboard. So too did more mainstream critics who had supported SALT II, especially those who opposed the drift toward abandoning a pure mutual assured destruction targeting posture, a development whose origins went back at least as far as James Schlesinger's tenure as secretary of defense in 1974.[12] Perhaps the best-known competition for the freeze was the educational organization Ground Zero, founded by former National Security Council staffer Roger Molander.[13] Together with his twin brother, Earl, Roger Molander raised over $285,000 in less than eighteen months during 1980 and 1981.[14] Molander also published the first in a series of easy-to-read, glibly written paperbacks about the nuclear danger, entitled *Nuclear War, What's in it for You?*[15] Within a month, the book had sold over a quarter of a million copies.[16] While Molander opposed the Reagan Administration on nearly every issue, he nevertheless opposed a freeze as well. He simply could not see how a freeze could lead to negotiated reductions, and he did not share the view of freeze advocates that all new weapons deployments had to be worse than present ones in their impact on deterrence, the arms race, and crisis stability. Molander believed that serious arms control was dependent mainly on the degree of comity in U.S.-Soviet relations, so he urged a broadly political route to arms control.[17]

George Kennan, too, made news by proposing sweeping, 50 per cent reductions across the board in all superpower arsenals.[18] The reaction to Kennan's proposal by strategic theorists and experts was interesting and ironic. Most judged that the proposed cuts were too deep, too radical, and non-negotiable, because the Soviets would not go along.[19] These same criticisms were made of the Reagan Administration's proposal for deep cuts when it was first broached in May 1982, though Kennan and Reagan saw eye to eye on little else. Some liberal critics, like Leon Sigal, pronounced both plans destabilizing and opted instead for a "selective freeze."[20]

The most popular initial response within the Left-Liberal Establishment and others further toward the center to both the Reagan Administration's policies and the challenge posed by the freeze movement was to find a middle ground by rallying around the negotiated but unratified SALT II Treaty. From the *The New Republic* to the editorial boards of the *New York Times* and the *Washington Post,* to the mainstream of Democratic congressmen and senators, this was the preferred option.[21] Even within think tanks and institutions not identified with "hawks" or even Republicans—the Arms Control Association, the Carnegie Endowment for International Peace, the Brookings Institution, the Council on Foreign Relations—the freeze was at first something of an embarrassment. Since the Democrats, soundly beaten across the board in the 1980 elections, were still groping for a party platform in opposition, and since SALT II was one thing that nearly all of them had agreed on back in 1979, it seemed the obvious choice. Persuasive pleas to reopen discussion and debate on SALT II and downplay the freeze were heard from Congressman Les Aspin, Senators Daniel Patrick Moynihan and Gary Hart, and from academics at Harvard, Columbia, MIT, and elsewhere.[22]

The argument was simple: While the freeze would (maybe) halt further weapons deployment at best, ratification of SALT would actually require the Soviets, according to the terms of the treaty, to dismantle over 100 existing systems. Besides, SALT had the benefits of comprehensiveness, prestige, the support of America's NATO allies, and a legal fullness and coherence totally absent from the freeze proposal. Turning the freeze from a vague declaration into a detailed negotiating proposal, and then actually negotiating it, might take months or even years. Why waste time on a freeze, therefore, when something better was already in waiting?

The problem with this argument, as far as some liberal politicians were concerned, was that SALT II was too complicated and too old an issue and therefore possessed only a limited capacity to motivate and mobilize voters against the Reagan Administration. On the other hand, the potential of the freeze in this regard was growing fast and seemed limitless. Besides, this suggestion would never get off the ground because the Reagan Administration had already come to terms with SALT II—albeit in a decidedly curious way, as most liberals saw it. It was clear that while the administration had announced as early as March 1981 that it would observe the terms of the treaty as if it were an executive agreement as long as the Soviets did the same, it did not favor Senate ratification.[23] As a formal instrument, it was the administration's firm view that, in Secretary of State Alexander M. Haig's words, "SALT II was dead."[24]

Advocates of the freeze from further left had other kinds of criticism of the SALT II revival campaign. First, SALT II was traditional arms control, conceived and negotiated by governments. This rendered it hopelessly compromised and irremediably flawed. The point of the freeze movement for its primary architects was that it was an anti-establishment cause and instrument; its ultimate aim was not arms control to perpetuate deterrence, but disarmament to transform political relations and security concerns among the powers. An unvarnished version of similar emotions was voiced by a California freeze supporter: "The real problem is that our governments have gone insane worldwide and the people are the only ones who have the sense that they're crazy. The governments don't think so. And so somehow or another we have to find a way to get through to the governments to say, 'We know what's going on, and what's going on is that you're crazy.' "[25] Such a point of view naturally considers conventional government-to-government methods of arms control, like SALT II, to be only slightly less menacing than the weapons they are supposed to control.

More radical freeze advocates were appalled by suggestions and speculations that the net effect of the freeze movement would be to put a liberal Democrat in the White House in 1984. Nick Seidita, a founding organizer of the California freeze campaign (from the Sepulveda Unitarian-Universalist Society in Los Angeles), told a journalist that: "What we have emphasized from the very beginning of the campaign is that this movement is not the creature of any political party. We invite all political parties to support it. But we are not going to be captive—the history of peace initiatives that have been taken over by the Democratic Party is that they have been co-opted."[26] Instead, Seidita and the other organizers envisioned the freeze campaign evolving into a broad-based and broadly ambitious political movement for economic and social change *outside* the formal structures of authority. Pressure on the politicians would come from the ground up; no deals would be made. And indeed, by January 1982 more than two dozen city councils, 300 towns, and six state legislatures in New England had passed freeze resolutions, and it was a ballot issue-to-be in at least five other states. Scores of churches and environmental and professional groups had voted pro-freeze resolutions, and by early 1982 it appeared that the freeze movement was pushing the calculations of politicians, and not the other way around.

The freeze movement grew so large and so wealthy so fast that changes in operation became inevitable. So too did disagreements over tactics, style, and personalities. The coalition of organizers and promoters, which by now centered around the AFSC, the FOR, Clergy and Laity Concerned, SANE, Pax Christi, WILPF, the Riverside Church Disarmament Program, Mobilization for Survival, and the Council for a Livable World, decided after a March 1981 meeting in Washington to set up a center and information clearinghouse.[27] It opened in St. Louis in January 1982. Randall Kehler was named national coordinator; operations opened with a paid staff of four.[28] A budget of $180,000 was projected, but with the sudden boost in popularity the freeze received in early March from Senators Edward Kennedy and Mark Hatfield, Kehler thought that an additional $100,000 might be raised. The clearinghouse used the direct mail solicitation method, but also received sizable seed amounts from a member of the Rockefeller family ($15,000), the Unitarian Church ($25,000), and Stewart Mott Enterprises ($3,000). Since then, the freeze clearinghouse and most other pro-freeze groups and their supporting casts of academics have benefitted from very generous foundation support. The C.S. Fund, one of many foundations run by the heirs of the late Charles Stewart Mott, has given over a quarter of a million dollars. Cleveland's Gund Foundation has given $200,000 a year for the past three years to freeze-oriented groups. The Carnegie Corporation announced in early 1984 its program to give away over $5 million to fund a variety of projects—mainly in the academic world—aimed at "preventing nuclear holocaust," and the Ford Foundation has awarded $33 million for similar purposes to pro-freeze and centrist antifreeze groups. Finally, the McArthur Foundation has given personal grants to both Randall Forsberg and H. Brian Hehir, the moving force behind the pastoral letter.[29]

As the freeze movement gradually acquired a broader base and more money, some of the original organizers of the Professional Left began to despair at being taken over by slick media types and the ideologically impure. The California campaign offered an illuminating example in this regard, and the mass demonstrations in New York in June 1982 were an even more vivid indicator of this head-on collision. What both these events illustrated, as well, was that as of early 1982 the freeze movement was a very mixed assortment of motives, interests, and power. On the organizational top sat the ideologues of the Professional Left. But mass support for the freeze, and the overwhelming bulk of new financial supporters of these organizations, did not share the views of their self-announced leaders and were largely unaware of them.

In September 1981, the California freeze campaign was joined by Harold Willens, a former anti-Vietnam War activist but also a millionaire businessman with ample media connections. In less than a year, Willens became state chairman of the campaign; Seidita failed even to retain a seat on the six-member executive committee. "Everybody bowed and scraped their foreheads on the floor when Harold Willens came into the campaign," said Seidita. "He's name, and he's money and he's connections. . . . Now that's important in the campaign. We can't do without it. But this campaign cannot succeed if it turns into a media debate between the haves and the have-nots. They'll beat our ass every time and I've told him that to his face. . . . The beginning of this campaign was an authentic, grassroots beginning. If it doesn't stay that way, it doesn't have a future."[30]

Seidita was wrong. The campaign did become a media-oriented business and it succeeded anyway. Willens hired media consultant Bill Zimmerman and direct-mail experts Craver, Mathews, Smith, and Company and raised "a gold-mine virtually unparalleled in the history of modern political fundraising."[31] This enabled the campaign to pay petition gatherers, among other things.

Political Interiors: The New York Rally
Preparations for the massive rally and demonstration in New York City on June 12, 1982 also had an interesting and fractious history. Original preparations for the rally, designed to coincide with the United Nations Second Special Session on Disarmament, were undertaken by various groups of the Professional Left and at first were entrusted to Benjamin Spock's umbrella group, Mobilization for Survival. There were also smaller, even more rad-

ical, organizations based in New York City that wanted—and got—a piece of the action. Together these groups went under the title of the Third World and Progressive People's Coalition, but the driving force was the Reverend Herbert Daughtry's Black United Front, a Brooklyn-based organization known for its rabid, overt anti-Semitism, among other things.

It was from the start a loose and uncomfortable coalition. Those without personal experience with leftist politics might assume that coalitions like the freeze coalition, made up of over a dozen separate groups, are capable of relative stability and unified action. But the farther toward the extreme left—or the extreme right—one goes along the political spectrum, the more fractured political relations tend to become. Fine points of Marxist theory that seem trivial to the uninitiated can be the cause of great upheaval in the politics of the Left. Tactical issues can rarely be discussed solely with reference to pragmatic criteria but must continually be linked back to some ideological base of *a priori* truth. Sören Kierkegaard was perspicacious indeed when he observed: "The most terrible fight is not when there is one opinion against another. The most terrible fight is when two men say the same thing—and fight about the interpretation."

The sudden upsurge of the freeze's popularity between January and April 1982 was so large that Mobilization for Survival and the local radicals could no longer handle the chore. Besides, Forsberg and Kehler believed that the rally was an excellent opportunity to broaden further the political base of the freeze, and other less radical, more liberal organizers were eventually brought on board. In March and April, as final plans were being made, a serious dispute broke out over how many speakers there would be at the rally and, more important, who those speakers would be. The more radical organizers of the Professional Left and their "Third-World-Within" New York City allies, as they sometimes called themselves, were determined to make the rally the biggest anti-establishment sensation since the heyday of the anti-Vietnam War movement. In particular, the most radical Left wanted the rally to call for *unilateral* nuclear disarmament by the United States, an end to U.S. military "aggression" in the Third World and Central America, and an end to racism in the United States.[32] They also insisted that the speakers include Daughtry himself, and others, like Ruben Zamora, a spokesman for the antigovernment guerrillas in El Salvador, who would not speak on nuclear issues per se. Their view was that "the political level of the disarmament movement must be raised and that Third World people must be involved in the leadership process." They feared, too, "attempts of the most conservative leadership, usually backed by huge sums of foundation money, to limit the political slogans to the most basic, to refuse to link one issue to another and, in the most treacherous fashion, to make the movement 'safe' for politicians to come and lead it."[33]

The more moderate latecomers desired a much less radical flavor to the whole affair. Indeed, as they came on board, they tried to displace the Black United Front and its allies from the official June 12 rally committee. The infighting became vicious, and doubt was thrown on just who constituted the committee. At one point it seemed that two separate organizations sponsoring two separate rallies might occur. The relative moderates, as a Greenpeace representative put it, wanted the crowd to "consist of as broad a cross-section of the American public as possible. To achieve this result, the rally must appear favorable to the new mainstream constituencies and this should be reflected in the sponsorship of the rally."[34] Mark Roberts, Greenpeace's National Freeze Campaign director, added: "A significant issue was trying to attract middle America. I think it's fair to say that if anything significant is going to happen on disarmament, this rally can't be too far Left." Roberts added, to the unabashed horror of the Third Worlders, that he would like to see even "right-wing and conservative groups involved."[35] This cast groups like Mobilization for Survival in the unlikely role of mediating between the ultra-Left and the merely Left.

It turned out that the more radical groups had taken special care to have in their own possession the parade permit, and the holder of this permit was legally bound to inform the City of New York about the particulars of the program. The radicals bulldozed through a list of speakers weighted in their favor, presenting the majority with a fait accompli. Quipped one dispossessed moderate: "Leave it to Lefty." Thus it was that Daughtry, Zamora, McReynolds, and others addressed the rally.

The crowd was confused too. A twenty-year-old college student told reporters at the rally: "I never thought I'd be at something like this. Demonstrations are usually a political issue—pro-Communist, pro-socialist. But this is pro-existence."[36] But a Quaker organizer from New Jersey was of a different opinion. "What we're really working for," she said to a roving journalist, "is a total transformation of the power structure."[37]

The point here is that what made the June 12 rally international news, and what passed the freeze in California, was the genuine, emotional, and not-too-specific support for the freeze in its simplest formulation, not the ideological churnings of the Professional Left, the grassrooters, or their troublesome Third Worlder allies. The question was: how long could the Professional Left hold on to a movement that had clearly exceeded first its expectations and now its control?

This raised another important issue: how to solidify and make permanent the power of the movement, and ensure that it was not just a fad that would pass as had other "ban the bomb" crazes before it. And here the self-assumed deacons and veteran politicos of the disarmament business were the most acutely critical of those latecomers who seemed to care more about symbolic petition drives, moral purity, and the size of occasional rally crowds than they did about sustaining the "movement." Alexander Cockburn and James Ridgeway, who together with Nat Hentoff comprise the literary-intellectual triumvirate of the *The Village Voice*, were not hesitant to attack their de facto freeze allies. They wrote:

Millenarian fear-mongering has become the idiom of the hour. Scarcely a Sunday newspaper supplement from Boston to San Francisco is without its little map of concentric bomb-impact and destruction zones stretching from ground zero downtown to the outer suburbs and beyond. Prophets of the apocalypse, such as Jonathan Schell with his interminable vaporings in *The New Yorker,* command vast audiences. Dr. Helen Caldicott's hysterical and demobilizing preachments—liberalism's answer to the hellfire sermons of the Moral Majority—are everywhere to be heard.[38]

Cockburn and Ridgeway counseled that the other "middle-class movements" of the past twenty years, the antiwar movement of the 1960s, and the environmental movement of the 1970s failed to reach their full potential because they did not "confront" or "change the economic and political underpinnings of the evils they were combatting."[39] Beware, they warned, the predatory politicians, "Schell's diffuse moralizing, and Caldicott's apoco-porn."[40]

In Mixed Company

The New York rally coup of the Professional Left in June 1982 seems to have been its final major victory. After the rally, the freeze's center of political gravity continued to move rapidly toward the center. Nick Seidita's conviction that the freeze would not be made captive and co-opted by the Democratic party turned out to be as misplaced as his predictions of doom in California. For while the majority of liberal congressmen—both Democrats and Republicans—at first eschewed support for the freeze proposal and backed a SALT II revival, some very important politicians did embrace and try to seize the freeze. The most significant turning point in the political evolution of the freeze came on March 10, 1982. On that day Edward M. Kennedy and Mark Hatfield introduced a resolution in the United States Senate calling for a bilateral nuclear freeze on testing, production, and deployment of all nuclear weapons, and subsequent reductions in nuclear arsenals thereafter. (See Appendix C for text.) A similar resolution was introduced simultaneously in the House of Representatives by Congressman Edward J. Markey (Dem., Massachusetts). With this, the freeze movement was well on the way to being lost to its originators. By the time a "freeze" resolution eventually passed the House in May 1983, it had been amended profusely, diffused programmatically, and interpreted widely. While the freeze had not quite become all things to all people, it did become many things to many people.

The support given the freeze by Senators Kennedy and Hatfield, and its quick endorsement by another twenty senators and over 120 congressmen, brought the freeze a respectability it had heretofore lacked. Before the Kennedy-Hatfield endorsement, the freeze had managed to attract the active support of a relatively small number of opinionmakers and former government officials. Among them were Philip Morrison, who had worked on the Manhattan Project; George Rathjens, an MIT physics professor who had served President Dwight D. Eisenhower as chief scientist in the Defense Department; and Jeremy Stone, director of the Federation of American Scientists (FAS).[41] But after the Kennedy-Hatfield episode, big names flocked to the freeze banner in droves, bringing their various organizations along with them.

By June 1982, individuals who supported the freeze included all of the following. There were religious leaders and organizations: Bishop James Armstrong, president of the National Council of Churches, and the National Council of Churches itself; Bishop James Crumley, president of the Lutheran Church of America; Theodore Hesburgh, president of Notre Dame; the Reverend Billy Graham; Archbishop Iakonos of the Greek Orthodox Diocese of North and South America; Eugene Pickett, president of the Unitarian Universalist Association; Archbishop Roberto Sanchez of Sante Fe; Rabbi Walter Wurtzberger, president of the Synagogue Council of America; the Fourteenth World Methodist Council; the Rabbinical Assembly; the Union of American Hebrew Congregations; the United Presbyterian Church, U.S.A.; and many more. There were women: Ruth Correll, mayor of Boulder, Colorado; Coretta Scott King; Eleanor Smeal, past president of the National Organization for Women; Mary Crisp, former co-chair of the Republican National Committee; and Gail Slocum Jones, executive vice president of the California Republican League.

There were blacks: Joseph Lowry, president of the Southern Christian Leadership Conference; and Andrew Young, mayor of Atlanta, as well as Mrs. King. There were scientists and Nobel laureates: Herbert C. Brown, Karl Menninger, Linus Pauling, George Wald, Jonas Salk, Carl Sagan, and others. There were academics: John Kenneth Galbraith, Jerome Weisner, Adam Yarmolinsky, Bernard Feld, Owen Chamberlain, and more. There were celebrities: Paul Newman, Meryl Streep, Celeste Holm, Stevie Wonder, Leonard Bernstein, and even the president's daughter Patti. There were environmentalists and their organizations: Russell Peterson of the National Audubon Society, Environmental Action, the Wilderness Society, Friends of the Earth, Greenpeace, and others. There were miscellaneous groups such as the National Council of La Raza; the Sisters of the Blessed Sacrament; the National Education Association; the National

Conference of Black Mayors; the Gray Panthers; and even the YWCA of the United States and a few isolated American Legion chapters.

Most impressive, however, were the former political and governmental notables that flocked to the freeze banner. These included George Ball, Hodding Carter, Warren Christopher, Clark Clifford, William Colby, William Fulbright, Averell Harriman, George Kennan, Townsend Hoopes, Henry Cabot Lodge, Donald McHenry, Gaylord Nelson, Paul Warnke, Thomas Watson, and other less well-known figures in large numbers. Supporters of the freeze pointed to this host of former senators, State and Defense Department officials, CIA figures, and ambassadors—two of whom had been posted in Moscow—as evidence that the freeze was not flaky but supported by "serious" people and "experts." Before long, the freeze was a household word, heard as often on the six o'clock news as in the meeting halls of the Professional Left.

The support for the freeze by big names who had formerly worked in government buoyed the movement and enhanced its respectability and saleability. But there was another kind of support given the freeze by former government employees of a different sort. When the Reagan Administration took office, one of the first things it did was clear out of the Arms Control and Disarmament Agency those whom it considered beyond the pale of realism on arms control issues. The Left-Liberal Establishment publicized these dismissals, charging that the Reagan Administration was trying to stack the bureaucracy along partisan political lines. The administration replied that it was only undoing such a partisan stacking undertaken by the Carter Administration, as was its prerogative. Whatever the truth, and regardless of who threw the first punch, the result was that dozens of liberal-minded arms control advocates who knew the government and who understood to some degree the technical issues involved suddenly became unemployed. More often than not, these were people who had fed at the public trough for decades either in government itself or as part of the orbiting bodies of think tanks and for-profit research organizations that depended heavily on government contracts. Not only were they out of a job, but their former organizations outside government were not recipients of federal contracts to the extent that they once were. Thus, many of them were naturally attracted by offers to "go into opposition" tendered by the organizations of the Left-Liberal Establishment. They formed a loose community of pro-freeze advocates, providing briefings and language for mass mail solicitors and their solicitations. They occasionally surfaced publicly as authors of ubiquitous op-ed pieces in the *Washington Post,* the *New York Times,* the *Christian Science Monitor,* and other like-minded publications.[42]

The Left-Liberal Establishment is no less organized than the Professional Left, only it is organized for less ideologically extreme, generally more pragmatic purposes. Like the organizations of the Professional Left, those of the Left-Liberal Establishment vary considerably and sometimes contend vigorously among themselves. Like the Professional Left, too, the organizations of the Left-Liberal Establishment publish an array of magazines, pamphlets, and newsletters, including *Arms Control Today, Breaking Point,* the *Bulletin of the Atomic Scientists, Defense Monitor, Disarmament Times,* and others.

Because of the ideological stratification and divisions in both "categories"—Professional Left and Left-Liberal Establishment—defining where one ends and another begins is an artificial exercise inherently open to dispute. One way to divide one group from the other, however, at least for the purpose of this narrative, is according to the strategic theory that guides the interpretation of the freeze proposal's intrinsic merit and broader uses.

The Old Orthodoxy

The strategic theory of the Professional Left, as outlined above, clearly sees the arms race as a symptom of the "constitutional deformity" of the modern American "national security state." Its goal is disarmament, not arms control, but disarmament is precluded by the corporate, Pentagon capitalism of the military-industrial complex. Thus, to stop the arms race and save the world, fundamental revolutionary changes in the U.S.—but not necessarily the Soviet—political system are necessary. But the individuals and organizations that hitched themselves to the nuclear freeze movement after the Kennedy-Hatfield initiative clearly do not share most, if any, of this worldview. Nor do they share the contemporary version of the Leninist theory of imperialism that makes up the basic foreign policy paradigm of the Professional Left.

The strategic theory of the organizations of the Left-Liberal Establishment—the Center for Defense Information, the Arms Control Association, the Union of Concerned Scientists, the American Federation of Scientists, the Lawyers Alliance for Nuclear Arms Control, most of the Physicians for Social Responsibility, and a host of other, smaller groups—is perhaps best defined by the term minimum, or finite, deterrence. This school of thought can be described with reference to six interlocking axioms:

(1) While total disarmament is an ideal solution to the nuclear dilemma, it is impractical. But since nuclear weapons have forever rendered traditional concepts of the relationship between military force and national defense both irrelevant and dangerous, a way must be found to prevent the military use of nuclear weapons and to quarantine their influence from international politics.

(2) The only way to ensure non-use, or deterrence, is to have a balance of power between nuclear weapons states up to a certain level of destructive capability. Beyond that level, additional increments of weaponry provide little or no military advantage and confer little or no political advantage.

(3) The saturation point of the capability needed to ensure deterrence is that required to inflict unacceptable damage on the enemy, defined as the destruction of certain levels of population and economy, beyond which nuclear capacity is wasteful and provocative "overkill."

(4) Since there is no defense against nuclear weapons targeted in a countervalue mode, that is, against cities and population, the adequacy of one nation's ability to inflict unacceptable damage on the other is *not* a direct function of the relative size and power of all opposing forces but *only* of the survivability of one's putative retaliatory forces.

(5) Therefore, most harmful to the stability of deterrence are attempts to undermine the confidence of both sides in their assured destruction capabilities, which include counterforce targeting, that is, against weapons and military assets, and counter-

94

force-oriented declaratory policies, measures for active or passive defense, and the pursuit of decisive superiority through technological breakthroughs and the militarization of new environments, like outer space.[43]

(6) Deterrence stability can be achieved informally through the continuing action-reaction sequences of superpower behavior, but it is safer, cheaper, and more certain to achieve this stability through formal arms control negotiations and treaties.

Within the school of minimum or finite deterrence advocates, there is much room for disagreement over many issues. For deterrence to work, is it necessary for both sides to accept these propositions, or are the inherent dynamics of the situation such that stability can be achieved by unilateral actions? Is "unacceptable damage" to the other side a knowable, quantifiable number, or a psychological condition certain to vary with circumstances and personalities? Is a triad of weapons, each capable independently of inflicting unacceptable damage, a reasonable and prudent hedge against future countermeasures, or is such redundancy more likely to appear provocative to the other side and thus weaken stable deterrence? If increments of additional strategic nuclear power beyond that required to maintain the credibility of one's second-strike force do not confer meaningful military advantage and have only modest and tentative political significance, can it ever be wise to add increments for political purposes alone?

Despite all these questions, there is no doubt that finite or minimum deterrence advocates agree on a number of major issues. First, to the extent that one deploys more than "enough" nuclear forces for deterrence, one clouds the certainty the other side has in one's defensive motives, impelling him to hedge similarly, this in turn casting doubt on *his* motives—the whole cycle of actions and reactions leading to a costly, destabilizing and unnecessary arms race. Second, a nuclear war cannot be "won" by any meaningful measure, and planning to fight one "just in case" is fruitless and even dangerous if it leads to an erosion of the perception of the strategic *discontinuity* between the pre-nuclear and the nuclear age.[44] Third, ballistic missile defense, civil defense, air defense, and antisubmarine and antisatellite warfare are all harmful to deterrence—especially if they work—because they can appear to be part of first-strike preparations even when they are not so intended. Fourth, counterforce targeting and declaratory statements, and all technological innovations aimed at increased ballistic accuracies and minimizing collateral damage, are destabilizing for identical reasons, and also because they encourage consideration of accident-prone launch-on-warning and launch-under-attack postures. Fifth, nuclear weapons generally cannot be used politically for purposes of extended deterrence because an aggressor cannot be persuaded easily that interests outside the United States are as important as interests inside the United States. It follows that the only way to defend such areas, like Europe, is either by conventional means or by independent nuclear forces.[45] Sixth, there is nothing immoral about targeting civilian populations because those populations will never really be harmed and because preventing nuclear war is a higher moral imperative anyway. Seventh, one can plan only to deter "rational" or marginally sane actors, and preparations to fight a war should deterrence fail because of an irrational act are not warranted because of the improbability of such an act and the destabilizing impact of such preparations on the stability of deterrence. Finally, even if the Soviet Union does not share these views now, it is wiser not to shift U.S. policy toward the Soviets' presumed war-fighting view because the Soviets might come to accept them later if the United States stands its ground. Even if they do not, the United States would still be worse off than it is today because a mutual counterforce world is even more unstable than a unilateral counterforce world.

Taken together, these axiomatic propositions and the analytic judgments that flow from them make up a serious, if arguable, strategic theory.[46] Indeed, this basic logic was the starting point for Robert S. McNamara's conception of deterrence through mutual assured destruction (MAD) and remains perhaps its ideal expression.

Once in the hands of minimum deterrence advocates, the debate over the nuclear freeze took on an entirely different aspect. At stake now were not raw emotions and the dialectics of revolutionary politics *sotto voce,* but tamer disagreements over the best way to prevent war. And it is easy to see how the tenets of minimum deterrence not only make the freeze an acceptable proposition but also make anything else unacceptable. Indeed, the sum of the advocacy of minimum deterrence theorists through the years over strategic modernization has added up to the same thing, at least on the U.S. side—support for a freeze.

Of course, not all kinds of advocacy are created equal. Debates over the freeze proposal on the intellectual level do not coincide with the simplifications and hyperbole one encounters in congressional floor speeches and mass-mail solicitations. But despite differences in tone, and occasional excesses of homiletic zeal, the arguments are really the same. They fall into three basic categories, trailed by other, more marginal considerations. The first category concerns the drift toward a "war-fighting" strategic posture for deterrence, and here the enemy is counterforce and all prospective weapons systems accurate enough to carry out counterforce missions. A freeze, it is claimed, would slay the counterforce dragon. The second category concerns the effects of a freeze on the action-reaction dynamic that is widely supposed to characterize the arms race: one must stop the forward momentum of the arms race before one can reverse it, and therefore the freeze will encourage eventual reductions in weaponry. Without a freeze first, arms control negotiations will, as always, lead to the transformation of bargaining chips into new, more destructive weapons. Technology will again outpace the negotiators. The third category of argument concerns both arms control in general and the specific attitudes of the Reagan Administration. So far, arms control has achieved too little; new developments have outpaced old constraints. Real arms control demands active public support, and without public activism the Reagan Administration will find it politically acceptable to ignore arms control, as is its real predilection.[47] The freeze movement is therefore *politically* useful in the current context even if a freeze is not achievable, and even if the freeze proposal itself is not the most logical, practical or prudent of available arms control programs.

Finally, there are usually a parade of ancillary benefits presumed to run after these three major ones. It is claimed that a freeze will help stem nuclear proliferation because, for the first time, the superpowers will have made good on their pledge in the Nonproliferation Treaty of 1967. A freeze, it is said, will allow the solution of other pressing global problems; nations will no longer be paralyzed by fear of nuclear war. A freeze, moreover, would have beneficial spillover effects in U.S.-Soviet relations, this proceeding from the view that arms agreements tend to promote improved political relations rather than the other way around. Finally, a freeze would supposedly "save money."[ ]

In the less dispassionate, more openly emotional espousals of the nuclear freeze, there is an another benefit. Not only are there arguments on behalf of the freeze, but there are also analyses of our broader predicament and even the placing of blame for it. There are two excellent sources for this sort of freeze advocacy: the congressional hearings on the freeze resolutions, and the ubiquitous mass-mail solicitations of the organizations of the Left-Liberal Establishment and the moderately toned literature of the nuclear freeze clearinghouse in St. Louis.

The Counterforce Bogy

Let us first review the main argument of nuclear freeze advocates, namely, that counterforce capabilities and the shift to war-fighting postures are sure to lead to nuclear catastrophe, and that for a proper mutual assured destruction deterrent, both the United States and the Soviet Union already have more than enough. In the first House debate on the freeze (Resolution 521) in August 1982, introduced by the late Representative Clement Zablocki (Dem., Wisconsin), freeze supporters returned frequently to these themes. At one point in the Hearings, Ronald Dellums (Dem., California) presented an encyclopedic tirade against the administration's strategic modernization program, lambasting "the absurdity of a military budget that includes crisis destabilizing weapons such as the MX missile, first-strike; Trident missile, first-strike; Pershing missile, crisis destabilizing."[48] Donald Pease (Dem., Ohio) stated the argument in more restrained terms: "The average American . . . believes that enough is enough, that we and the Soviets already have far more nuclear weapons than we need, and that it is time to get on with the job of a mutual, verifiable nuclear freeze to be followed by substantial reductions."[49] Thomas Downey (Dem., New York), leader of the anti-MX forces in the House of Representatives, was downright folksy and anecdotal: "I see this as two old adversaries locked in a room knee-deep in gasoline. One has nine matches and the other has seven matches, and it really does not matter who strikes the first match because the consequences for both would be the same—total annihilation."[50] James Jeffords (Rep., Vermont) was just as graphic: "Who has the advantage when two men, one with a 12-gage shotgun and the other with a 20-gage, have guns to each other's heads?"[51] John Sieberling (Dem., Ohio) waxed mystical: "We have built them up beyond all reason, beyond all necessity, and there is an evil genius propelling the arms race that somehow makes it a self-propelling vicious cycle."[52] Finally, Mervyn Dymally (Dem., California) arrived at a new definition of parity, sweeping aside considerations of who strikes first and the requirements, acknowledged even by minimum deterrence supporters, of being able to ride out a Soviet first-strike and still be able to retaliate with adequate force:

We continue to debate over how many nuclear warheads we have as opposed to how many they have, or whether or not we can trust the Soviets to observe a freeze. Are these questions truly relevant? The point is, we each have the capacity now to destroy each other and the world at least one time. That is parity, because once is all that counts.[53]

Mass-mail solicitations of the Left-Liberal Establishment echo the same sentiments. The Union of Concerned Scientists (UCS) presented the most eloquent and intellectually honest arguments. The main problem is not counterforce capable weapons but rather "the doctrine of limited war" in which counterforce weapons would be used. The UCS believes that " 'limited war' proponents ignore, at our ultimate risk, the warnings of leading military authorities who believe that a nuclear exchange could not be terminated until it had escalated into a global catastrophe." The UCS also believes that the "advent of new nuclear weapons that are most threatening heightens the risk of an attempted preemptive strike"—clearly a reference to counterforce. This is why, according to the UCS, "we are entering a new age of instability. We are moving into a time in which nuclear war is becoming increasingly probable." However, the freeze, to the UCS is only a part of a broader program for a "new national security policy." In this new policy, of which there are five parts, the freeze is played down and the need for major reductions is emphasized.

Moreover, the UCS solicitation goes out of its way to emphasize the reality of Soviet policies, mentioning Afghanistan and Poland, and says plainly, "we do not call for unilateral arms reduction." At base, the UCS wishes to reverse U.S. nuclear weapons policies back to pure assured destruction doctrine, and to a purely conventional defense of Western Europe, as well.

The Council for a Livable World (CLW) sent out a solicitation in 1983 asking support for candidates dedicated to arms control. The CLW is an organization with a specific political action committee, called PeacePac, headed by Paul Warnke. The gist of the solicitation was pro-freeze and anti-MX, which the CLW describes as "a dangerous first-strike weapon." A Philadelphia Nuclear Freeze Campaign flyer stated simply: "WE NEED JOBS— NOT MORE BOMBS! THE MX MISSILES WILL COST MORE THAN $20 BILLION. THEY ARE FIRST STRIKE WEAPONS AND WILL MAKE US LESS SECURE—NOT MORE SECURE."

The U.S. Committee Against Nuclear War (USCANW) is a "political action committee for a nuclear freeze" established by nine congressional co-sponsors of the freeze resolution. Its main pitch is signed by Congressman Edward T. Markey, who is also chairman of USCANW. First of all, the solicitation mimics official congressional stationery, using the same typeface and style. In the solicitation, the description of the MX remains constant, here with an ostensibly evenhanded twist:

And while our Committee is hard at work seeking passage of the freeze, both the United States and the Soviet Union are hard at work deploying or planning new missile systems like the Russian SS-18 and the American MX. These are deadly, first-strike weapons that are used to *start nuclear wars,* not deter them.

A final example of a solicitation that repeats this general theme is that of the Nuclear Weapons Freeze Campaign headquarters in St. Louis:

With the developments of new first-strike weapons like the MX, Trident II, Pershing II missiles, and their Soviet counterparts—the nuclear arms race is taking on more and more suicidal developments. These faster and more accurate weapons being developed by both the U.S. and the

100

U.S.S.R. can attack and wipe out military targets in a surprise first-strike. *They are designed not just to deter a nuclear war, but also to fight one. And therefore they make nuclear war more likely.*

In the Nuclear Weapons Freeze Campaign Fact Sheet Number 1, we have perhaps the fullest exposition of the counterforce argument: "The nuclear arms race is moving to new kinds of weapons known as 'counterforce' or *first-strike weapons*." The same fact sheet repeats verbatim the language of its solicitation and adds that counterforce weapons "make both sides more vulnerable to surprise attacks. This could tempt either side, in time of crisis, to launch a first-strike before the other side has a chance to. The result is that the new weapons are adding a hair-trigger to the balance of terror."

Freezing the Arms Race

The second argument for the freeze is that in order to reverse the arms race one first has to stop its forward momentum. Other arms control attempts, like SALT, have failed at this. During the freeze hearings in the House of Representatives, Claudine Schneider (Rep., Rhode Island) said it perhaps most simply: "One cannot dispute that the more nuclear weapons one builds, the other side will also build. The result guarantees less security in the world."[54] Berkley Bedell (Dem., Indiana) went a bit further, implying that the action–reaction cycle was fueled by unjustified fears: "Clearly, the history of the arms race is fraught with examples of one side responding to a perceived, or real, advantage of the other. Each deadly action initiated by one side sets off an equally deadly reaction by the other side and upward pressures of the arms race continues unabated."[55] Senator Mark Hatfield elected to present the argument with a simple metaphor: "We have to stop the arms race before we de-escalate it. If the elevator's going up and you want it to go down, you have to stop the elevator first."[56]

Both Schneider and Bedell believe that the freeze will kill this action–reaction sequence dead in its tracks. Underlying their arguments is the criticism that other attempts at arms control have failed because they were too complicated. The simpler and the more unambiguous the prohibitions are, the reasoning goes, the more likely they will be successful and loophole-proof. Jonathan Bingham (Dem., New York), however, let the beauties of simplicity overcome his sense of logic: "The beauty of the freeze idea, which came from the grassroots of Middle America, was its common sense, its simplicity. The way to stop the arms race is to stop it."[57] Applying this assessment to other pressing public policy problems, we now know, thanks to Congressman Bingham, that the way to stop unemployment is to stop it, the way to stop crime is to stop it, the way to stop the Arab-Israeli dispute is to stop it, and so on.

Mass-mail solicitations also speak to this point. The Union of Concerned Scientists put it this way:

Time and time again, we have seen unrealistic proposals put forth which seem plausible to a public unaware of the intricacies of weapons technology and the complexity of the strategic balance, but which one knows in advance to be unacceptable to the other side. New weapons systems have been advanced as "bargaining chips," but all too often they have become integral parts of the nuclear arsenal, never to be traded away. Thus, with every passing day we are driven closer to the brink.

In other words, old-fashioned arms control negotiations have allowed the competition to continue, and in the end we have larger, not smaller, nuclear arsenals. The UCS believes that a freeze can stop this process and create the preconditions for reductions. Without the freeze, the UCS fears that arms control as usual will again fail to *reduce* anything.

Edward Markey's U.S. committee Against Nuclear War makes only a glancing remark in this direction in its mass mail solicitation. Among the enemies of the freeze it enumerates is "the entrenched bureaucracy of arms strategists and nuclear war theorists . . . who have been saying that we must 'arm to disarm' for the past thirty years." Markey and his colleagues evidently see no relationship between the prospects for fair and meaningful arms control negotiations on the one hand and the balance of negotiating assets on the other.

The St. Louis nuclear freeze clearinghouse fact sheets give the most reasonable argument for this view. Fact Sheet Number 1 praises the existing arms control treaties we have with the Soviet Union, saying "they have worked well." "But *these treaties don't go far enough,*" claims the Fact Sheet, written by David Riley.

"They do not stop the technological improvements in nuclear weapons which make the arms race more and more dangerous. During the many years of negotiations, both sides develop new weapons that often create more problems than the treaties solve." The Fact Sheet then proceeds to offer undebatable evidence of this from SALT I and SALT II—in language that even the Reagan Administration could love—and notes that during the present START (Strategic Arms Reductions Talks) negotiations, "both sides are developing first-strike weapons, which present us with the most dangerous nuclear arms race ever." According to the Fact Sheet: "The Freeze is the only way to truly stop the nuclear arms race in its tracks, rather than just change the rules a little so it can go on again to another tack. *The Freeze stops both sides from making new weapons while they talk about reducing old ones.*"

Freezing the Reaganauts

The third category of argument, that the freeze is good politics and helps keep the Reagan Administration "honest" about arms control, has lived a double life. As to honesty, the "tactical" political argument on behalf of the freeze was often sincere, based on a pragmatic reading of the political climate, but sometimes it was not. Many politicians who lacked mature views about arms control, and even some who recognized the flaws of the nuclear freeze proposal, seized on the tactical argument as an excuse not to risk the displeasure of their newly mobilized constituents. This dilemma was not limited to individual politicians. Many organizations of the Left–Liberal Establishment that deal specifically with arms control issues were at first embarrassed by the nuclear freeze. For example, a man of experience and erudition like William H. Kincade, executive director of the Arms Control Association, could hardly have been enthusiastic about the nuclear freeze proposal based on its substantive merits alone. But the Arms Control Association risked alienating its own broad constituency if it did not board the freeze bandwagon. Caught between its private assessment of the freeze and the political cost of opposing it, the tactical argument provided an enticing temptation. Still, the Arms Control Association managed to avoid a formal endorsement of the freeze despite the presence of many prominent freeze activists on its board of directors.

Sincere or not, the tactical argument on behalf of the freeze has

103

had its share of the debating stage. In the congressional hearings over the freeze resolution in August 1982, Les Aspin (Dem., Wisconsin) said: "If we had a President who was genuinely interested in arms controls . . . who would negotiate in good faith . . . we would need no [freeze] resolution at all."[58] Harold Hollenbeck (Rep., New Jersey) was more diplomatic: "Those of us who cherish life on earth must encourage our Government to act in harmony with the demands of peace rather than out of narrow self-interest."[59] James Florio (Dem., New Jersey) contrasted the Reagan Administration's "irrational and casual approach to confrontation" with the "the reaction of the American people," which has been "rational and sober."[60]

Leon Panetta (Dem., California) was the most straightforward of all in accusing the administration of disingenuous behavior. We need the freeze, said Panetta, because "the fear is that all of the assurances, all of the words, all of the resolutions are really just so much political pabulum to try to respond to the fear. It is not a real commitment to try to limit arms."[61]

The mass-mail solicitations are more careful on this point, but the message comes through. A Common Cause solicitation tells the reader that only "action in Congress . . . forced the President to deal with the question of extricating ourselves from Vietnam" back in the 1970s—the logical presumption being that the president otherwise would have had no such interest. Now, "it's up to an organization like Common Cause to commit itself— for long periods of time—whatever is necessary—to *force* the duly elected representatives of this country, the President and the Congress of the United States, to face these issues and to take into consideration the well-being of our country and the people of the world," again, presumably things that the president and the Congress would otherwise never imagine doing. If you give them money, Common Cause promises to be "relentless" in this.

The U.S. Committee Against Nuclear War did not say directly that support for the freeze can make the Reagan Administration more "honest" about arms control. "Arms control" is never even mentioned in Congressman Markey's letter. It is not arms control that hangs in the balance, but the earth. The point is not to influence the administration's politics but to defeat them. Markey went to great lengths to draw a Manichean picture of the choices:

104

Once again, our movement is at the crossroads. . . . The House will be forced to publicly decide between two paths: the resolution I have sponsored calling for an immediate, verifiable *nuclear weapons freeze,* or President Reagan's plan to continue a massive nuclear arms build-up . . . calling for a $1.7 trillion rearmament program that will build 17,000 new nuclear bombs.

The organizations of the Left-Liberal Establishment, like those of the Professional Left, are not above counter-red-baiting in order to drive home a point or raise money. In a solicitation distributed in January 1984 by an organization founded by Norman Lear calling itself People for the American Way (a "project of the Citizens for Constitutional Concerns, Inc., a nonprofit tax-exempt organization"), opponents of a nuclear freeze are, essentially, collectively accused of being members of the Moral Majority and admirers of Jerry Falwell. Anthony T. Podesta's letter as chairman of People for the American Way begins:

Recently Jerry Falwell proudly announced that he is launching 'the most massive campaign in the history of the Moral Majority.' Its sole objective: to block any possibility of a nuclear freeze. After reviewing some of the initial programs in this campaign, I consider it one of *the most shameful exploitations of the media for the purpose of mass intimidation ever conceived.*

It is not long before Podesta states: "Unfortunately, all these efforts are directly encouraged by the Reagan White House." On the little card enclosed in the solicitation, used to send money back to the source, the message commences, in large, bold red type: "I will not be intimidated! Nor will I allow the Far Right to intimidate millions of Americans into believing that because they are for a nuclear freeze or a smaller defense budget they are un-American and un-patriotic!" The envelope supplied for sending money is also emblazoned in red in the upper left-hand corner: "RUSH: NUCLEAR FREEZE T.V. SPOT CAMPAIGN." People for the American Way claims it is defending everyone's right to his or her own opinion about the nuclear freeze, without fear of intimidation and innuendo. But those who wish to help People for the American Way uphold the sanctity of the First Amendment are going to have their money used to promote a nuclear freeze, whether they like it or not.

Saving Money

One other point of debate is relevant here, since it is repeated in endless variation. It is that we cannot afford a nuclear arms race, and that a freeze would save money for more worthy causes. The cost of the arms race is perhaps the oldest complaint about it, even though strategic nuclear forces, in the era of the All-Volunteer Force and high manpower costs, usually take up less than 20 per cent of the defense budget in any given fiscal year. Nevertheless, in times of large deficits and unpredictable economic trends, the defense budget in general, and the strategic budget in particular, is an irresistible target for other, competing budget constituencies.

In the House debate of August 1982, the late Congressman John Burton (Dem., California) made the following, exaggerated claim: "The money spent on a nuclear arms race would balance the budget in a minute. The money spent on the nuclear arms race if it was spent on helping people would solve our problems in a minute."[62] The exaggeration derives from the fact that spending for strategic weapons was about $25 billion in fiscal year 1982, while the deficit exceeded $110 billion. As for the second part of Burton's claim, spending money on "helping people" totaled well *over* $110 billion in fiscal year 1982, in transfer payments for medicare, medicaid, welfare, workmen's compensation, and special programs, and yet our problems are still not solved.

The mass-mail solicitations of the Union of Concerned Scientists, Common Cause, and others do not hit hard on the money argument, but Markey's U.S. Committee Against Nuclear War does. One enemy of the freeze, says Markey, is the "powerful weapons lobby, whose arm twisting tactics are well known on Capitol Hill. Their repudiation . . . has not stopped them from asking the Congress to *approve in your name* one billion dollars *a day* over the next four years for the purpose of human destruction." Later, Markey adds, "It would take less than *one-fifth* of the Reagan five-year arms budget to cover the [Social Security] systems shortfall through 1982." And finally, Markey claims that "the cost of the MX missile is more than a quarter of the Administration's projected deficit for next year," and that the cost of the B-1 bomber program alone "nearly matches all our spending for *all the job training programs* enacted by Congress over the past twenty years."

Markey's statistics remind one of Lord Palmerston's remark that there are three kinds of liars: big liars, little liars, and statisticians. First, 20 per cent of the budget taken away from the military for five years running would do very serious damage, for most of the budget is not for new weapons but for manpower, operation and maintenance of existing equipment, and so forth. It is not discretionary, or extra, money. Second, the total, multiyear costs of the MX may be one-quarter of the fiscal year 1983 deficit, but money spent for the MX in the *next* fiscal year is more like 8 per cent. Finally, the B-1 program, figured on a multiyear basis, is matched appropriately to job training programs calculated on a multiyear basis. But the B-1's costs are future costs adjusted for inflation, while the total multiyear spending for job training, some of it in the 1960s, is not adjusted for inflation, which taken together has been very considerable over the past twenty years.

On the issue of money, the freeze headquarters in St. Louis again provides the more complete argument. Under the title "The Arms Race Hurts Our Economy," a Freeze Fact Sheet argues that while defense spending stimulated the economy during World War II, today's weapons are so capital intensive that "a billion dollars spent on military programs provides an average of 20,000 fewer jobs than the same amount spent in most other areas of the economy." The Fact Sheet also avers that large weapons programs "use up scarce capital, research talent, and raw materials that could be invested in our civilian economy to make it more efficient, more competitive with other countries and less inflationary." Finally, heavy military spending "keeps the federal budget high, and drains away urgently needed funds for human services. Military spending also contributes to the highest national debt in our history." The Fact Sheet claims that the freeze would save $20 billion a year for ten years—this based on a pamphlet issued by SANE and the Coalition for a New Foreign and Military Policy. Senator Kennedy is fond of using the figure $100 billion as the expected savings from a freeze; the Coalition claims savings of $84.2 billion over the next five years.

Another organization of the Left-Liberal Establishment which hits hard on the money issue—indeed, that has made the economic implications of the "arms race" its raison d'être—is Harold Willens's organization, Business Executives for Nuclear Arms Control (BENAC). Willens argues that the arms race is not rational, economical, or conducive to good business. Moreover, he asserts that proper "management techniques" can solve the problem. Willens likens the business community to a trimtab rudder (which refers both to the small flaps on the stabilizers on airplanes and to the small rudder which activates a large one on ocean-going ships) that can steer U.S. military policy onto a safer course. As with SANE, there is a discrepancy between Willens's beliefs and the kind of target audience that BENAC aims to capture. Willens's arguments resemble in part those of Seymour Melman and Marcus Raskin, who speak of the U.S. economy as a war economy, and also the "nuclearism" and "exterminism" arguments of Richard Falk and E. P. Thompson. Yet clearly the businessmen Willens seeks to bring into support for the freeze do not share such radical notions. Willens has had a good deal of experience, however, in maneuvering these differences; BENAC seems to be the natural successor to Willens's older organization, Businessmen Against the War in Vietnam. One can read the full exposition of Willens's views in his book, *The Trimtab Factor*. For a shorter version of the same argument, the Center for Defense Information's *Defense Monitor* (vol. 12, no. 8) is devoted entirely to Willens's new campaign. This is not surprising for Willens is one of the Center's most generous patrons, sitting on its board of advisers along with Alan F. Kay, Paul Newman, Joanne Woodward, Earl Ravenal, Jonathan Bingham, and others.

There is something else that is not surprising. Willens advocates a "step-by-step program of American initiatives aimed at slowing, stopping, and reversing the Soviet-American nuclear arms race," that calls for *unilateral* American initiatives, beginning with a halt to all U.S. nuclear weapons testing. This is identical to the program adopted by the freeze movement at its February and December 1983 conventions in St. Louis, after it became clear that the "halt in the tracks" maximal version of the freeze would not pass muster in Congress. In reviewing Willens's book, Alton Frye, father of the "build-down" concept, says that "most interesting is Mr. Willens's advocacy of a different approach to a nuclear freeze [that] reflects a degree of pragmatism that may open the way for a wider coalition, linking freeze proponents with other Americans who favor a step-by-step approach."[63] What Frye reads as pragmatism can also be interpreted as unilateralism, however, for Willens's definition of the degree of Soviet reciprocity needed to move on to new U.S. initiatives is ambiguous.

The arguments about money carry with them a number of assumptions, all of them arguable. The first tacit assumption is the absurd proposition that the amount of money the United States spends on defense ought to be judged by its economic spin-offs rather than on the kind of national security it purchases. On reflection this is ludicrous, but many freeze supporters simply assume that any money spent on strategic weapons does nothing to enhance U.S. security regardless of what potential enemies may do. This makes it much easier to look at tangential considerations like economic effects. A second assumption is that military spending starves the civilian economy of capital, talent, and raw material. To some degree, this is true, but there is no solid evidence that U.S. economic doldrums are in any way caused by capital scarcity. It is too bad that things are not that simple. Here, ironically enough, freeze supporters join hands with George Gilder and the supply-side economists, although for the supply-siders excessive taxation, not military spending, is the main culprit. Both are wrong.

A third assumption is that military spending contributes to the high federal budget deficit in a way somehow more pernicious than other kinds of spending. But spending is spending, no matter what is bought. Department of Defense spending, from fiscal year 1974 through the present, has represented roughly 25 per cent of the federal budget (between 5.0 and 5.9 per cent of the gross national product), while transfer payments to individuals in entitlement programs have run in excess of 45 per cent of the federal budget.[64] Logically, it is safe to conclude that welfare entitlements have contributed a larger share of the federal deficit than defense spending, even though some entitlements are financed by a special tax. Freeze advocates are not likely to note such a relationship, however, because most nuclear freeze supporters believe that spending on defense is inherently bad and wasteful while spending on "human needs" is inherently good. Never mind the consequences, it's the thought that counts.

Finally, the claim that the freeze would save $20 billion a year is difficult to understand, unless it is based on an inadvertent error. The entire strategic forces budget for fiscal year 1984 was just slightly more than $20 billion, but less than half of that goes to procure new weapons that the freeze would prohibit. The rest goes for operations and maintenance; command, control, and communications improvements; strategic defense (non-nuclear), and the like.[65] Some freeze supporters evidently do not know how the budget works and so assume that a freeze would simply eliminate the *entire* strategic forces budget.

It is also assumed that no conventional force build-up would be required to offset a build-down in strategic capabilities. But even those who advocate no first use of nuclear weapons in Europe and support the freeze—like McGeorge Bundy, Robert S. McNamara, George Kennan, and Gerard Smith,[66]—admit that a conventional build-up would be required to maintain stable deterrence, and that politically this offset would be inevitable. Since conventional forces cost *more* than nuclear forces because of manpower requirements, a freeze probably would not save any money at all, and certainly not $20 billion a year.

Forsberg on the Freeze

Even some avid supporters of the freeze admit that most of the popular support for the freeze is highly emotional and based on a very superficial understanding of most of the issues.[67] But this does not mean that more sophisticated arguments on behalf of the freeze do not exist. For a more sedate articulation of these basic themes, it is best to turn to the originator of the freeze, Randall Forsberg. In a *Scientific American* article timed to appear just before the November 1982 midterm elections, Forsberg provided for the first time in print detailed arguments on behalf of the freeze. This begs examination because even if one grants certain assumptions for the sake of argument, parts of Forsberg's presentation are remarkably weak.

As to the evils of counterforce, Forsberg claims that "the bilateral freeze would preclude the production of a new generation of 'counterforce' weapons by the U.S. and the U.S.S.R."[68] This is good because, as Forsberg states it so simply, "the production of counterforce weapons would increase the risk of nuclear war" because their "deployment would put pressure on leaders to launch their weapons first in time of crisis, before they were attacked."[69] Forsberg also illustrates her dedication to the minimum assured destruction paradigm for deterrence by claiming: "More

110

important than comparisons of numbers of weapons is the fact that both countries have acquired enormous 'overkill,' that is, each has many times the number of weapons to annihilate the other's urban population."[70] Thus, Soviet advantages in missiles, launchers, throw-weight, and counterforce-capable MIRV'd ICBMs do not have any real meaning and are in any case offset by U.S. advantages in non-counterforce-capable submarine-launched-ballistic-missile (SLBM) warheads and bombers. A freeze would prevent a counterforce world and ensure basic assured destruction parity.

The second basic freeze argument, that one must stop the forward momentum of the arms race before one can contemplate reductions, is represented in Forsberg's article in the form of an attack on the Reagan Administration's original START proposal of May 1982. "Under the Administration's proposals the technological arms race would continue indefinitely. . . . Under the freeze proposal the nuclear part of the military industry would be closed down and there would be no future generations of nuclear weapons. . . . The freeze represents a modest but significant step toward abolition."[71] Forsberg claims that the original U.S. START proposal would have sanctioned new U.S. systems that would have led to an *increase* in the number of U.S. warheads, a *reduction* only in the number of launchers. "The U.S. nuclear weapons to be built during the 1990s have been mistakenly characterized as 'bargaining chips'," wrote Forsberg, who said that neither the MX, Trident II, the B-1 bomber, U.S. cruise missiles, or new battlefield weapons were on the START on INF (Intermediate-range Nuclear Forces) negotiating agendas.[72] The implication here is that the administration's opening position was its only and last position—which has never been the case in the history of the SALT process.

Forsberg is much more concerned with stopping new *U.S.* systems than she is with reductions, because she denies that the Soviet Union enjoys a counterforce advantage and because she is convinced that the present balance is "roughly stable." By making a series of assumptions about present Soviet and U.S. ballistic accuracies *installed,* and discounting the next half-dozen years entirely, Forsberg concludes that "a hypothetical U.S. first-strike conducted . . . in late 1982 would be more devastating than a U.S.S.R. first-strike against U.S. ICBMs."[73] By making addi-

111

tional assumptions positing the relative *invulnerability* of U.S. bombers and submarines and the relative *vulnerability* of *Soviet* bombers and submarines, Forsberg concludes further: "Even if U.S. land-based ICBMs are or are becoming more vulnerable to pre-emptive attack than those of the U.S.S.R. (a disputable point), this could be offset by the invulnerability of U.S. bombers and submarines. On the U.S.S.R. side the high vulnerability of its strategic bomber and submarine force is offset by the size of its ICBM force. Without a bilateral freeze this *relatively stable balance* will be eroded by the weapon programs planned for the next decade."[74] Specifically, Forsberg says that a freeze "would prevent the emergence of a new, destabilizing U.S. advantage in counterforce capability, projected in the build-up planned by the Reagan Administration."[75]

In other words, we have to "abolish" nuclear weapons, but the real problem is not the "relatively stable balance" we have at present, but refinements and technological advances in counterforce accuracies planned *by the United States.* Soviet counterforce advantages at present are not destabilizing because they *do not exist,* according to Forsberg.

Whatever one thinks of this logic, it is consistent and clear, at least until we come to the question of intermediate-range nuclear forces. Forsberg notes that the freeze would prevent deployment of the Pershing II missiles in Europe, a plan adopted jointly at the behest of NATO-Europe on December 12, 1979. But this does not matter because Soviet SS-20s are already offset by French, British, U.S., *and Chinese* forces.[76] (This is the same argument that Moscow puts forth.) Besides, writes Forsberg, "The new SS-20s actually reduce the nuclear threat to Western Europe compared with the old SS-4s and SS-5s they are replacing."[77] The reasons she gives are interesting. "The older missiles carried bigger warheads" and "were 'sitting ducks' for a pre-emptive attack. The U.S.S.R. has thus replaced a destabilizing 'first-strike' force, which would have had to be used first if it were not to be destroyed, with a less vulnerable force that can be held back."[78] Moreover, the SS-20 is more accurate and therefore its use would cause less collateral damage: "The greater accuracy of the SS-20s gives them a higher 'kill probability' against the few hardened targets in Western Europe."[79] Somehow, when the Soviets introduce a new weapon suitable for protracted war-fighting missions

112

by reducing its yield, lowering its vulnerability to pre-emption, and increasing its accuracy, this "reduces the nuclear threat," according to Forsberg. But when the United States attempts to do the same thing with the neutron bomb or with ground-launched cruise missiles, this is destabilizing and provocative.

It cannot be asserted on the basis of this inconsistency that Forsberg consciously holds Soviet objectives dear to herself. But it is difficult not to conclude that Forsberg has in common with the more politically radical of the freeze's promoters the inclination to judge U.S. and Soviet behaviors by two rather different standards, giving Moscow every benefit of the doubt and giving Washington none. Only her written espousal of the freeze in a liberal-oriented journal is moderate. The same inclination shows through in another way: Forsberg hopes that the freeze movement can be expanded into a more broadly based political movement— and here Forsberg has much in common with the War Resister's League and its like-minded allies. In May 1983, Forsberg was in Berlin. She told a rally there: "Delay of the deployment of new missiles in Europe should be part of our strategy." Forsberg also told journalists that the nuclear freeze drive would be expanded in 1985 to other issues, particularly "intervention in third countries." The focus would be Central America, but also the U.S. military presence in Greece and Spain—two nations with Socialist governments.[80] No mention was made of *Soviet* intervention and direct or proxy military presence "in third countries" such as Afghanistan, Poland, Ethiopia, Syria, Angola, Cambodia, and so on and on and on. Some European "activists" responded to this notion accordingly. Mary Kaldor, a prominent antinuclear activist in Great Britain, urged "the American freeze movement to look beyond the nuclear issue and focus on their country's aggressive foreign policy."[81]

Forsberg did not, in her *Scientific American* article, discuss the freeze as a political tactic, but she did claim that a freeze would help stop nuclear proliferation and "save billions of dollars."[82] Still, it is difficult to believe that any non-NPT adherent would view a U.S.-Soviet freeze as sufficient rationale to sign the Non-proliferation Treaty, especially considering the build-up in U.S. and Soviet arsenals since 1967. It is even more difficult to believe that anything the superpowers do could deflect nations who see themselves under pressure—like Pakistan or Israel—or who see themselves as uniquely righteous—like India and Libya—from the pursuit of nuclear weapons. As for saving money, it is widely believed that nuclear weapons are cheaper than conventional weapons for accomplishing similar broad tasks. Those who propose a lesser reliance on nuclear weapons for NATO acknowledge that the price is a conventional build-up and that this would not save billions but *cost* billions.[83] But Forsberg had an answer for this one, too: no extra money need be spent on European conventional defense because NATO is in no way disadvantaged conventionally in Europe.[84]

NOTES

1. See Clifford Geertz, "Ideology as a Cultural System" in his *The Interpretation of Cultures* (New York: Basic Books, 1973).

2. For details, see *The Three Per Cent Solution and the Future of NATO* (Philadelphia: Foreign Policy Research Institute, 1981), esp. pp. 38-48, 58-61, 80-84.

3. See "Should Federal Spending on Defense Be Increased?" *CBS News/New York Times Poll,* April 30, 1981.

4. This criticism has been voiced in Adam Garfinkle, "Dense Pack: A Critique and an Alternative," *Parameters,* December 1982; Colin S. Gray, " 'Dangerous to Your Health': The Debate over Nuclear Strategy and War," *Orbis,* Summer 1982, esp. pp. 329-31; and Colin S. Gray, "Wanted: An Arms Control Policy," *Arms Control Today,* February 1982, pp. 1-2, 8-9.

5. See the documentation in "Public Opinion and the Defense Debate," *National Security Record,* February 1983. The reference to "limited nuclear war" is the president's remark of October 16, 1981, reported in the *New York Times,* October 17, 1981. Reagan later tried to clarify the statement, but the damage had been done (see *New York Times,* October 22, 1981). The reference to a "nuclear shot across the bow" refers to a remark made by former Secretary of State Alexander Haig on November 4, 1982 (see *New York Times,* November 5 and 6, 1981). Finally, leaks about Pentagon plans to achieve war-fighting strategic superiority did not help either. See Richard Halloran, "Weinberger Said to Offer Reagan Plan to Regain Atomic Superiority," *New York Times,* August 14, 1981; and Gerald F. Seib, "Atomic Angst," *Wall Street Journal,* December 9, 1981.

6. This started at Caspar Weinberger's nomination hearings, where he predicted at least a six-month delay in SALT. See Richard Halloran, "Weinberger, Expects Six-Month Delay for Renewal of Talks on Arms Control," *New York Times,* January 7, 1981. Then, on June 24 at his confirmation hearings, Eugene Rostow said that SALT and Euro-strategic talks might be "a year away." See *New York Times,* June 25, 1981.

7. See, for example, Gary Hart, "For Arms Talks Soon," *New York Times,* July 22, 1981.

8. The pivot of this school was said to be Richard Perle, assistant secretary of defense for international security policy. Perle was a former aide to the late Senator Henry M. Jackson (Dem., Washington). For hints of Perle's attitudes even before he was confirmed by the Senate, see the article by George Wilson in the *Washington Post,* April 14, 1981.

9. Author's estimate based on interviews and earlier statistical estimates. See Peter Pringle, "Putting World War III on Ice," *Inquiry,* July 1982, p. 16. See also Melinda Fine and Peter Steven, *American Peace Directory: 1984* (Cambridge, Mass.: Ballinger, 1983); this book has a foreword by Randall Forsberg. See also the paperback *The Whole Freeze Catalog: Resources for Peace* (Salem, Ore.: CALS, 1983). I have purposely avoided citing polling data on the popularity of the freeze within the text because of their inherent fungibility. On an issue like the freeze, the answers one gets depends almost entirely on the questions one asks. See "Committee Releases New National Poll on Attitudes Toward Nuclear Freeze and Nuclear Arms Issues," Committee on the Present Danger, April 19, 1984.

10. See Pringle, "Putting World War III on Ice," p. 18.

11. Helen Caldicott's Physicians for Social Responsibility was reported to have increased its membership sevenfold in a ten-month period in 1982. Ibid., p. 17.

12. See here Thomas Wolfe, *The SALT Experience* (Cambridge, Mass.: Ballinger, 1979), chap. 7, esp. pp. 135-53.

13. See the feature on Molander by Judith Miller, "New Look at Stopping Nuclear War," *New York Times,* April 17, 1982.

14. Pringle, "Putting World War III on Ice," p. 18.

15. Published by Pocket Books in 1982.

16. Pringle, "Putting World War III on Ice," p. 18.

115

17. Molander's views are reported in Miller, "New Look," and Fox Butterfield, "Anatomy of the Nuclear Protest," *New York Times Magazine,* July 11, 1982. See also Ground Zero, *What About the Russians—and Nuclear War?* (New York: Bantam, 1983), and *Hope: Facing the Music on Nuclear War and the 1984 Elections* (New York: Pocket Books, 1983).

18. See George Kennan, "A Modest Proposal," *New York Review of Books,* July 16, 1981.

19. See Leon V. Sigal, "Kennan's Cuts," *Foreign Policy,* Fall 1981, pp. 70-81.

20. See Leon V. Sigal, "Warming to the Freeze," *Foreign Policy,* Fall 1982, pp. 54-65.

21. *The New Republic* has been especially active in opposing both the freeze and the administration; see, for example, "Nuclear Fantasies," April 18, 1983. See also "Reheating SALT," *New York Times,* June 29, 1982, and "Add SALT to the Freeze," *New York Times,* November 5, 1982.

22. See, for example, Les Aspin, "Freeze? Why Not Just Okay SALT II?" *Washington Post,* April 15, 1982, and Charles Krauthammer, "The Real Way to Prevent Nuclear War," *The New Republic,* April 28, 1982, pp. 1, 15-20.

23. For an explanation of this view, see Eugene V. Rostow, "The Great Nuclear Debate," in Adam M. Garfinkle, ed., *Global Perspectives on Arms Control* (New York: Praeger, 1984), pp. 9-10.

24. Michael Getler, "Haig Says SALT II Is Dead," *Boston Globe,* May 12, 1982.

25. Cited in Carol Polsgrove, "The Freeze Heats Up," *Inquiry,* July 1982, p. 16.

26. Ibid., p. 17.

27. The March 1981 meeting at Georgetown University was funded in large part from a $5,000 grant supplied by Alan F. Kay, a wealthy retired businessman who holds a Ph.D. in mathematics from Harvard. Since then, Kay has contributed over a quarter of a million dollars to various "peace" and "freeze" groups. See Butterfield, "Anatomy of the Nuclear Protest," p. 14.

28. Nathaniel Sheppard, Jr., "Center for Nuclear Freeze Set Up in St. Louis," *New York Times,* March 23, 1982.

29. Ibid.; see also Howard LaFranchi, "A More Thoughtful Path to Preventing Nuclear War," *Christian Science Monitor,* March 9, 1984, and Kathleen Teltsch, "Philanthropies Focus Concern on Arms Race," *New York Times,* March 25, 1984.

30. Quoted in Polsgrove, "The Freeze Heats Up," p. 16.

31. Alexander Cockburn and James Ridgeway, "How the Freeze Is Big Business," *The Village Voice,* April 20, 1982, p. 11. Willens is also a member of the board of advisers of the Center for Defense Information, another pro-freeze group of which he is the main financial backer. He is chairman of the board of Factory Equipment Corporation in Los Angeles. The more complete analysis of the freeze from Cockburn and Ridgeway's perspective can be found in their "The Freeze Movement Against Reagan," *New Left Review,* January/February 1983, pp. 5-21.

32. See the fascinating insider's account of all this by David Lindorff, "War in Peace," *The Village Voice,* April 20, 1982; and Ronald Radosh, "The 'Peace Council' and Peace," *The New Republic,* January 13, 1983, esp. pp. 17-18.

33. Quoted in Lindorff, "War in Peace," p. 13.

34. Ibid.

35. Ibid.

36. Quoted in Anne Quindlen, "About New York," *New York Times,* June 13, 1982.

37. Quoted in Robert D. McFadden, "A Spectrum of Humanity Represented in the Rally," *New York Times,* June 13, 1982. As usual, many people went simply for the love of crowds and rock music. See Michael Levin, "The Springsteening of Disarmament," *New York Times,* June 19, 1982.

38. Alexander Cockburn and James Ridgeway, "Will the Freeze Movement Be More Than a Fad?" *The Village Voice,* April 13, 1982, p. 6.

39. Ibid., p. 7.

40. Ibid.

41. Stone was not particularly well liked by other relative doves, including sponsors of the American Federation of Scientists, because he had opposed SALT II back in 1979 as being inadequate and urged its renegotiation. This was also the view of the treaty's most effective opponent, General Edward Rowny. Stone's views earned him the honor of a personal attack by the arms controller's pantheon: Marvin Goldberger, Herbert Scoville, Ruth Adams, Hans Bethe, Paul Doty, George Kistiakowsky, Sidney Drell, Charles H. Townes, Richard Garwin, Gerard Piel, Jerome B. Weisner, and Abram Chayes. See Jeremy Stone, "SALT in Perspective," *New York Times,* March 11, 1979, and "Why the Senate Should Ratify SALT II," *New York Times,* April 3, 1979.

117

42. The following examples should suffice: David Linebaugh, formerly deputy assistant director of The Arms Control and Disarmament Agency (ACDA), is now a member of the Committee for National Security. Anne H. Cahn, another former ACDA official, directs the committee. Alan Neidle, another former ACDA official, also works now for the committee. See David Linebaugh, "Last Fifteen Minutes in Geneva," *Christian Science Monitor,* August 10, 1983; Anne Cahn and James F. Leonard (a former State Department official during the Carter Administration), "Don't Accuse Moscow," *New York Times,* April 26, 1983; Alan Neidle, "A Freeze Benefits Both of Us," *New York Times,* March 15, 1983; and Paul Warnke and David Linebaugh, "It's Time for a Summit," *Washington Post,* October 23, 1983. See also the views of yet another former ACDA official, Stefan H. Leader, "The Nuclear Freeze Movement," *Christian Science Monitor,* November 10, 1982. Warnke, former director of the ACDA, heads PeacePac, a pro-freeze political action group organized under the aegis of the Council for a Livable World. His writings are ubiquitous, from the discursive to the brusque. See, for example, "Can 18,000 Warheads Be Wrong?" *Human Rights,* Winter 1983, pp. 14-17, 51-53; and "Deadlier Arms Move World Closer to War," *U.S.A. Today,* July 8, 1983.

43. On this, for example, see Jennifer Leaning, Matthew Leighton, John Lamperti, and Herbert L. Abrams, "Programs for Surviving Nuclear Wars: A Critique," *Bulletin of the Atomic Scientists,* June/July 1983, pp. 1-16; and "Militarizing the Last Frontier: The Space Weapons Race," *Defense Monitor,* vol. 12, no. 5, 1983, the broadside of the Center for Defense Information. A solicitation from the Union of Concerned Scientists, received by this writer in January 1984 dated "Thursday Afternoon," describes the prospective militarization of space as "dragging heaven into hell."

44. For example, see the views of Leon Wieseltier, *Nuclear War, Nuclear Peace* (New York: Holt, Rinehart and Winston, 1983), pp. 44-45; Sir Solly Zuckerman, *Nuclear Illusion and Reality* (New York: Random House, 1982); Arthur Macy Cox, "End the War Game," *New York Times,* November 8, 1983; and Theodore Draper, "Nuclear Temptations," *New York Review of Books,* January 19, 1984, pp. 42-48.

45. Some minimum deterrence theorists must be given credit for logical consistency when they argue that the United States should disengage strategically from Europe because the United States *cannot* defend it without running unacceptable risks to ourselves. This new variety of isolationism is championed at the Center for Defense Information. See Morton Kondracke, "Nuclear Innocents Abroad," *The New Republic,* May 9, 1981, pp. 16-19; and Earl Ravenal, "Counterforce and Alliance: The Ultimate Connection," *International Security,* Spring 1982.

46. Recent defenses of finite deterrence views are not difficult to find. See, for example, Spurgeon M. Keeny and Wolfgang Panovsky, "MAD Versus

NUTS," *Foreign Affairs,* Winter 1981-82; and Louis René Beres, *Mimicking Sisyphus: America's Countervailing Nuclear Strategy* (Lexington, Mass.: D. C. Heath and Co., 1983). Perhaps the classic exposition of this position is McGeorge Bundy's "To Cap a Volcano," *Foreign Affairs,* October 1969. One of the first expositions was by P. M. S. Blackett, *Studies of War* (New York: Hill and Wang, 1962). Explicit linkages between finite deterrence theory and the freeze are also plentiful. See Eugene J. Carroll, Jr., "Nuclear Freeze: Yes," *New York Times,* October 31, 1982; W. Averill Harriman, Clark Clifford, William E. Colby, and Paul C. Warnke, "Nuclear Freeze: The Case for an American 'Yes'," *New York Times,* October 3, 1982; and especially "America's Nuclear Ferment: Opportunities for Change," *Defense Monitor,* vol. 12, no. 3, 1983. The latter source states: "A much smaller, *retaliatory* nuclear force is the only useful arsenal that the U.S. and the Soviet Union can hope to possess." If the Center for Defense Information could only convince the Soviet General Staff of this principle, we should all be grateful.

47. This charge has been leveled almost constantly since January 1981. For an example that picked on Richard Burt, then-assistant secretary of state for European affairs, see "Dissension in the Ranks," *The New Republic,* June 6, 1983, p. 9.

48. U. S. House, *Congressional Record,* August 5, 1982, p. H5321. Dellums is one of few congressmen who deserve to be classified as members of the Professional Left rather than of the Left-Liberal Establishment. In the summer of 1983, Dellums convened the Special Congressional Ad Hoc Hearings on the Full Implications of the Military Budget and invited over forty witnesses in six days to present the view that the United States is militaristic in its approach to the world, that U.S. nuclear policy is now geared toward war-fighting *instead* of deterrence, and that military spending should be cut by 20 or 30 per cent. Some "witnesses" included Richard J. Barnet, Paul Warnke, Robert Aldridge, Herbert Scoville, Philip Berrigan, and William Winpisinger. A book emerged from these hearings. See Ronald V. Dellums, *Defense Sense: The Search for a Rational Military Policy* (Cambridge, Mass.: Ballinger, 1983). It is not without irony and interest that Dellums's opponent in the 1984 election is none other than Eldridge Cleaver, author of *Soul on Ice.*

49. U. S. House, *Congressional Record,* August 5, 1982, p. H5178.

50. Ibid., p. H5257.

51. Ibid., p. H5824.

52. Ibid., p. H5332.

53. Ibid., p. H5325.

54. Ibid., p. H5261.

55. Ibid., p. H5347.

56. Freeze Fact Sheet No. 1.

57. U.S. House, *Congressional Record,* August 5, 1982, p. H5227.

58. Ibid., p. H5257.

59. Ibid., p. H5350.

60. Ibid., p. H5255.

61. Ibid., p. H5296.

62. Ibid., p. H5320.

63. Alton Frye, "Weaponry Is Theft," *New York Times Book Review,* March 18, 1984, p. 25.

64. See Department of Defense Annual Report to the Congress, Fiscal Year 1983, p. iv-10; and Joseph A. Peckman and Barry P. Bosworth, "The Budget and the Economy," in Joseph A. Peckman, ed., *Setting National Priorities: The 1983 Budget* (Washington: Brookings, 1982), p. 37.

65. See the relevant data in U.S. Senate, *Strategic Force Modernization Programs, Hearings before the Subcommittee on Strategic and Theater Nuclear Forces of the Committee on Armed Services,* 97th Cong. 1st sess., 1981, p. 118.

66. The reference here is to "Nuclear Weapons and the Atlantic Alliance," *Foreign Affairs,* Spring 1982.

67. See, for example, the report of the second conference on "Public Opinion and Disarmament Priorities," Stanley Foundation, February 1983, p. 8.

68. Randall Forsberg, "A Bilateral Nuclear Weapons Freeze," *Scientific American,* November 1982, p. 52.

69. Ibid.

70. Ibid.

71. Ibid., p. 61.

120

72. Ibid.

73. Ibid.

74. Ibid.

75. Ibid., p. 52.

76. Ibid., p. 60.

77. Ibid. Forsberg makes the same point in *Seeds of Change: The First Real Hearings on the Nuclear Arms Freeze* (Andover, Mass.: Brick House, 1983), pp. 28-29.

78. Forsberg, "A Bilateral Nuclear Weapons Freeze," p. 60.

79. Ibid.

80. See "An Atlantic Alliance for Freeze Activists," *Business Week,* June 13, 1983, p. 64.

81. Mary Kaldor, "Alternative Alliance," *New York Times,* December 15, 1983.

82. Forsberg, "A Bilateral Nuclear Weapons Freeze," p. 52.

83. Bundy, et al., "Nuclear Weapons and the Atlantic Alliance."

84. Forsberg, quoted in *Seeds of Change,* pp. 34-35.

Chapter 4

THE PRAGMATIC CENTER

There is a simple answer to every complex problem—neat, easy, and wrong.

—Henry Louis Mencken

A Different Strategic View

Supporting a policy proposition for a reason having little or nothing to do with its intrinsic merit smacks of dishonesty, and indeed the partisan tactical argument for the nuclear freeze—that it would force the Reagan Administration toward "serious" arms control—has been used dishonestly by some politicians for whom their own political ambitions outweighed all other considerations. But one also found honest uses of such unabashedly pragmatic arguments coming from those professional politicians and policy analysts who are accustomed to compromise, to horsetrading, and to the humbling reality that, as the poet Wallace Stevens once put it, "our paradise is the imperfect." Wherever results are more important than nobility of intention, one will find members of the Pragmatic Center.

For those in the Pragmatic Center, the tactical argument on behalf of the freeze—that supporting it would force the Reagan Administration toward the center, help Democratic electoral prospects, or both—was really the *only* argument. And even on pragmatic grounds it was not an unassailable position; some members of the Pragmatic Center supported the freeze and voted for it, and others did not. The reason that some members of the Pragmatic Center could support the freeze for tactical reasons while others could not is that the beliefs of the Left-Liberal Establishment and the strategic theory derived from them are unevenly shared by the Pragmatic Center. The Pragmatic Center accepts some but not all of the basic axioms of minimum deterrence, but those that are not shared make a very big difference. In essence, the dominant assured destruction views of the Kennedy, Johnson, and pre-1974 Nixon Administrations, as they evolved, form only the starting point of the strategic theory of the Pragmatic Center, but both the starting and *ending* points of the strategic theory of the Left-Liberal Establishment. Where the beliefs and policies of the Pragmatic Center differ from minimum deterrence views, they do so in three basic ways.

First, the view that incremental advantages in numbers of weapons short of decisive military advantage casts no political shadow is rejected. More specifically, the inapplicability of using nuclear weapons for purposes of extended deterrence is rejected less for logical reasons than for reasons of political exigency. We *cannot* abandon Europe politically even if the military logic of flexible response is imperfect. We have substituted *uncertainty* about what we would do in the event of war for the unconvincing "certainty" of massive retaliation in order to ensure deterrence in Europe. Few were ever completely satisfied with this solution even in the days of substantial U.S. central strategic preponderance. When that substantial preponderance turned to marginal advantage in the 1960s, to rough parity in the 1970s, and then to clinging parity in the 1980s, what had been a very abstract problem became far more worrisome and proximate. It still is.

Second, the rapid pace of technological innovation, combined with the long lead times involved in developing, testing, and deploying strategic weapons systems, is such that constant vigilance is required even to maintain *assured* destruction capabilities. So even if the *logic* of minimum deterrence were true, the technological dynamism of the arms competition still renders "enough" a constantly moving target.[1]

Third, the relationship of arms races to war and the different effects of different kinds of arms races are also topics wherein the strategic theory of the Pragmatic Center differs from that of the Left-Liberal Establishment. In the Left-Liberal Establishment, there tends to be a somewhat indivisible view of arms races. In other words, accumulations of new arms—of whatever kind—beyond retaliatory sufficiency are provocative, destabilizing, and rob the budget of funds sorely needed for human services. There is also an implicit assumption, based on a generalized "learning from history," that arms races lead to wars by magnifying fears and exacerbating tensions. Edward Kennedy put it directly: "Anytime you get an expansion of nuclear capabilities in a dramatic

124

way you increase the possibility of a nuclear confrontation and war."[2]

The strategic theory of the Pragmatic Center disputes the inevitability of arms races leading to war, admitting instead only the possibility of such a relationship. This is because, on the matter of the provocative nature of arms races, the strategic theory of the Pragmatic Center differentiates between weapons. Some weapons *are* destabilizing, putting in jeopardy the surety of survival of an adversary's retaliatory force. But some new developments can enhance survivability, reduce payload, or enhance command and control, so as to reduce the risks of war by provocation or accident. While the strategic theory of the Left-Liberal Establishment worries little about incremental differences in static indices of nuclear power beyond the threshold of sufficiency, that of the Pragmatic Center is concerned that numerical imbalances can press the disadvantaged side into less prudent postures, such as launch-under-attack or launch-on-warning, in order to compensate for weakness. Numbers alone may mean little, true enough, but such hair-trigger (and hair-raising) postures may mean quite a lot.

A Historical Aside

Perhaps the best way to trace the evolution of the strategic theory of the Pragmatic Center from its early origins in a more pure version of mutual assured destruction logic to its present more nuanced state is to review the evolution of U.S. strategic doctrine in the post-1974 Nixon, Ford, and Carter Administrations. Despite differences among and within these administrations over strategic issues, it is still accurate to say that both the Ford and Carter Administrations, taken as a whole, were representative of the Pragmatic Center when it came to their views of deterrence strategy. When "real conservatives" criticized the Nixon and Ford Administrations in this regard and today assail the Reagan Administration for bringing aboard "all the Nixon-Ford retreads," as Richard Viguerie put it, speaking of Henry Kissinger, Alexander Haig, Donald Rumsfeld, Brent Scowcroft, William Ruckelshaus, and George Shultz, to name but a few, they were not far wrong.[3] While there were in the Carter Administration many well-placed advocates of minimum deterrence, the Carter Administration, was nevertheless the creator of a document known as Presidential Directive 59 (PD-59), which signaled an accelerated shift in U.S. strategic targeting doctrine away from assured destruction requisites. This revision in U.S. strategic doctrine was the culmination of years of doctrinal turmoil, and, as is evidenced by the freeze movement, the sources of that turmoil have yet to disappear. The root of the turmoil lies mainly in the different assessments of Soviet strategic culture and intentions adopted by the Left-Liberal Establishment and everything to its left on the one hand, and by the Pragmatic Center and almost everything to its right on the other hand. To see how this schism developed, we must consult the historical record.

During the early post-World War II period—before Sputnik—when the United States possessed a nuclear monopoly, the problem of strategy did not really arise. Until the Korean War, U.S. policy had to negotiate only with itself on what to do with nuclear military power. Even after Soviet attainment of nuclear weapons, the absence of effective Soviet countervailing power led the United States to feature prominently U.S. atomic power in its Cold War diplomacy. The posture of "massive retaliation" was implicit U.S. policy before it was announced by Secretary of State John Foster Dulles in 1954. Curiously enough, the official doctrine began its life only a few years before its logic began to wane. After Sputnik in 1957, "massive retaliation" devolved into an effort to maintain maximum political benefit from a strategic balance that no longer provided unequivocal military advantage. Despite the bluster of "massive retaliation," the reluctance of the United States to use or threaten to use nuclear weapons remained intact. With a single possible exception (in Korea in 1953), the United States never threatened the use of its nuclear monopoly for political purposes. Moreover, during the eight years of the Eisenhower Administration, U.S. military forces intervened abroad only one time—in Lebanon in 1958—and they did not fire a shot. The doctrine of massive retaliation was something of a bluff, dependent on a ghoulish uncertainty for most of its existence. But it projected an image of toughness which, though it gave rise to Gaullism, was nevertheless a creditable backdrop to early U.S. Cold War diplomacy.

The declining credibility of the massive retaliation posture eventually led, during the Kennedy Administration, to a new theory altogether. The notions of "flexible response," "assured destruction," and "damage limitation" were born under the tenure of Robert S. McNamara at the Pentagon. At about the same time that nuclear strategy became a serious matter because of developing Soviet capabilities, a remarkable liaison between the U.S. government and social science academia took shape.[4] The intellectual power that forged U.S. military strategy during the Kennedy Administration came not from the professional military but from intellectuals for the most part bereft of any military experience. As critics of mutual assured destruction see it, David Halberstam's account of the tragedy of the "best and brightest" in the Vietnam War is no less true with regard to matters of nuclear strategy.[5] The same secretary of defense, Robert S. McNamara, and the same "whiz kids" who gave us "controlled escalation" in Vietnam also gave us "assured destruction." Camelot was indivisible.

Strategies developed by the United States during this period were primarily theories of bargaining. Cognizant of the sharp distinction between diplomacy and war that had existed in the United States prior to World War II, and aware perhaps to a fault of the advent of "limited war" like that in Korea, McNamara set about to integrate military posture with what he conceived to be the politically possible.[6] The goal was to provide the president with military options on every level of conflict commensurate with the challenge. Not only would this prevent a situation where a U.S. president would be forced to choose between major war and capitulation, but it would also create material bargaining assets in the way of forces in place to deal with a wide array of circumstances.

Despite this praiseworthy ambition and its high-powered logic, things did not work out as planned. What had begun as an effort to integrate force and political tasks degenerated into a technocratic exercise. The great efforts undertaken to build up U.S. conventional forces with the newest and most sophisticated military technologies, and to expand and modernize U.S. strategic forces, effaced the calculus of political prudence. With respect to strategic forces, Henry Kissinger retrospectively described what occurred:

According to [assured destruction doctrine] deterrence was assured so long as we possessed the ability to destroy a predetermined percentage of Soviet population and industrial capacity. Strategy thereby turned into an engineering problem, an economic analysis essentially independent of the size of the opposing forces.[7]

Nuclear weapons were for deterring other nuclear weapons and nothing more. The point of nuclear doctrine was not to plan the use of these weapons in an ultimate contingency, but rather to quarantine them altogether from international politics. The consistency of this perspective with the longstanding U.S. view that nuclear war was immoral and "unthinkable," as President Eisenhower once put it, is clear. On this basis, McNamara looked forward to the day when assured destruction might be made mutual. While the United States busied itself with diversifying its forces for the sake of survivability, creating the triad, it ceased building new intercontinental ballistic missiles after 1967. It allowed the Soviet Union to manage itself into a position of essential strategic equipoise under the belief that, once attained, there would be no military or political incentive for either side to build up more forces. At the time of the beginning of the SALT process at Glassboro State College in 1967, President Lyndon Johnson and his advisers still believed that, having attained parity with the United States in most measures of nuclear capability, the Soviets would slow down and eventually stop their building program, assuming that we did the same. The absence of political motive, it was hoped, would help sustain a technological plateau in the arms race, which would in turn contribute to permanent parity.[8]

The doctrine of mutual assured destruction assumed, logically, that U.S. weapons would be targeted against Soviet cities and industry, and not against Soviet weapons. Moreover, the U.S. government assumed that Soviet missiles would be targeted in a similar fashion and for a similar set of reasons. McNamara and most of his associates became so convinced of the correctness of this paradigm they had created that they never gave serious thought to the possibility that the Soviets believed something quite different about the use of nuclear weapons. To some extent, the tightness of mutual assured destruction logic was one of its problems: it was so methodically articulated and so cognitively

128

symmetrical that McNamara and others took Soviet silence on its precepts as matter-of-fact agreement. This concept was reinforced by the technical "fact" that accurate, reliable counterforce targeting was either not possible at all or easily counteracted by silo-hardening.

Disenchantment with the doctrine of mutual assured destruction emerged in the late 1960s. Early in the Nixon Administration there was a general consensus in the National Security Council and the Department of Defense that the concept was inadequate as it stood, and this found clear expression in President Nixon's first two foreign policy reports.[9] Yet the doctrine of mutual assured destruction made an improbable comeback mainly because of SALT I, the Anti-Ballistic Missile (ABM) Treaty in particular. Many took the Soviet agreement to sign an ABM treaty as a sign that they had come to accept the concept of mutual assured destruction. The chairman of the Senate Foreign Relations Committee, William Fulbright, exemplified this belief as he castigated Secretary of Defense Melvin Laird in 1972:

You sought to give the impression in public session to this committee and to the public that the Soviets were probably going for a first-strike capability. It scared everybody to death and you got your appropriations. . . . I think the record will show that you were wrong in your estimate. . . . They have not gone for a first-strike capability; *the very fact that we have the ABM Treaty is evidence of that* and your hunch or whatever you want to call it was not correct.[10]

National Security Adviser Henry A. Kissinger was most explicit of all about what SALT I meant in doctrinal terms. On June 15, 1972, he said:

By setting a limit to ABM defenses the treaty not only eliminated one area of potentially dangerous defensive competition, but it reduces the incentive for continuing deployment of offensive systems. As long as it lasts offensive missile forces have, in effect, a free ride to their targets. *Beyond a certain level of sufficiency, differences in numbers are therefore not conclusive.* . . . In the absence of significant defenses, even relatively small forces can do an enormous amount of damage.

Therefore, too, if we can move into the second phase of SALT, into an explicit recognition that both sides will stay away from counterforce strategies, from the one danger that now exists, or the overwhelming danger, that they will try to destroy each other, then perhaps the premium on MIRVs will be reduced, because, as you remember, Mr. Chairman [Senator Fulbright] MIRVs were developed at first as a hedge against ABM.[11]

These remarks, and countless others like them at the time, illustrate something very important about the hold that Secretary McNamara's theories continued to have over U.S. strategic thinking. The ABM treaty was supposedly a sign of Soviet acceptance of mutual assured destruction logic, because in order to mount a first strike one had to be able to limit damage to oneself to "acceptable levels." Since Soviet counterforce capabilities in their ICBMs were incapable of destroying U.S. submarines or bombers, it stood to reason that a first strike required some additional means of protection. The Soviets had an extensive air-defense system arrayed against U.S. bombers, but against U.S. SLBMs only some form of ballistic missile defense could be effective. The treaty therefore indicated, supposedly, that the Soviets had given up trying to protect themselves against the U.S. sea-based deterrent and therefore did not seek a first strike.

But this logic made sense only if the alternatives were limited to deterrence through mutual assured destruction, or the absence of deterrence represented by a first-strike capability, the latter being the symmetrical logical opposite of the former. The mistaken assessment of Soviet intentions that Senator Fulbright and others made at the time was based on their inability to rise above the sterile couplet of the mutual assured destruction (MAD) concept and its logical opposite. Fulbright is no longer in the Senate, but others who are remain locked in this same conceptual prison, as do some hawkish critics on the Far Right who continue to assume that the Soviets seek, and think they can obtain, classical first-strike posture.[12]

Serious scholars of Soviet military thinking have long since risen above this sterile dichotomy. While there is no firm consensus on all points as to what the Soviets are up to, the outlines of a plausible alternative view that accounts well for our observations of Soviet building programs and negotiating strategy has emerged, and it is this alternative view that undergirds the strategic theory of the Pragmatic Center. Its most fundamental

130

premise is that the Soviet Union does not even view
in the same way the United States does.[13] The Sovi
appear to have theories per se about deterrence, crisis e
or bargaining. For the United States, deterrence is an
intellectual construction, "invented by civilians and rooted   y-
chological or game theory, not the organizational theory of military science." But, writes Robert Legvold,

For the Soviet Union, it is a residual concept, an effect produced by
performing other primary tasks well. . . . It is inexplicit, it has no texts,
it even lacks an adequate name in Russian, and it is without authors,
only overseers, and these are military leaders whose first concern is with
success in war.[14]

So whereas the U.S. view of deterrence is captured in a
formal theoretical framework established by civilians, for the Soviets it is a residual concept without a theory that instead substi-
tutes the science of war. In this regard, the Soviets have a very
traditionally minded view of military strategy; they do not share
the conclusion that bargaining, that is, *inducing* choices rather than
eliminating choices (coercion), will dictate the course of war in
the nuclear age. Instead, they assume that by preparing to pros-
ecute war successfully they are both deterring war and putting
themselves in the best possible position to win a war should deterrence fail. Moreover, they appear to see war as total. The more
abstract idea that the outcome of a nuclear war can be decisively
shaped by limited counterforce strikes followed by informal or
formal bargaining is alien to Soviet thinking. Consequently, the
Soviets see U.S. doctrines about bargaining, escalation dominance, and the like as ways to extract political benefit from nuclear
weapons, which the Soviets had been reluctant to do. As Legvold
describes it: "We tend to start with deterrence, pressing on to
defense, ultimately subordinating defense to deterrence; they skip
the issue of deterrence and concentrate on defense, assuming deterrence will follow."[15] The United States, then, has or aspires to
have a strategic doctrine. The Soviet Union does not. It is interested only in the *operational* concepts of war. The Soviets not only
reject specific U.S. doctrines, they reject the very *idea* of a "strategic doctrine" as it is understood in the West.

Therefore, Soviet ideas about nuclear deterrence can be aptly

131

described as a "war-fighting" strategy, but it is important to distinguish what this does and does not mean, for the issues are sometimes confused by emotional inclinations. The sense of the Pragmatic Center is that the Soviet Union aims to practice damage limitation on the grandest of scales. In the Soviet view, preventing war is the job of politics and diplomacy; winning wars is the job of the military. Soviet civil defense and their massive—though perhaps futile—investment in air defense is *not* a prolegomenon to a "first-strike" capability defined according to classical U.S. doctrinal precepts, but rather reflects the traditional task of reducing damage so that general war can be waged on all levels.

Here we must address another significant difference between traditional Western and Soviet strategic thinking. For the Soviets, the central nuclear balance seems not nearly as important a factor in war as it is for the United States. The Soviets believe that the "decisive feature of any general war will be the ability of one side to triumph on *all* levels, from conventional to nuclear."[16] The Soviets are therefore much less worried than we are about the precise calibration of the nuclear balance. Similarly, they (thankfully) ascribe less significance than do most Western analysts to the incipient vulnerability of U.S. ICBMs and much more significance than do most Western analysts (not so thankfully) to their growing advantages in conventional and theater forces in Europe and elsewhere. All together, the Soviets are less concerned than the United States about the central strategic balance, not only because that balance is now much more favorable to them than it ever was in the past, but also because they have a much more integrated view of how various levels of military forces are likely to be used, and *should* be used, in a war.

Since the Soviet Union tends to substitute operational fighting concepts for strategic doctrine, it places ahead of all other goals the reduction of the damage that the U.S. nuclear arsenal can do to the Soviet Union. This may well be a historically conditioned reaction to the melancholy experience of the Russians with a parade of devastating Mongol, French, and German invasions over the years. Nevertheless, we must distinguish what this does and does not mean in contemporary terms. It *does* mean that the Soviets are bent on putting the U.S. ICBM force in jeopardy, and they seem to have come close to doing so.[17] It also *does* mean that the Soviet Union does *not* accept the proposition that, despite the enormous devastation that would be inevitable in a full nuclear exchange, nations cannot recover to the point of being able to wage war on other levels. "Winning" such a war is by no means attractive to the Soviets, and it is false to assert that the Soviet Union believes that political objectives can be plausibly advanced by recourse to nuclear war. But winning is preferable to losing. What it does *not* mean is that the Soviet Union has a formal strategic doctrine that deliberately aims for a classic first strike; it does *not* mean that the Soviet Union believes that a preclusive, unambiguous nuclear superiority is attainable.

The Soviet view of deterrence and military power in the nuclear age has important implications for arms control. One of the reasons that the Soviet Union is so intent on an extension of traditional damage-limitation war strategies is that these kinds of measures are completely within their control and do not depend on inducing the other side to exhibit restraint. Specifically, they do not depend on notions of "shared liability" in the population-hostage relationship; this the Soviets have consistently rejected.[18] They have been, and remain extremely reluctant to trade measures in arms control that are under their own control for those that are not, even if such measures lead to increased "stability." Unless promised a greater degree of damage limitation within arms control proposals than could be had unilaterally, they are not likely to be interested. This explains both why the Soviets have refused to reduce their SS-18 silo-killers *and* why they did accede to the ABM treaty. The United States had an enormous, perhaps insuperable, lead in ABM technology. If successful, a U.S. ballistic missile defense system would have severely limited the penetrability of Soviet ICBMs long before the reverse would have been true. It was this interest, and not any concern with conditions of stability under the mutual assured destruction (MAD) paradigm, that recommended the ABM treaty to Moscow.

Because the Soviets are primarily concerned with damage-limitation measures, they worry less than the United States does about the destabilizing effects of a counterforce race—especially when they are winning it. Indeed, their sense of "stability" is quite different from ours. The United States has traditionally viewed "stability" as something that must be achieved by *mutual* restraint or agreement; again, it is a concept based on tacit or formal bargaining. The Soviet view is much simpler: the more power "we" have, the more "stable" the situation is from "our" point of view. Stability for them is a unilateral concept. Living for so many years in a position of manifest inferiority, and fearing constant "machinations" of the United States to reap maximum political and psychological benefit from its declaratory nuclear policies, this notion of stability is understandable. So long as military trends favor the Soviet Union, any arms control agreement the Soviets sign will increase "stability" from *their* point of view. Only if and when Soviet ICBMs become equally vulnerable to U.S. counterforce capabilities—which is a far more serious problem for Soviet planners because more than twice as much of the Soviet nuclear arsenal is in land-based forces—will the matter become a likely issue for arms control. Before then, there is little hope that the United States can convince the Soviets to reduce their capabilities against Minuteman through negotiation, *even if* Moscow is convinced that they could never achieve a certain capability of eliminating U.S. ICBMs. This is why most members of the Pragmatic Center support the MX and Trident II programs.

Finally, because the strategic balance is less important to the Soviet Union than it is to the United States, the Soviets have tended to see the SALT process, and now the START process, less as a way to shape the military balance and more as an exercise in political relations. The Soviets have always been interested in less radical, almost cosmetic, agreements that leave the strategic balance essentially intact; they have also been sensitive to failure less for military and more for political reasons. This partly is why they were so upset at the Carter Administration's comprehensive proposal of March 1977 and the Reagan START proposal of May 1982. The greater the push by the United States to achieve deep reductions, the more these fundamentally different views of what arms control is all about become clear—or should become clear.

The Schlesinger Innovations

While these Soviet views, with these same implications for arms control, existed in 1972, it was not until 1974–75 that the cloud of euphoria that descended with SALT I began to lift. This was one consequence of a conjunction of new blood in the Nixon

134

Administration and unmistakable intelligence information that the Soviet strategic programs were not eschewing counterforce capabilities, as had been hoped in 1972. By 1975, Soviet ballistic accuracies were beginning to worry U.S. planners. Indeed, it was becoming clear that the Soviet Union intended to target U.S. military forces to the extent that their technology permitted.[19]

By 1974–75 it was becoming clear that there were at least three things wrong with McNamara's still-reigning theories. First, the assumption of the mirror-image turned out to be completely wrong. The Soviets evidently did not share the theory of mutual assured destruction, they did not ascribe the kind of importance we did to "stability" under this doctrine, or even mean the same thing by "stability." Second, as a result, the mutual incentive to create and maintain parity—and thereby to find the elusive technological plateau that would eviscerate the momentum of the arms race—never existed and there was little hope that it ever would. What was not possible in the mid-1960s—reliable counterforce—had become very possible, and ironically this was as much due to U.S. technological advances as to Soviet ones. Third, the doctrine of mutual assured destruction was never sensitive to the psychological inhibitions of implementing such a strategy, which in turn seriously degraded its credibility. It depended on raising the nuclear threshold as high as possible through the "unthinkability" of invoking the mutual hostage relationship. This was fine so long as the other side saw things the same way. But if the other side did not, then the deterrent power even of an invulnerable U.S. countervalue second strike was not a sure thing. The "engineering" problem referred to by Henry Kissinger, which *could* be undertaken without concern for the other side's *forces,* could *not* be undertaken successfully without concern for the other side's *understanding.*

Starting in 1974, the United States began to consider what became known as "limited nuclear options," in other words, ways to engage in nuclear exchanges short of all-out war. Ironically, this was a logical extension of McNamara's NATO doctrine of "flexible response" to levels of violence *beyond* the nuclear threshold, and for the same reason—the search for maximal deterrent credibility. But Secretary of Defense James Schlesinger's doctrinal revisions were not born mainly out of a better theoretical appreciation of Soviet strategy and military doctrine. Nor was the desire to build up "limited counterforce options" a new intellectual bolt out of the blue; while it was official doctrine to avoid counterforce targeting, the military had always included in the SIOP (single integrated operating plan) options to attack purely military targets.[20] What really led to the Schlesinger innovations was mounting evidence that the Soviet Union intended to take full advantage of the numerical disparities allowed them under SALT I. With greater numbers and larger payloads, the extensive MIRVing of Soviet ICBM forces might eventually allow them to pass the United States in every static indicator of strategic power, including warheads. Schlesinger worried that these asymmetries favoring the Soviet Union might tempt the Kremlin into thinking it could exploit a military imbalance for diplomatic purposes. Worse than the problems of political perceptions were the military implications of the large Soviet counterforce advantage that seemed likely to emerge if nothing were done to prevent or offset it.

There were two closely related problems here. First, the stability of mutual assured destruction, after all, depending on the mutual inability to threaten the forces of the other side. If the Soviets could improve their relative military position with a preemptive counterforce first strike to the point where the United States could retaliate in a countervalue mode only at the risk of total destruction, then deterrence would be seriously undermined. Schlesinger suggested that if the Soviets would not abandon their counterforce weapons in SALT, it was only prudent to make sure that the president had the option, after riding out a counterforce first strike, to deprive the Soviet Union of its residual ICBM force holding U.S. cities hostage, so that things would be "even" again. To do less was to call the stability of deterrence, especially in crises, into serious question. Second, Schlesinger was concerned about degradation of the U.S. commitment to Western Europe under conditions of central strategic parity. He reasoned that unless the United States developed options other than all-out war, the U.S. umbrella over Western Europe would appear fully credible only to the extent that the Kremlin believed that a suicidal maniac resided in the White House.

Schlesinger went to great pains to point out that what he

proposed did not diverge much from past practice. He simply wanted to enhance the credibility of deterrence by giving the president a broader range of employable options, and by ensuring that the weapons required to implement those options became available. Schlesinger did not advise that the United States necessarily required equity in counterforce, nor did he seek a degree of counterforce capability that the Soviets could construe as preparation for a disarming U.S. first strike. Still, Schlesinger's doctrinal innovations were the first formal breach in the mutual assured destruction paradigm, and, as such, they evoked much debate about the problem. The weapons programs initiated under his tenure—including MX— signaled a recognition that SALT II probably would fail to prevent mutual counterforce postures, as Kissinger had hoped it would after SALT I, and introduced new, complicating variables into the SALT process. Finally, Schlesinger's reformulations made it more difficult for any subsequent administration to retreat to a simple posture of "mutual assured destruction."

So it remained, though not without considerable debate until 1979–80, that is, throughout the entire period during which SALT II was being negotiated and beyond. Early that year, President Carter authorized a further shift in U.S. strategic doctrine—PD-59—that was basically an extension of Schlesinger's "limited nuclear options" under new technical conditions.[21] Not only would the United States develop limited nuclear options within an assured destruction framework, but from now on U.S. targeting posture would emphasize counterforce targeting to strengthen deterrence.

If there is any single text of the strategic theory of the Pragmatic Center, it is PD-59 and the "countervailing strategy" that accompanied its unveiling. In April 1979, Secretary of Defense Harold Brown spoke to the Foreign Policy Association on behalf of the SALT II treaty. There he repeated the basic requirements of mutual assured destruction, calling it "the bedrock of nuclear deterrence." But, he continued, assured destruction is not

sufficient in itself as a strategic doctrine. Massive retaliation may not be appropriate, nor will its prospect always be sufficiently credible, to deter the full range of actions we seek to prevent.

137

We need capabilities convincingly able to do, and sure to carry out, under any circumstance the Soviets consider realistic, whatever damage the Soviets consider will deter them. Put differently, the perceptions of those whom we seek to deter can determine what is needed for deterrence in various circumstances. For fully effective deterrence, we need to be able to respond at the level appropriate to the type and scale of a Soviet attack. Fully effective deterrence requires forces of sufficient size and flexibility to attack selectively a range of military and other targets and to enable us to hold back a significant reserve.

This ability to provide measured retaliation in response to less-than-total attacks—and thus to prevent the Soviets from imagining that they can gain meaningful advantage at some level of nuclear conflict—is essential to credible deterrence. Moreover, whatever doubts one may have about whether a nuclear war could be kept limited—and I have severe ones—it would be the height of folly to put the United States in a position in which uncontrolled escalation would be the only course we could follow.[22]

The Pragmatic Center and the Freeze

Now that the strategic theory of the Pragmatic Center has been laid out and its origins explicated, the attitude of the Pragmatic Center toward the main arguments of nuclear freeze proponents becomes much easier to understand. Let us start with the freeze movement's attack on counterforce. The argument advanced by Forsberg, Markey, and others that counterforce weapons and targeting doctrines are crisis-unstable and give rise to the "use'em or lose'em" dilemma is not new, and may even be correct under some circumstances.[23] But the problem confronting U.S. planners today, say the members of the Pragmatic Center as well as the Conservative Mainstream, is not *whether* to abjure a counterforce world; it is, rather, what *kind* of counterforce world will it be, for the Soviet Union has already foreclosed the prior option. The Soviet ICBM force is already designed and targeted in a counterforce mode. A freeze even in 1975, or in 1980 or 1982, would not have prevented a counterforce world, nor would a freeze today prevent one. What a freeze *would* prevent is a counterforce world in which there is *rough parity* between U.S. and Soviet counterforce capabilities. The question is, then, what are the implications of inequity in counterforce capabilities favoring the Soviet Union? Honest people can and do disagree about whether an imbalanced counterforce world is more unstable

138

or less unstable than a mutual counterforce world, or whether *equity* in counterforce is necessary to negate the counterforce capabilities of the other side, or rather something less than that.[24] But to frame the issue—as the freeze movement does—as being about *whether there will be* a counterforce world is to blink at reality. As to the questions about Soviet strategic culture and the crisis implications of counterforce imbalances, Forsberg does not mention these at all, nor have other supposed "experts" who support the freeze seriously addressed these issues.

The U.S. Committee Against Nuclear War distorted the matter even more by implying, as Markey's letter did, that the MX presents the world with the same problem today that Soviet counterforce systems bring. But Markey did not mention that there were already over 300 Soviet SS-18s currently deployed, not to mention SS-19s and SS-17s in large numbers, while the fate of the MX was still uncertain, and that the United States would not have been able, in any event, to deploy even 100 MX missiles before 1989. Moreover, the categorical distinction Markey made between weapons that deter and weapons that fight is disingenuous. Many analysts of the Pragmatic Center argue that only weapons that appear to be usable in militarily logical ways can successfully deter war in times of great crisis and stress. Threatening to do illogical and militarily senseless things with weapons of mass destruction seems less likely to deter a determined adversary and more likely to lead to self-deterrence.

The claim made by pro-freeze groups that the MX is a "first-strike weapon" is a more complex matter. The MX *is* planned to be a counterforce-capable weapon and therefore a weapon theoretically suited to pre-emptive, damage-limiting strikes against the Soviet Union. The mere existence of such capabilities makes such an option possible. But the MX was never intended as a first-strike weapon, and the current strategic doctrine that would govern its use, as developed over the last four administrations, does not call for its use first. It is rather designed as a second-strike counterforce weapon that can ride out a Soviet first-strike and retaliate against Soviet weapons held in reserve to such a degree that after the exchange the Soviets will have gained no relative military advantage. Foreknowledge of the MX's capability and mission would presumably help persuade the Soviet

Union that nothing could be gained by their striking first and so would contribute to deterrence. Clearly, for a first-strike weapon to provide a first-strike capability, it must be deployed in numbers large enough to cover a wide target set. The decision to acquire only 100 MX missiles falls far short of a first-strike capability. Moreover, the United States would not have spent many years and many billions of dollars trying to find a survivable basing mode for the MX if it were intended to be fired first. In a speech in April 1982, Secretary of State Haig essentially restated the basic argument of PD-59: "Deterrence depends upon our capability, even after suffering a massive nuclear blow, to prevent an aggressor from securing a military advantage and prevailing in a conflict. Only if we maintain such a capability can we deter such a blow."[25] Such a capability, Haig explained, included second-strike counterforce weapons capable of hitting residual Soviet forces holding U.S. countervalue targets hostage.

As simple and logical as the concept of second-strike counterforce is, pro-freeze groups insist on equating counterforce capability with first-strike intentions. And while the true radicals of the Professional Left were not hesitant to make this claim when Harold Brown was a spokesman for a Democratic administration, many people seem to find it much easier to do so when there is a Republican in the White House.

It is only when one comes to the question of whether *matching* Soviet counterforce capabilities or throw-weight advantages is necessary for military purposes that policy differences arise between the Pragmatic Center and the Conservative Mainstream. Supporters of PD-59 would argue that military adequacy must be measured according to mission, not according to some numerological abacus. The Reagan Administration, on the other hand, wishes not only to be able to deny the Soviet Union the potential to improve its military position with a first-strike, but also to put Soviet counterforce systems *at equivalent risk* in the belief that the risks of such a posture are offset by potential benefits, notably in the leverage such a capability can bring to promote serious arms control negotiations. We will return to these matters in chapter 5.

On the general question of linkage, most members of the

Pragmatic Center have trouble with the assertion that arms control agreements necessarily have benign influences over political relations more broadly conceived. Most would agree energetically with Seweryn Bialer's observation that while arms agreements *can* aid political relations, such agreements themselves tend to follow rather than precede an improved political relationship. "The error of the various peace and 'freeze' movements," wrote Bialer, "is to think the process works the other way around."[26]

As to the positive correlation between arms races and war, the Pragmatic Center admits only the possibility, depending on the nature of the race. Clearly, an arms race could lead to war. Some technologies *are* destabilizing and lead to increased fears and the temptation to pre-empt in a crisis. Arms races can eventually create more powerful military bureaucracies that might be less reluctant to go to war or resort to violence. Arms races can make the search for political accommodation more difficult and contribute to a war-prone psychology. Arms races can lead inadvertently to technological innovations that could increase the allure of war-fighting postures and raise the risk of accidental war. Arms races can consume money that might otherwise be spent on human needs to reduce social tensions that can contribute to international friction. Arms races can stimulate proliferation and thus cause war by indirection. Finally, arms races can lead to one side or the other winning the race, thus inviting international blackmail and the consequent possibility of angry armed resistance. But none of these things has to happen. Arms races can be stabilizing if they end up righting an imbalance. They can be stabilizing if, as a result, launch-on-warning or launch-under-attack postures are obviated. They can be stabilizing if obsolete, high-yield warheads are replaced by more controllable, less accident-prone, smaller-yield weapons. They can be stabilizing, too, if competition heads off in a direction likely to minimize the incentives for a first strike—like a competition to deploy non-MIRV'd, small ICBMs.

The key to this perspective is the capacity to distinguish between the implications of various developments rather than to assume, as does the Professional Left, that all new U.S. weapons are bad or that all new U.S. weapons are good, as the Far Right assumes. This capacity to distinguish is a hallmark of what may be the most persuasive and mildly toned argument against the freeze, that of the Harvard Study Group.

Harvard Weighs In

In the current debate, the Pragmatic Center has been well represented intellectually by the Harvard Study Group report. The group's findings first appeared in summary form in *The Atlantic Monthly* in June 1983 under the title "The Realities of Arms Control" and later appeared in book form as *Living with Nuclear Weapons*. The report was authored by a committee of well-known and highly respected scholars: Albert Carnesale, academic dean of the Kennedy School of Government at Harvard and a member of the U.S. SALT I delegation; Paul Doty, director of Harvard's Center for Science and Public Affairs and a member of the Science Advisory Committee in the Kennedy and Johnson Administrations; Stanley Hoffmann, chairman of the Center for European Studies at Harvard; Samuel P. Huntington, director of the Center for International Affairs and coordinator of security planning for the National Security Council from 1977–78; Joseph S. Nye, Jr., former deputy undersecretary of state from 1977–79; and Scott Sagan, a teaching fellow in Harvard's government department. While this august group did not see eye to eye on everything— no surprise to those who know the views of Hoffmann and Huntington—they did close ranks on a number of important issues, placing the report squarely in the Pragmatic Center.

One of the more philosophic points that *Living with Nuclear Weapons* takes up is the chimera of disarmament, whose prospects, the authors note, are bound up with broader political conditions. "While complete disarmament may be a worthy long-term goal, trying to achieve it before the requisite political conditions exist could increase the prospects of war."[27] In other words, in the absence of a sturdy political agreement to abjure the use of force, disarmament is an inherently unstable arrangement, for it tempts the would-be aggressor with disproportionately great rewards for mischief. Until the world progresses to such an arrangement, arms control is in order, and indeed is perhaps necessary even to allow us to reach such a stage of international relations. By rejecting disarmament as an immediate objective but accepting its ultimate desirability and possibility, the Harvard Study Group differs sharply from the Professional Left and from those on the right for whom talk of disarmament in the distant future either evokes disdain or conjures religious visions of the "second coming."

The main point that the Harvard Study Group makes is that the aim of arms control should be military stability, of which there are three types: deterrence stability, arms race stability, and crisis stability. Arms control proposals—of which there are four types (more of this below)—should be judged according to the degree to which they contribute to stability, variously defined. Of the four types of arms control delineated by the study, two are obviously designed with stability in mind: force restructuring to reduce the dangers of accidental war or impetuous war, and stabilizing measures, that is, the banning or limiting of tests, better facilities for crisis communications, like the hotline, and other confidence-building measures.

But the other two types of arms control—reductions and freezes—can have and have had uneven effects on stability. In other words, similar proposals for deep reductions or deployment freezes can have dissimilar effects, depending on the circumstances. *Living with Nuclear Weapons* has little difficulty gleaning the history of arms control for examples:

Certain types of proportional cuts, such as cutting all existing categories by 50 percent [as George Kennan has suggested], could also be destabilizing. It might be dangerous, for example, to cut in half the number of strategic submarines. Because we keep half of our nuclear submarines in port, fewer than ten submarines would then have to be tracked and destroyed for a successful surprise attack against what is now the most invulnerable part of our force.[28]

As to freezes, "A freeze in 1959 would have stopped deployment of our invulnerable Polaris submarine-based missiles, which would have made the 1960s *less* safe."[29] The authors conclude that a nuclear freeze, as proposed by the freeze movement, would pose difficult problems of verification, especially in regard to a production freeze, would "require extensive and elaborate negotiations" lasting "several years," and might in the end prove destabilizing:

It is an open question whether a freeze today would enhance crisis stability or not. Some threatening systems would be stopped. But a freeze could also prevent such developments as the new small single-warhead land-based missile that many experts, including the Presidential Commission on Strategic Forces, believe is the best way to remedy the problems created by MIRVs.[30]

In other words, "there is a strong case for pursuing discriminating restraints on weapons technology rather than a total freeze."[31] The Harvard study pointedly chides those in the nuclear freeze movement who "find refuge in simplistic, unexamined solutions."[32]

Living with Nuclear Weapons is specific about what sorts of freezes or reductions would be stabilizing. In the study's view, a warhead ceiling, or some version of a build-down, could be useful. Freezing MIRVs would be useful; freezing single-warhead missiles or, effectively the same thing, the number of launchers would be bad. A ban on the militarization of space is also a stabilizing feature, according to the study, as are limitations on air defense, ballistic missile defense (BMD) and antisubmarine warfare (ASW). Here, the authors adhere to at least one basic theorem of the mutual assured destruction school of deterrence: to assure the other side's forces a "free ride," as it is often called, by abjuring all efforts at defense, is to guarantee mutual vulnerability. This is a hallmark of the strategic view of the Pragmatic Center and most strategic views to its left. Indeed, the attitude taken toward defensive measures may be the surest litmus test of the contemporary division of views over deterrence theory. In the case of antisatellite weapons, therefore, the only possible rationale for building such a capability, according to the Pragmatic Center, is to persuade the Soviet Union, which developed a crude antisatellite (ASAT) capability first and which is what kindled U.S. interest, to negotiate a ban on further deployment.

Finally, on the crucial question of how much counterforce is enough, the Harvard study backs PD-59 and backs away from the Reagan Administration's approach. What each superpower "needs" for the deterrence of nuclear or major conventional attacks on itself and its main allies is the capacity for assured destruction (which requires a moderate number of survivable but not particularly accurate weapons), *and a limited* capacity for actual warfare. A complete counterforce capability would be disastrous

144

for crisis stability if it consisted of vulnerable forces; and even a completely invulnerable counterforce capability might incite the opponent to strike first in order to use his vulnerable weapons. As Joseph Nye put it in another forum: "A sensible nuclear policy has to make clear to people that the weapons are usable enough to be credible and deter the Soviets, but not so usable that they are actually used. We have a very narrow box in which to work."[33]

By saying that the freeze proposition, however simple its formulation and ostensibly parsimonious its impact, was really very complex as one anticipated implementation, and not as benign as claimed, the Harvard study flew directly in the face of the freeze movement's most cherished assumptions and arguments. Negotiations would be long and difficult, not short and sweet. Stability may or may not be enhanced. The United States is *not* solely responsible for the pace and character of the arms race. "Overkill" is a misleading, simple-minded notion as used by the freeze movement, "redundancy" can be stabilizing and prudent.[34] It is not surprising that these challenges to the catechism of the freeze movement touched off a wrathful attempt at rebuttal, not all of it very polite.

In his review of the Harvard study, Richard J. Barnet likened the study's conclusions to those of the Reagan Administration and, having produced guilt by association, spent most of his time in an attack on the "irresponsibility" of the study's authors and on Harvard University.[35] Robert K. Musil, director of SANE's "education" fund, was also fond of *ad hominem* attack, but he went Barnet one better, claiming that the Harvard study shows that "U.S. nuclear policy would not be much different with a moderate or liberal administration in Washington."[36] To some, this description would suggest that the Reagan Administration is pursuing a realistic, consensually supported strategic nuclear policy, but this is not at all what Musil was trying to say. He meant that the entire U.S. political spectrum to the right of himself is wrong on the question of nuclear weapons and nuclear deterrence. Musil accuses the authors of the Harvard study of justifying the building of nuclear weapons "because they offer distinct worldwide political advantages to the United States,"[37] a twisted reading of the study by any measure. Perhaps Musil assumed, as Mark Twain once quipped, that "classics" are books more often reviewed than read and that he would therefore be saved because far more people would read his review than would read the book he was reviewing. Musil's finale, claiming that 'informed public opinion' in America and around the world sees those weapons as horrendous and unnecessary,"[38] seems to imply that the majority of the American body politic is with him rather than with "conservative, moderate, or liberal administrations," supported by elitists from Harvard, who are said to favor nuclear weapons because of their "political advantage."

Andrew Kopkind, writing in *The Nation,* was even less generous to the Harvard study. He ridiculed the authors for failing to note that "American nuclear strategy may be marshalled to advance imperial interests, rather than deter Soviet aggression."[39] He also criticized the authors' "reverential" treatment of President Kennedy's management of the 1962 Cuban missile crisis, citing instead "Kennedy's hostile and aggressive policy toward the Cuban revolution" and his "crusade to open the Third World to American influence and control."[40] Only after such ritualistic references to the Leninist interpretation of U.S. foreign policy does Kopkind get down to business. The real reason for the Harvard study's conclusions is that the reinvention of world politics proposed by Schell "would reinvent them out of jobs, identities, positions of power. . . . Harvard is hip-deep in the intellectual apparatus of the national security state. . . . If an institution can *want,* Harvard wants to own the debate over nuclear weapons."[41]

The Pragmatic Center and Congress

As noted above, many scholars associated with the views of the Pragmatic Center have opposed the freeze as intellectually shallow, strategically irresponsible, and a throwback to the naiveté of an unregenerate mutual assured destruction mentality. But those in the Congress itself have not had the luxury of making judgments about the freeze from the safety of an ivory tower. They have to run for re-election, to stay on working terms with their party colleagues, and to consider the net effects of their actions on national policy. It is fortunate that some members of the Pragmatic Center supported the freeze in the House of Representatives. Otherwise, the freeze movement would have had less an incentive to moderate its views, and the floor debates would have been even more vacuous than they were. It was perhaps not coincidental that those members of the House who found themselves in the Pragmatic Center on this issue were also among the most knowledgeable of their number on nuclear matters.

One supporter of the freeze on the floor of the House was Wisconsin Democrat Les Aspin. Aspin admitted that he had difficulty with some aspects of a freeze, depending on what was to be frozen, but he supported any measure that kept the issue of arms control alive and well and that forced the Reagan Administration to consider the political price for arms control foot-dragging.[42] For his pragmatic support of the freeze, Aspin was assailed by freeze opponents. Later, for his support of the Scowcroft Commission compromise package—which included the MX missile— he was pilloried by freeze supporters. Noting the twin attack, Aspin concluded that he must be doing something right.[43]

Another prominent congressman with praise for the freeze movement but not necessarily the freeze proposal was Albert Gore, Jr., of Tennessee, who in 1981 introduced his own arms control proposition. Unlike most, this one actually contained some new ideas. Gore, like Aspin, was determined to find a way to build a consensus between Congress and the administration so that partisan politics would not ultimately diminish nationl security. Part of his proposal included the suggestion of building smaller, single-warhead missiles, an idea that later found its way to a prominent place in the Scowcroft Commission report. Gore's attitude toward the freeze reflected his basic concern for a broad, bipartisan base for arms control and in his view the administration moved in the right direction because of it. Said Gore: "Because Congress proposed to choose between . . . [President Reagan's] conduct of arms control and the audacious freeze, it was imperative for him to make his conduct in arms control and arms planning more persuasive. That led him," added Gore, "to expand the charter of the Scowcroft Commission to encompass arms control, and to embrace its recommendations, even though they are in many ways contrary to his original goals."[44] The debate over the freeze in Congress, concluded Gore, provided "the basis for a durable bipartisan consensus. That, too, should be counted as a victory for the freeze."[45]

Gore was more generous in praising the positive accomplishments of the freeze than many strong freeze supporters themselves claimed. The "durable consensus" to which Gore pointed included support for the MX missile, which had become a symbol of pure evil—the very harbinger of Armageddon—for avid freeze supporters. Actually, there was only one way to explain how many congressmen could support *both* a version of the nuclear freeze proposal and the MX missile: politics.

What befell the freeze movement once it became the political property of the House of Representatives had less to do with the frailties or merits of the freeze proposal itself and more to do with three crosscutting political struggles. The first struggle was within the freeze movement between the more radical groups who wanted to guide the freeze into anti-MX, anti-Trident, and anti-defense spending lobbies, and the more pragmatic group who wished to keep the freeze a single-minded proposition and not risk the divisions that specific weapons witch hunts would cause.[46] The second struggle was within the Democratic party, between those who wanted to make the freeze part of the party platform and image and those who, whatever their attitude to the freeze itself, wished to avoid making the issue so partisan that arms control would in effect be crippled.

The third struggle was between the Congress as a whole and the Reagan Administration. The Congress, ever sensitive to public opinion, was driven to a pro-freeze majority, and this included many Republican congressmen as well. The administration, which fought the freeze idea from the start, wished to force Congress away from the freeze. In the end, both parties moved toward each other. The administration moved toward the Congress through the Scowcroft Commission compromise, the incorporation of the "build-down" concept into the U.S. position in START, by adjusting its positions in the INF (Intermediate-range Nuclear Forces) talks, and by solemn promises about "seriousness" and "flexibility" in arms control. The Congress moved toward the administration by diluting the freeze in the House, defeating it in the Senate, and by voting up the MX and the B-1 bomber programs—the latter finally accomplished in early November 1983. None of this could have taken place without the mediating services of the politicians of the Pragmatic Center. One

148

can argue about the merits of the resulting compromise, and about the MX compromise of May 1984, but it at least had the semblance of a national policy. Better an imperfect national policy than no policy at all.

NOTES

1. For a good discussion of this point, see William R. Kintner and Harvey Sicherman, *Technology and International Politics: The Crisis of Wishing* (Lexington, Mass.: D. C. Heath and Co., 1975), chap. 4.

2. Kennedy is quoted in Judith Miller, "Reagan's View on Lag in Arms Being Disputed," *New York Times,* April 2, 1982.

3. Viguerie is quoted in Daniel Southerland, "Signals of Change in Mideast," *Christian Science Monitor,* November 4, 1983.

4. See Colin S. Gray, *Strategic Studies and Public Policy: The American Experience* (Lexington, Ky.: University of Kentucky Press, 1982), esp. chaps. 4 and 5. See also Irving Louis Horowitz, *The Rise and Fall of Project Camelot* (Cambridge, Mass.: MIT Press, 1967).

5. David Halberstam, *The Best and the Brightest* (New York: Random House, 1972).

6. See Robert S. McNamara, *The Essence of Security: Reflections in Office* (New York: Harper and Row, 1968).

7. See U.S. Senate, *The SALT II Treaty, Hearings before the Committee on Foreign Relations,* 96th Cong., 1st sess., 1979, part 3, p. 163.

8. See Kintner and Sicherman, *Technology and International Politics,* pp. 58-60.

9. In President Nixon's first message, he raised the question of whether a president should "be left with the single option of ordering the mass destruction of enemy civilians." See *U.S. Foreign Policy for the 1970s: A New Strategy for Peace, a Report to the Congress by Richard M. Nixon, President of the United States,* February 18, 1970, p. 122. In the second message, Nixon wrote that a "simple 'assured destruction' doctrine does not meet . . . the requirements for a flexible range of strategic options." See *U.S. Foreign Policy for the 1970s:*

The Emerging Structure of Peace, a Report to the Congress by Richard M. Nixon, President of the United States, February 9, 1972, p. 158.

10. U.S. Senate, *SALT I, Hearings of the Committee on Foreign Relations,* 92nd Congress, 2nd sess. 1972, p. 111. (Emphasis added.)

11. U.S. Senate, *Military Implications of the Treaty on the Limitation of Anti-Ballistic Missile Systems and the Interim Agreement on Limitation of Strategic Offensive Arms, Hearings of the Committee on Armed Services,* 92nd Cong. 2nd sess., 1972, pp. 121, 128-29, 137. (Emphasis added.)

12. See, for example, R. J. Rummel, "Will the Soviet Union Soon Have a First Strike Capability?" *Orbis,* Fall 1976, pp. 579-94.

13. The following discussion borrows from Robert Legvold, particularly his testimony and prepared statement for the Senate Foreign Relations Committee (in *SALT I, Hearings,* part 3, pp.79-83); and his "Strategic 'Doctrine' and SALT: Soviet and American Views," *Survival,* January/February 1979.

14. Legvold, "Strategic 'Doctrine'," p. 8.

15. *Salt I Hearings,* part 3, p. 80.

16. Ibid., p. 82. See Adam M. Garfinkle, "SALT and International Stability: An American View," *Disarmament,* May 1981, pp. 27-29.

17. This is almost universally accepted by Soviet specialists. See David Holloway, *The Soviet Union and the Nuclear Arms Race* (New Haven: Yale University Press, 1983); Robert L. Arnett, "Soviet Attitudes Toward Nuclear War: Do They Really Think They Can Win?" *Journal of Strategic Studies,* September 1979; Fritz Ermath, "Contrasts in American and Soviet Strategic Thought," *International Security,* Fall 1978; Richard Pipes, "Militarism and the Soviet State," *Daedelus,* Fall 1980; Richard Burt, "Brown Says Soviet Sought to Knock Out U.S. Missiles," *New York Times,* May 31, 1979; and especially Legvold, "Strategic 'Doctrine'." Arthur Macy Cox, a freeze supporter, wrote in November 1983 that the opposite was true, that the Soviet Union targeted cities, but offered no evidence. See his "End the War Game," *New York Times,* November 8, 1983.

18. For a discussion and some examples, see Thomas Wolfe, *The SALT Experience* (Cambridge, Mass.: Ballinger, 1979), p. 111.

19. Legvold, "Strategic 'Doctrine'," p. 9; and Garfinkle, "SALT and International Stability," p. 28.

20. In fact, mention has been made of at least limited counterforce options in

the annual report of the secretary of defense every year since 1963. See Lynne E. Davis, *Limited Nuclear Options: Deterrence and the New American Doctrine,* Adelphi Paper no. 121 (London: Institute of International Strategic Studies, 1976), p. 3; Wolfe, *The SALT Experience,* p. 136; Gray, *Strategic Studies and Public Policy,* p. 133; Aaron Friedberg, "A History of U.S. Strategic 'Doctrine'," *Journal of Strategic Studies,* December 1980; and Jan M. Lodal, "Deterrence and Nuclear Strategy," *Daedelus,* Fall 1980. To get a feel for the sense of change in U.S. strategic thinking, see the following articles, all from the Fall 1974 issue of *Orbis:* William R. Van Cleave and Roger W. Barnett, "Strategic Adaptability"; George Rathjens, "Flexible Response Options"; Donald R. Westervelt, "The Essence of Armed Futility"; Colin S. Gray, "Foreign Policy and the Strategic Balance"; Robert H. Kupperman, Robert M. Behr, and Thomas P. Jones, Jr., "The Deterrence Continuum"; John M. Collins, "Maneuver Instead of Mass: The Key to Assured Stability"; and Conrad V. Chester and Eugene P. Wigner, "Population Vulnerability: The Neglected Issue in Arms Limitation and the Strategic Balance."

21. For a discussion of PD-59, see the contending views of Louis René Beres and Colin S. Gray in *Parameters,* March 1981.

22. Harold Brown, "SALT II and the National Defense," Department of State Publication 8979, General Foreign Policy Series 313, Bureau of Public Affairs, Office of Public Communication, April 5, 1979, p. 7.

23. One then–well-known articulation of this argument dates back to 1970. See Herbert York, *Race to Oblivion* (New York: Simon and Schuster, 1970). It should be noted here that while counterforce weapons that *are* vulnerable to pre-emption may be crisis-unstable, those that are *not* vulnerable to pre-emption can be crisis-*stabilizing.* Moreover, this argument says nothing about the longevity or logic of deterrence based on countervalue retaliation, where problems abound.

24. See, for example, Alexander M. Haig, Jr., "Judging SALT II," *Strategic Review,* Winter 1980; and Victor Utgoff, "In Defense of Counterforce," *International Security,* Spring 1982.

25. Alexander M. Haig, Jr., "Peace and Deterrence," *Current Policy,* no. 383, U.S. Department of State, April 6, 1982, p. 3.

26. See Seweryn Bialer, "Danger in Moscow," *New York Review of Books,* February 16, 1984, p. 9.

27. See "The Realities of Arms Control," pp. 39-40; and *Living with Nuclear Weapons* (Cambridge, Mass.: Harvard University Press, 1983), p. 190. There is also a Bantam paperback edition of *Living with Nuclear Weapons.*

28. "The Realities of Arms Control," pp. 45-46.

29. Ibid., p. 46.

30. Ibid.

31. Ibid., *Living with Nuclear Weapons*, pp. 208-9.

32. *Living with Nuclear Weapons*, p. 4.

33. Nye is quoted in "For and Against a Nuclear Freeze," *Time*, March 29, 1982, p. 17. See also *Living with Nuclear Weapons*, p. 250.

34. *Living with Nuclear Weapons*, pp. 104-5, 107-8.

35. Richard J. Barnet, "Viewing the Bomb Through Crimson-Colored Glasses," *Washington Post*, July 3, 1983.

36. Robert K. Musil, "From Harvard: Advice on Living with the Bomb," *Philadelphia Inquirer*, June 26, 1983.

37. Ibid.

38. Ibid.

39. Andrew Kopkind, "Living with the Bomb at Harvard," *The Nation*, June 15, 1983, p. 695.

40. Ibid.

41. Ibid.

42. See Judith Miller, "House Takes Up Nuclear Freeze and Rival Plan Reagan Supports," *New York Times*, August 6, 1982.

43. See, for example, Alexander Cockburn and James Ridgeway, "How Liberal Les Aspin Saved the MX for Reagan," *The Village Voice*, May 31, 1983; Mary McGrory, "Freeze Backers Set to Call Congress to Account in Next MX Vote," *Washington Post*, July 14, 1983; Steven V. Roberts, "A Shrewd Insider Battles for the MX," *New York Times*, July 18, 1983. For Aspin's own views, see his "It's a Good Deal—and It's in Trouble," *Washington Post*, July 17, 1983.

44. Albert Gore, Jr., "Beyond the Freeze," *Washington Post*, May 9, 1983, p. 11; and Flora Lewis, "For Nuclear Consensus," *New York Times*, August 24, 1982.

45. Gore, "Beyond the Freeze," p. 11. This was also the attitude of Alton Frye, the originator and most energetic exponent of the build-down. See his "Divisions Imperil Arms Control," *Los Angeles Times,* April 7, 1983, and his "Strategic Build-Down: A Context for Restraint," *Foreign Affairs,* Winter 1983-84, pp. 293-317. See also Morton Kondracke, "Arms Control—Plus," *Baltimore Sun,* December 9, 1983.

46. See Judith Miller, "Advocates of Arms Control Ponder Some New Moves," *New York Times,* December 5, 1982.

Chapter 5

THE CONSERVATIVE MAINSTREAM

The concessions of the weak are the concessions of fear.

—Edmund Burke

Is Reagan Being Reagan?

The compromise package that congressional members of the Pragmatic Center like Congressmen Aspin and Gore tried to assemble between the Reagan Administration and the Congress made sense and had prospects of stability to the extent that the administration shared many of the basic strategic views of the Pragmatic Center. But if the administration was instead faithful to the New Right image of the Soviets, of military power and arms control, then no stable *modus vivendi* was possible. Freeze advocates and avid freeze supporters in Congress tended to view the Reagan Administration as beyond hope on these questions— an administration of the New Right. As far as most freeze supporters were concerned, Reagan was being Reagan when and where it most counted. Most congressional Democrats of the Left-Liberal Establishment, and those few even further Left, saw the administration as an evil to combat without respite, not a respectable force with which to confer. In the interests of national security and unity, Aspin, Gore, and their colleagues either thought the opposite or hoped to push the administration toward the center by lifting the potential political costs of immobility beyond acceptable limits.

The Reagan Administration has supplied ample evidence for each of these views. But is the administration representative of the strategic theory of the Far Right outlined in chapter 2, as most freeze advocates claim? Is the moderation of deeds and inclination toward arms control evidenced by the administration merely public relations maneuvering, forced on the president and the Pentagon by an aroused and mobilized public holding up the nuclear freeze as its banner? Or is the administration—at least on these issues—in possession of another set of views that are far closer to the political Center, views here identified as those of the Conservative Mainstream? The answers to these questions are not obvious because the administration has not spoken with a single voice on these matters.

Those who insist that the Reagan Administration is an administration of the Far Right point first to the 1980 Republican campaign platform, which called for "a margin of safety" in strategic weapons. Critics of the platform immediately claimed that by seeking nuclear superiority the Republicans were engaging in a dangerous and quixotic nostalgia for days forever gone—and so much the better that they *were* gone. Clearly, "a margin of safety" was a euphemism for nuclear advantage, and Republican supporters did not deny that. They denied only that seeking such an advantage was a futile goal and said that in any case it was an ideal more laudable than that of the Democrats, which amounted in their eyes to an acquiescence in an inferior military capability garbed in high-sounding proclamations about human rights and the "inordinate fear of communism."[1]

The strategic modernization program proposed by the Reagan Administration did not have as its most proximate goal the attainment of nuclear superiority, as critics charged. The obverse of the desirability that the United States attain nuclear superiority is the president's persistent belief that the United States is *inferior* to the Soviet Union in strategic nuclear power. The first goal, the president has said many times, is to "achieve parity."[2] By taking a worst-case view of the current strategic balance characteristic of the New Right, the administration sought to portray its proposed build-up as defensive in nature. Irritated and anxious critics of the administration were uncertain whether the president was more clever than sincere or more sincere than clever.

The inclusion of the nuclear superiority plank in the Republican platform of 1980 reflected the growing influence of the New Right in the Republican party. The desire for nuclear superiority, even if quixotic and impossible, nonetheless represented the sentiment of the party professionals who nominated and supported Ronald Reagan, and it also reflected Reagan's belief that regaining a strategic edge for the United States was not so far-fetched a notion given his understanding of technological trends.

156

Not long after the inauguration, Defense Secretary Caspar Weinberger offered the president a "plan for regaining nuclear superiority," though it was not clear whether that meant an effort to attain preclusive first-strike capability or merely to achieve advantages in some static indices of strategic nuclear power far short of such a capability.[3]

Secretary Weinberger was also cited as evidence of the Far Right character of the Reagan Administration. Aside from planning for nuclear superiority, Weinberger also ordered planning for a protracted nuclear war with a mind to winning, or "prevailing," in such a conflict.[4] Adding to the perception that something had changed radically were reports about the "extreme" views of certain administration officials, like Major General Robert Schweitzer and Dr. Richard Pipes, both at the National Security Council, and T. K. Jones at the Pentagon. They were said to believe in the inevitability of nuclear war with the Soviet Union and the possibility of winning it. In other words, they were suspected of planning for nuclear war not for the sake of deterrence but for actual war-fighting.[5] Planning to fight a nuclear war also seemed to fall in line with the Far Right's notion that nuclear war was likely because the Soviets were satanic and implacable. It was also harmonious with the certainty, as far as the religious Right was concerned, that such a war would result in the defeat of satanic forces by the forces of good. Later on, the president's "star wars" speech of March 23, 1983 and his depiction of the Soviet Union as an "evil empire" filled with liars and cheats, whose only sense of morality was of the most sinister self-serving variety, reinforced the view of those who saw the administration as beyond rational thought on these and other matters.[6] This was not all. James Watt, former secretary of the interior, told a House Interior Committee that there was no urgency about preserving natural habitats and mineral resources for future generations because there might not be many generations before "the Lord returns."[7] Fearful critics imagined high-level administration officials dismissing the dangers of nuclear war in the belief that reality itself was about to be transformed by a divine act.

Moreover, the president's accusations that the Soviets were violating a passel of arms control agreements already in force were taken by some to reflect a basic New Right orientation. In the president's long-awaited presentation of his START proposal on May 9, 1982, he said:

I do not doubt that the Soviet people, and, yes the Soviet leaders have an overriding interest in preventing the use of nuclear weapons. The Soviet Union within the memory of its leaders has known the devastation of total conventional war and knows that nuclear war would be even more calamitous. And yet, so far, the Soviet Union has used arms control negotiations primarily as an instrument to restrict U.S. defense programs and, in conjunction with their own arms buildup, a means to enhance Soviet power and prestige.

Unfortunately, for some time suspicions have grown that the Soviet Union has not been living up to its obligations under existing arms control treaties. There is conclusive evidence the Soviet Union has provided toxins to the Laotians and Vietnamese for use against defenseless villagers in Southeast Asia. And the Soviets themselves are employing chemical weapons on the freedom-fighters in Afghanistan.[8]

As if all this were not enough to persuade the already suspicious about the nature of the Reagan Administration, at the height of the midterm election campaign the President brought forth a favorite theme of the New Right: the freeze movement was a KGB plot.

On October 4, President Reagan said that there was plenty of evidence that the nuclear freeze movement was made up of "honest and sincere people" who were being manipulated by "some who want the weakening of America." Some of these people, the president said, were "foreign agents."[9] This charge evoked a cascade of accusations that the president was red-baiting the nuclear freeze movement—never mind if the charge were true or not. An FBI report on the subject which concluded that the Soviet Union had indeed *tried* to influence the U.S. peace movement, but without appreciable success, did not settle the matter.[10] Each side took from the FBI report what it wished to take and ad-libbed the rest. The president claimed that the Soviets had both tried and succeeded; freeze defenders, that they had neither tried nor succeeded. (It is not often that the FBI finds itself in the role of sophisticate in such matters.) In response to the FBI report, the president backtracked only a little. On December 10 he said, "One must look to see whether, well-intentioned though it may be, this movement might be carrying water that they're not aware of for another purpose."[11] He added: "We know that the originator, the originating organization, of that was the World Peace Council, which is a Soviet organization supported and maintained by them."[12] Freeze supporters were again appalled by these remarks and denied them. One representative of the Nuclear Weapons Freeze Campaign in St. Louis, Reuven McCornack, swore that he did not know anything about the World Peace Council. "They're not associated with our organization," he said.[13]

Ronald Reagan's extemporaneous remarks, more likely to pour forth at news conferences and on other less formal occasions, do seem to reflect more than coincidentally the New Right's perspective on these subjects. But, for better or for worse, one man— even the president—is not an entire administration. Every new administration is a coalition in fact if not by intent, and this is particularly so of new administrations that are, and consider themselves, unconventional political forces in one sense or another.

The Carter Administration was one such creature. Candidate Carter built his image around being an outsider to the Washington establishment, a man who would come to town without a backlog of personal and institutional obligations that would work to limit his mandate for making changes. And at first Carter's "Georgia Mafia," as it became known, did act with a certain amount of contempt for the Democratic party establishment in the Congress. Although President Carter was forced for political reasons to work closely with Senator Henry M. Jackson on arms control matters in the first half of 1977, his chief of staff, Hamilton Jordan, never introduced himself to Senator Jackson, one of Senate's most senior Democrats.[14] On the other hand, "outsider" administrations simply do not have the means or the inclination to supply the key staffing of jobs in the foreign policy and national security bureaucracies. In the case of the Carter Administration, this staffing job was left primarily with the vice-president, Walter F. Mondale, who had been well acquainted with the bevy of academics and analysts formerly close to the late Senator Hubert H. Humphrey, from Mondale's own state of Minnesota. When the dust settled, the Carter Administration's appointed foreign policy and national security staff resembled an out-of-town administration not at all. When one adds to this the presence and influence of career professionals at the Departments of State, Defense, and

Treasury, the Arms Control and Disarmament Agency, and so on, the Carter Administration never had much of a chance of displacing established policies, even if President Carter had wanted to do so.

The Reagan Administration faced similar problems after November 1980 and did not fare much better in solving them. The New Right may have helped put Ronald Reagan in the White House, but could it run the government? There were some important appointments that pleased the New Right—James Watt, for example. But most of the rest were either personal friends of the president (Weinberger and William French Smith) or holdovers from the Nixon–Ford–Kissinger era—Haig, in particular. Still others were out-of-work senators and governors who were party mainstreamers, not "real conservatives," like Richard Schweiker, David Stockman, Ray Donovan, and James Edwards. And still others were card-carrying Democrats like Eugene Rostow, Jeane Kirkpatrick, Paul Nitze, and Richard Perle who though hawks on defense were hardly the advanced guard of the New Right. George Bush, now vice-president but formerly Reagan's most serious challenger for the nomination, had been a congressman and director of the Central Intelligence Agency. Bush knew a lot of people, and through White House personnel director A. Pendleton James he found jobs for many of them. James Baker, Bush's closest aide, joined the president's White House staff and soon rose to rival Ed Meese in stature and power. Add a good measure of professional bureaucracy to this mixture, and what emerged was hardly a New Right administration. It has been, on balance, an administration of the Conservative Mainstream.

The Strategic Theory of the Conservative Mainstream

Unlike the strategic theory of the Far Right, which is uncomfortable with the very concept of nuclear deterrence to the point of exasperation, the strategic theory of the Conservative Mainstream is a *deterrence* theory, and in a sense a classical one. In almost every respect, the strategic theory of the Conservative Mainstream accepts the critique of mutual assured destruction offered by the Pragmatic Center, as discussed in chapter 4, and the various implications that flow from that critique. The strategic theory of the Left-Liberal Establishment—and of most of the nuclear freeze movement—is one in which deterrence is assured through the threat of unacceptable countervalue retaliation, a strategy based on deterrence by punishment. The strategic theory of the Pragmatic Center—best typified by PD-59 and the "countervailing strategy"—rests on a mix of countervalue and counterforce strategy that may be termed a strategy of both punishment and denial—denial of any opportunity for the other side to contemplate any net military advantage from an attack at any level of violence. The strategic theory of the Conservative Mainstream tends toward a strategy of deterrence that emphasizes victory-denial over everything else and thus emphasizes overwhelmingly a counterforce targeting posture. The threat of enormous societal damage clearly remains, but it is not the *intent* to punish that is held to be the deterrent. Indeed, since a victory-denial strategy is sensitive to threats at many levels, its ideal success should deterrence fail is the *restoration* of deterrence at the earliest possible time at the *lowest* level of violence—this being the opposite ideal of a strategy that means to punish.

Advocates of pure mutual assured destruction—and of the freeze movement, too—speak as though "deterrence" were synonymous with a pure countervalue deterrent based on the threat to punish. But this is not so. Deterrence can be achieved as well in theory and practice through a mixed targeting posture, or one that clearly emphasizes war-fighting options. It is more sensible to think of deterrence as a kind of continuum on which there are a great many shades of gray between opposite ends. Today the most sophisticated analyses of deterrence tend to view deterrence through punishment and deterrence through victory-denial not as mutually exclusive options but as mutually reinforcing aspects of a deterrence posture. A countervailing strategy such as that envisaged in PD-59 demands greater effort in readying both plans and capabilities to end a nuclear conflict and establish intra-war deterrence as soon as possible. The availability of an array of options minimizes the prospects of uncontrolled escalation, giving some hope that the end of deterrence need not be the same as the end of civilization. But on the other hand, the inevitable disaster that would attend any nuclear exchange, and the uncertainty of controlling it once it began, still functions to deprive an adversary of the option of a controlled use of nuclear weapons—he cannot be emboldened by any *surety* of intra-war deterrence.

The differences between the strategic theories of the Pragmatic Center and the Conservative Mainstream are not in their critique of mutual assured destruction—for here the two schools are almost fully compatible—but in their views of the mix of targeting postures most likely to strengthen deterrence. Those of the Pragmatic Center are reluctant to leave the certainty of unacceptable punishment too far behind and to adopt a victory-*denial* posture to the extent that it could look at the other side like a victory-*seeking* posture, thus raising the prospect of a destabilizing arms race. Those of the Conservative Mainstream worry less about how a victory-denial posture looks to the other side. They wish to maximize the *rationality* of the U.S. deterrent posture in the sense of retaining or building into the arsenal not a single weapon bereft of a militarily logical function. Note that both assured destruction and victory-denial varieties of deterrence theory depend on rationality of some kind—the former on the obvious senselessness of committing suicide and the latter on the obvious senselessness of starting a war at any level of violence that one cannot win. The problem is that both forms of rationality are vulnerable to erosion. The key question is, therefore, on which kind of rationality is it least irrational to depend?

Implicit in denying victory to an opponent, should he be so foolish as to start a war he cannot win, is the prospect that the aggressor might indeed lose such a war in narrow military terms, if not also in others. And here lies the main problem with the strategic theory of the Conservative Mainstream. The force posture of victory-denial can be very difficult to distinguish from preparations for a first strike. Improving one's ability to fight a war enhances an adversary's belief that war might actually happen and this renders the deterrent more credible. But it is possible that the adversary might view the deterrent enhancement not as a defensive but as an offensive measure designed to secure victory in a nuclear war. This is probably how the Soviet Union and the United States perceive each others' counterforce weapons programs. Clearly, neither effort can be wholly explained on the basis of assured destruction postures.[15]

Another way of stating the differences in emphasis between

the Pragmatic Center and the Conservative Mainstream is that the former worries most about what might push an *inferior* power into attack, while the latter is more concerned about what might tempt a *superior* power to attack. Of course, advocates of mutual assured destruction worry about neither of these problems because *incremental* inferiority or superiority short of a decisive first-strike capability or decisive vulnerability is blithely dismissed as meaningless.

Practical Implications

The strategic theories of the Pragmatic Center and the Conservative Mainstream really differ in degree of emphasis. Both of them differ *in kind* from the strategic theory of the Left-Liberal Establishment so dear to nuclear freeze advocates. Nevertheless, when it comes down to practical matters—questions of specific weapons systems, numbers of warheads and delivery vehicles, budgetary implications, and questions of active and passive defenses—differences abound. And these differences are no less trivial than the differences between the core strategic programs and intentions of the Carter Administration and those of the Reagan Administration. [16] There are four significant implications of these differences, each one flowing from the one before.

First, while the countervailing strategy calls for counterforce in excess of the limited amount provided by Minuteman II and III, it does not demand counterforce equity. The strategic goal of the Reagan Administration is just that—counterforce equity. The rationale for counterforce in the countervailing strategy was well described by Alexander Haig in 1980. Some members of the Carter Administration, he wrote:

do recognize the need for the United States to muster a prompt, hard-target kill capability in order to ensure that the Soviet Union cannot improve its relative military position with a first strike. Counterforce capabilities, according to this view, are required for stable deterrence because we need to demonstrate that an American second strike could destroy not only urban and industrial targets, but also a residual Soviet third-strike capability that could otherwise hold American cities hostage.[17]

But this was not the best solution to the problem of Soviet advantages in prompt hard-target kill capabilities. According to

163

Haig, the United States needs "hard-target kill capabilities beyond those necessary to attack a residual, third-strike Soviet force."[18] Two reasons are cited: the first is perceptual, the second and more important one is purely military. Haig wrote:

A significant imbalance in counterforce capabilities is profoundly de-stabilizing militarily, particularly in times of intense international crisis. . . . If the Soviets should come to believe, in a given situation, that the probability of war was very high, then the incentive for Moscow to preempt in order to limit the damage that the United States could do might become irresistible, especially if the Soviets were confident that an American retaliation would be either completely deterred or limited to a counterforce strike for fear that, otherwise, the Soviet Union would strike at American cities. Clearly, apprehensions by the Soviets that the United States could destroy Soviet cities would not deter them under such circumstances, for they would believe that such damage would occur anyway, and would probably be much worse if they did *not* preempt.[19]

To eliminate the possibility that the Soviet Union might contemplate pre-emption, the Soviets must not imagine themselves able to deprive the United States of a full range of response options. Limited counterforce is less likely to get this point across than equity in counterforce. If the United States fails to achieve counterforce equity through either negotiated reductions or unilateral action, then "it invites dangerous political trends, as well as a degree of crisis instability that neither we nor the rest of the world can afford."[20]

Second, since counterforce equity is a desirable goal, the huge Soviet counterforce-capable force of ICBMs is the main problem for U.S. planners and also the main target of U.S. arms control negotiators. President Reagan said as much in the May 9, 1982 address at which he presented the U.S. START proposal:

The main threat to peace posed by nuclear weapons today is the growing instability of the nuclear balance. This is due to the increasingly destructive potential of the massive Soviet buildup in its ballistic missile force.

Therefore, our goal is to enhance deterrence and achieve stability through significant reductions in the most destabilizing nuclear systems, ballistic missiles, and especially the giant intercontinental ballistic missiles, while maintaining a nuclear capability sufficient to deter conflict,

164

to underwrite our national security, and to meet our commitment to allies and friends.[21]

It stands to reason that any future arms control treaty that leaves unchanged the inequity in counterforce in favor of the Soviet Union must be unequal and unworthy. This is why much of the Pragmatic Center could support SALT II in 1979, because *equity* in counterforce was not a requirement of the countervailing strategy. It is also why the principles of the Reagan Administration could not and did not support SALT II because their conception of strategic parity *does* require counterforce parity and, in their view, the measure of worthy arms treaties lies in providing at least reasonable movement in that direction.[22]

Actually, the Reagan Administration's case against SALT II was not only that it failed to right the counterforce imbalance, but also that it failed to constrain strategic expansion in any meaningful way, and was therefore reduced to a cosmetic palliative that could only give arms control a bad name in the long run. Assistant Secretary of Defense for International Security Policy Richard Perle was subjected to accusatory questioning by *New York Times* reporter Leslie Gelb, an architect of SALT II in the Carter Administration. Gelb asked: "Why are you observing a treaty that your president and many of the senior officials in this Administration believe is fatally flawed? And if you're observing it, why don't you sign it?" Perle answered:

We're observing it in practice, Mr. Gelb, because when one looks at the programs that we presently have under way and the programs that the Soviets presently have under way, there is not at this moment a practical concern. Nevertheless, we believe the treaty to be fatally flawed not only because it fails to constrain the growth of strategic forces . . . but because it would represent the ratification of a treaty that we believe is essentially cosmetic in nature, that does not meet the fundamental purposes of arms control.

Gelb persisted: "If the treaty is fatally flawed . . . why observe it at all?" Perle responded:

The point is we are proceeding with our programs and our programs are not, in a fundamental sense, now inhibited by the treaty, nor are Soviet programs in any fundamental sense inhibited by the treaty. And that's precisely the point about the failure of this treaty. It does not significantly alter the course of weapons development and deployment that is now taking place or that would take place in the absence of the treaty. . . . *Les, I think the point is that the difference between no agreement and the SALT II agreement is so minuscule that Soviet behavior and American behavior are essentially unaffected.* [23]

This distinction between criteria of adequacy in arms control between the Pragmatic Center and the Conservative Mainstream reflects yet another gradation of concern along the deterrence continuum, this one having to do with numbers. A strategy of deterrence by punishment is likely to be little concerned about numerical balances of weapons; all that matters is the survivability of a countervalue retaliatory force, and this can in theory be maintained without reference to any balance of numbers at all. A countervailing strategy *is* concerned with numbers, but mainly with respect to cost/exchange ratios. Counterforce balances matter, but only in the context of military mission. Since the Soviets would greatly deplete their counterforce capabilites with a first strike, U.S. equity in counterforce is not the most relevant measure of adequacy. A strategy of victory denial, however, is sensitive to crisis dynamics and more concerned with fielding a deterrent that is as convincing as possible than in computing cost/exchange ratios, depletion and attrition rates, and so forth. In a crisis, victory-denial advocates argue, such arcane computations have no psychological reality, while a perception of checkmate—total equity—does. In this sense, the argument goes, the countervailing strategy suffers from a kind of hyper-rationalism. "But is it any wonder?" Conservative Mainstreamers might ask. After all, Harold Brown was one of Robert McNamara's original "whiz kids."

A third point in the strategic theory of the Conservative Mainstream is that while arms control treaties that leave the counterforce imbalance untouched are ipso facto unequal and inadequate, treaties that limit meaningful defenses—like the ABM treaty of 1972—might actually be harmful. A full strategy of victory denial has a place for measures of active and passive defense—ballistic missile defense (BMD) and civil defense (CD). Damage limitation is not, as mutual assured destruction adherents claim, necessarily a prelude to first strike preparations. It can also be seen as a way to make it more expensive and less certain for

166

the *other* side to achieve a military advantage from striking the United States.[24] Here a critical distinction must be made. The BMD of the victory-denial school is primarily a BMD that protects U.S. weapons from pre-emptive attack by making their destruction so complicated as to be impossible. This is referred to as "point defense." It is only secondarily a BMD designed to protect population (area defense), and such an area defense is acknowledged to be leaky even under the best circumstances. This is quite a contrast from the High Frontier panacea of the New Right, which is unenthusiastic about point defenses except as a technological and political "bridge," but holds out the promise of a hermetic national seal against Soviet ICBMs.

The Reagan Administration has not regarded the ABM treaty as sacrosanct, but neither has it abrogated the treaty. It has not abrogated the treaty for two reasons: political prudence at home, and the likelihood that Soviet BMD technology is better situated today to take advantage in the near term of an unrestrained competition. The administration's lack of enthusiasm for the ABM treaty is based on the erosion of the basic assumptions that undergirded the treaty when it was signed in 1972. The ABM treaty was predicated on the eventual diminution of offensive forces; this is written into the treaty as Article XI and mentioned as well in the preamble. Guided at the time by an assured destruction mentality, it was assumed that if there were no defenses to impede the penetrability of offensive forces, then there would be no justifiable incentive to build more of them. For this reason Eugene Rostow, first director of the Arms Control and Disarmament Agency in the Reagan Administration said: "I do not regard the abrogation of the ABM Treaty, or its substantial modification as, in any sense, a catastrophe in itself. The ABM Treaty is part of the old MAD doctrine and it suffers from all the weaknesses of that doctrine."[25]

Similarly, the Reagan Administration has had much sympathy for civil defense preparations. There is no illusion that through civil defense measures we might somehow convince ourselves that nuclear war could be waged without excessive muss and fuss. Freeze advocates have claimed repeatedly that civil defense and contingency planning for nuclear war makes war more likely by trivializing its impact. A variety of pro-freeze scientists—physicists, meteorologists, medical doctors, and even psychiatrists—have tried to "prove" that a nuclear war is not survivable and so have counseled resistance to all civil defense measures as psychologically dangerous and financially imprudent. But the rationale for CD, argues the Conservative Mainstream, is nothing so grandiose. It is merely to demonstrate to a potential adversary that American society is not so lax and potentially hysterical that a single nuclear bomb could touch off utter social chaos. If attacking a nation's command, control, and communications facilities can be aptly dubbed "decapitation," then victory by inciting social collapse might be called "detruncation."[26] There has been much too little thought given to the strategic significance of social vulnerability in the broadest sense of the term.[27] The point of U.S. civil defense in the United States is to offset *psychologically* the massive Soviet CD program. This would still be worth doing, it is argued, even if the programs of both nations are probably futile.

A fourth and final implication of the strategic theory of the Conservative Mainstream is that deterrence is not solely a military matter, but one that engages foreign policy writ large. Arms control negotiations with the Soviet Union are a part of the broader context and cannot be divorced from it. To use the political shorthand, "linkage" is a fact of life. This has two aspects, one having to do with the relationship of arms control negotiations to U.S.-Soviet relations generally, the other with the relationship between U.S. consistency and determination around the world and the stability of deterrence itself.

Eugene Rostow once told an interviewer that the most likely danger of a nuclear imbalance was not nuclear war but nuclear blackmail.[28] Prospects for nuclear blackmail are only partly predicated on the nuclear balance per se; they are also predicated on a balance of political willpower and resolve. Being serious about arms control "has to mean being serious about foreign policy as a whole."[29] Peace must be indivisible in the nuclear age; it is not just nuclear war that must be prevented, but all major war, because little wars might grow large indeed. Here the main source of danger is the Soviet Union; the main source of restraint is a firm U.S. policy. This point of view rests on the argument that the political relationship between the United States and the Soviet Union is of a single fabric and that it is the total unraveling of that relationship, not stockpiles of this or that weapon, that is the harbinger of war. The ultimate deterrent to war between the superpowers does not depend primarily on the physical balance of strategic forces, but on the mutual realization that (a) persistent attempts by one side to gain unilateral advantage at the other's expense inevitably increase the risk of war, and (b) that given the inherent uncontrollability of tense international crises and the morbid impact of nuclear war on the biosphere, deliberately running such risks on behalf of a political program or aspiration is immoral and irresponsible. According to this view, the major problem is that as long as the Soviet Union works to increase its influence worldwide, refusing to forswear any particular means to do so, and as long as those efforts are but fitfully resisted, the outbreak of major war will remain a disaster waiting to happen.[30]

As to arms control more specifically, the Conservative Mainstream ridicules the logic of liberals who at once say that arms control is too important to be disrupted by other matters *and* that successful arms control will have positive spillover effects on U.S.-Soviet relations as a whole. But, so the argument goes, we have learned that spillovers run both ways. It is illogical to argue that if arms control can have benign effects on U.S.-Soviet relations in general, then arms control can or should be protected against political backlash arising from other sources. It is not too much to ask that restraint in arms be accompanied by restraints on political and military behavior. To argue otherwise breeds the illogical proposition that arms control is more important, and its failure more dangerous, than the larger political relationship of which it is a part.[31]

The Conservative Mainstream and the Freeze

It follows from the foregoing discussion that the freeze is an anathema to the Conservative Mainstream, including the Reagan Administration. Its opposition can be grouped under four general principles:

(1) A nuclear freeze would remove any incentive for the Soviet Union to negotiate major, equitable reductions in nuclear weapons, would lock in Soviet strategic superiority by preventing U.S. programs designed to restore effective parity, and thus would foster a strategic imbalance that makes war more likely. In

particular, a freeze would doom the INF negotiations in Europe, lock in NATO theater-nuclear inferiority, and contribute to the deterioration of NATO's political cohesion and the advance of "Finlandization."[32]

(2) The Soviet Union does not share traditional U.S. strategic concepts of stability, parity, and deterrence, as freeze advocates claim, but instead has an aggressive, pre-emptive war-winning strategy that the United States must acknowledge and address. Therefore Soviet support for a freeze is a function of its desire to maintain or enhance its advantageous situation, and not an expression of a willingness to accept parity with the United States or U.S. definitions of "stability."

(3) A freeze is not verifiable without on-site inspection and, lacking that, the Soviet Union may be expected to cheat on a freeze as it has cheated on other arms control agreements.

(4) Arms races in and of themselves do not cause wars, as freeze advocates insist, but failing to run in a race with a persevering opponent often does.

Each of these principles merits some comment. With respect to arms control, both the administration and the Conservative Mainstream as a group believe that the kind of serious arms control agreement needed to enhance U.S. security cannot be obtained unless the United States has assets in being or assets in preparation with which to bargain. This is particularly true with respect to the MX. Proceeding from the observation that the Soviet Union is unlikely to seriously consider reducing its ICBM force until that force too becomes vulnerable, Colin Gray observed: "To give the Soviet Union a very persuasive incentive to negotiate seriously, the United States must have a program [the MX ICBM] in train which, potentially, places much of the Soviet strategic-forces payload at immediate risk."[33] But the MX was *not* conceived by the Reagan Administration or by previous administrations as a first-strike weapon that would help achieve U.S. superiority. Rostow was once asked, "How do we get an agreement that will concede to us nuclear superiority?" He answered, "I've never used the phrase nuclear superiority. I've talked of credible second-strike capability."[34]

The use of the MX as bargaining leverage in negotiations with the Soviet Union was an early, and has been a constant, justification for building the system. But critics in the Pragmatic Center have put forth a useful warning for the president on this subject. For a weapons system to be useful as a bargaining chip, it must be a system that one would want to keep if it could not be traded for valuable reductions on the other side. Leslie Gelb, who was instrumental in the conception of SALT II, gave his advice:

Do we need "bargaining chips" in our negotiations with Moscow— new weapons projects we might be prepared to scrap in return for Soviet concessions?

Yes. Moscow is impressed by American technology and will bargain to curtail our inventiveness. But our chips must be weapons we would really want to keep if we did not get a worthwhile quid pro quo. And here you have a problem.

The one new system that worries the Russians most is the MX missile, because of the threat it would represent to their land-based missiles. It is also the system that faces the greatest skepticism in Congress, because of the difficulty of making it any less vulnerable than our present land-based Minuteman missiles. If you don't divine some better scheme for basing the MX, it looks as though Congress won't appropriate the money. If you don't cash this chip with Moscow soon, it may not be around to cash later.[35]

Putting MX missiles in unprotected silos, which the administration proposed not once but twice, almost cost Reagan the missile itself. Some who were otherwise in favor of the MX claimed that such a scheme committed the United States to a first-strike policy.[36] Even Rostow acknowledged the problem of finding a relatively invulnerable basing mode for the MX lest the United States be forced into a launch-on-warning policy. "Nobody in the administration," he said, "favors launch-on-warning; indeed, we regard it as one of the strongest destabilizing elements."[37]

Nevertheless, despite the administration's fumbling with the MX, the principle remains intact that negotiations with the Soviets cannot solve the main problem—the counterforce imbalance—if the United States slows or stops its own strategic programs. As early as July 13, 1981, Secretary Haig stated: "There is little prospect of agreement with the Soviet Union that will help solve such a basic security problem such as the vulnerability of our land-based systems until we demonstrate that we have the will to and the capacity to solve them without arms control, should that be necessary."[38] Rostow applied this principle to the likely effects of a nuclear freeze. A nuclear freeze, even a mutual one, "would 'freeze-in' a Soviet advantage of great importance, namely the Soviet advantage in ground-based ballistic missiles."[39] He added:

The peace movements would have a profound effect if they are carried forward and if we get a binding nuclear freeze joint resolution—which would have a force of law in the United States—freezing our nuclear arsenal at current levels or providing that it could not be increased. Then I think the nuclear arms negotiations would simply cease to exist.[40]

The same general analysis applied to the Intermediate-range Nuclear Forces negotiations. With respect to the nature of the problem, Rostow said, for example:

The Soviets have built up an enormous force of intermediate range missiles which are causing panic and terror, and the potentiality of a crisis directed against Europe, which would be paralyzed by the threat of intermediate range weapons, when the United States nuclear umbrella would lack credibility because we allowed the number to become adverse.

The modernization program the President has ordered is to restore our credibility. We want reductions that will give each side equality in deterrence and to use the negotiations as a catalyst for moving the Soviet Union toward acceptance that there's no safety in expansion.[41]

But a freeze would make this impossible. Richard Perle put forth the administration's case. The ultimate goals of the freeze are good, wrote Perle,

but a freeze now would be dangerously irresponsible. It would perpetuate the current imbalance in nuclear forces, undercut the long-term deterrent value of our nuclear forces, and doom to failure our efforts to achieve deep and meaningful reductions in the START and INF negotiations. . . .

Perhaps most importantly, by reneging on the NATO dual-track decision to deploy Pershing II and GLCM in Western Europe while we try to negotiate an agreement that would substantially reduce the Soviet nuclear threat to our allies, we would be undermining the military basis of NATO and our own credibility as an ally.[42]

172

Being Serious about Arms Control

The freeze movement has claimed repeatedly that had it not been for public pressure, the Reagan Administration would never have entered negotiations of any sort because it opposed U.S.-Soviet arms control on principle. Even after negotiations commenced, freeze advocates charged that the administration was not "serious" about arms control (and often implied that the Soviets were serious), and that both the INF and START proposals were designed to be non-negotiable, leading to the same outcome as if no proposals were ever set forth. Randall Kehler spoke on behalf of the nuclear freeze movement when he charged:

> The Reagan negotiations are simply smoke screens for achieving military superiority over the Soviet Union. This stems from a basic, unshakable belief on the part of radical right-wingers in this administration that we can, No. 1, achieve that strategic superiority and that, No. 2, once having achieved it, we can bully the Soviet Union into behaving as we wish. Both assumptions are absolutely wrong.[43]

The culprit in the Reagan Administration said to be largely responsible for this "smoke screen" was Richard Perle, whom Alexander Cockburn has called "the Great Satan of the arms race."[44]

Many of the charges made by the freeze movement and its supporters annoyed the Reagan Administration, either for their being wholly false or for their being half true. But none was so false nor so annoying as this charge, and the demonizing of Richard Perle. In July 1983, Perle got a chance to reply to his critics.[45] His remarks point up the differences between the Conservative Mainstream and others as to what it means to be serious about arms control. Perle said:

> I believe that the principal difference between this Administration and its critics on the subject of arms control lies in the standard we each set for the reaching of agreement. I confess that I believe we set a higher standard than our detractors: we are searching for arms control agreements that will significantly constrain the growth of Soviet military power while limiting our own proportionately. We are searching for negotiated arms limitations which, if agreed to, would provide for greater stability at sharply lower levels of weapons. We are trying, as the Congress has directed, to obtain agreements that are based upon the principle of equality between the United States and its main adversary,

173

the Soviet Union. We are attempting to achieve agreements that are sufficiently precise so that we can verify compliance with them. And in attempting all this we are mindful that there are some agreements that are better than others, all too many that convey the appearance—but not the reality—of militarily meaningful restraint and some that are worse than none at all.[46]

For the slippery subject of what is and is not serious, Perle saved he best barrage:

In all of the confusion that surrounds the subject of arms control there is none so serious as the issue of seriousness. . . . But what does seriousness in arms control mean? Is it a sign of seriousness to make concessions to the Soviet desire to accumulate and preserve significant advantages in nuclear weapons? Is the ease with which we abandon our objectives and make "progress" toward an agreement—any agreement— a sign of seriousness? Is there any relationship between seriousness and the content of the agreements we seek to negotiate?

The burden of advice we are receiving from many of our critics amounts to little more than that we should modify our proposals so as to permit the Soviets to retain a vastly larger strategic arsenal than the levels the administration has proposed. According to this view seriousness is to be found on the side of the big guns—or, in this case, the big missiles. Demand too much restraint on the part of the Soviets, even though the levels we have proposed would be equal for both sides—and you are not serious. Hold out for an agreement worthy of our children's respect (and with some chance of protecting their safety and liberty) and you are not serious. Seriousness resides with those who don't worry too much about the terms of an agreement as long as something gets signed.

That is, needless to say, not our view of what constitutes being serious about arms control. In our view seriousness requires clear-sighted objectives, militarily significant outcomes, agreements that are equal and verifiable—and the patience and courage to achieve results. It can't be done quickly or easily. Our adversaries won't permit it. They prefer to wait for terms more to their liking—terms which, like those to which they have become accustomed, leave their military programs largely unimpeded, their build-up undiminished.[47]

The second principle—that the Soviet desire for a freeze is a desire to lock in advantages and play propaganda games with U.S. and West European publics—has been expressed widely, though less bluntly. Still, Reagan Administration officials have been quick to point out the sources of Soviet support on both counts. The president put the essence of it in a light-hearted quip to a pro-freeze Presidential Scholar, Ariela Gross: "If the Russians support it, there must be something wrong with it."[48] In a more serious vein, officials have noted the regularity with which Soviet official statements about the freeze and "no first use" of nuclear weapons regularly followed their appearance and popularization in the United States. Among many examples that could be cited, the no-first-use episode is a good case in point.

In the spring of 1982, Robert McNamara, McGeorge Bundy, George Kennan, and Gerard Smith made news by proposing in *Foreign Affairs* that the United States forswear first use of nuclear weapons, notably in the European theater.[49] Almost immediately the network of former ACDA officials and freeze organizations got in line behind the proposal, even though U.S. allies in Western Europe were alarmed by the entire affair. The "no-first-use" plank became a corollary to the freeze itself by the time of the June 1982 New York demonstration. Like clockwork, Andrei Gromyko's speech before the United Nations Special Session on Disarmament on June 15 included a dramatically staged Soviet announcement that it would adhere to the no-first-use principle.[50] This thrilled members of the freeze movement, some of whom fantasized that they had had a decisive impact on the Kremlin. Fewer noticed that two days earlier Soviet police had unceremoniously shut down the only legitimate, small Soviet peace group led by a modern day man of La Mancha, Sergei Batovin.[51] Batovin himself was incarcerated in a "mental institution" for "treatment." He was said to be suffering from antisocial delusions and disorientation. Nevertheless, Robert Scott of the Arms Control Association called the Soviet UN announcement "historic." State Department officials more appropriately described Soviet behavior as "old hat" and "a clever public relations gimmick that is perfect for the U.N."[52]

As to the problem of verification, the Reagan Administration has a mixed record. It has not been as forthright as it might have been about Soviet treaty violations, as we shall discuss below, but it has put the Soviet Union on notice that it is not considered a trustworthy partner. The administration played up supposed Soviet treaty violations of biological and chemical warfare pacts in Southeast Asia and Afghanistan. State Department Counselor James L. Buckley said, for example:

But the critical reason why we cannot rely on trust is that the Soviets so constantly prove themselves unworthy of trust. We have conclusive proof that the Soviets are currently violating international arms control agreements by using chemical weapons in Afghanistan and supplying biochemical weapons for use in Southeast Asia. Ask an Afghan if Soviet agreements on arms control can be trusted.

In March, the Soviets announced a temporary unilateral ban on further deployment of intermediate-range missiles—a not so grand gesture considering that the Soviets have raced to an advantage of over 600 missiles to none. Even so, we have conclusive evidence that the Soviets promptly violated even this announcement.

In other areas the Soviets have proven themselves no less unreliable. Soviet violation of the Helsinki accords are only the most visible recent instances of Soviet disregard for international accords.[53]

On the subject of arms races, the administration dismisses freeze rhetoric as a clever canard. For example, Buckley said that freeze proponents "assume that changes in nuclear forces make the balance less stable and more destructive." Not so, says Buckley, at least not necessarily. In the present program of U.S. strategic modernization:

technology has actually resulted in a net decrease in the destructive power of our strategic forces. In the past 10 years, technological advances have allowed us to reduce our total megatonnage by almost 30% and by roughly 60% since the peak levels of the early 1960s; reductions, incidentally, a freeze 10 years ago would have made impossible.

Other advances that we contemplate would make weapons safer and less vulnerable to attack or to unauthorized or accidental use. The freeze movement, for example, would have us forego more survivable land-based missiles, the deployment of less vulnerable submarines, and other measures designed to insure their survival and hence the credibility of deterrence.

By condemning all technological advances, in short, the freeze movement throws out the baby with the bathwater.[54]

To this account, Perle added the following comment addressed directly to the sense of anxiety behind the freeze:

176

The most prominent expression of this anxiety is found in the two words "arms race" and in the awesome image these words conjure in our minds—an image of the endless piling of weapon upon weapon, an ever upward spiral without end, a race to the apocalypse. Yet the reality is more mundane, and quite elusive. It is this: the United States has today deployed worldwide some 8,000 fewer nuclear weapons than we had deployed in the later half of the 1960's. For fifteen years or more we have been engaged in a sustained program of unilateral arms reductions while the Soviet Union has been adding constantly to its arsenal of strategic and theater nuclear weapons.[55]

Last of all, many administration officials, whatever their disagreements with each other over details, tend to see unabashed partisan political motives in the freeze movement. This is not so much directed from the freeze's mass support but from the architects of the Professional Left and the politicians of the Left-Liberal Establishment who have tried their best to make the administration's relations with the Congress as difficult as possible. Once a policy debate leaves the realm of the cerebrum and descends to this viscera, logic is often an early casualty. To the Reagan Administration's credit, it has for the most part eschewed personal attack on the freeze movement. And it has not unleashed the Justice Department, the FBI, and the Internal Revenue Service against its domestic enemies as was the wont of certain of its predecessors.

NOTES

1. A reference to a phrase in a speech given by President Carter in 1977 which he lived to regret. Incidentally, the first reference to the phrase "margin of safety" that this writer has been able to find is that of the late Hans Morgenthau, prince of the realist tradition in the study of international relations. Morgenthau thought that the idea of military "parity" contradicted historical reality. See Arthur Herzog, *The War-Peace Establishment* (New York: Harper and Row, 1967), p. 111.

2. See Leslie Gelb, "Reagan Says That Peace Depends on Support for U.S. Arms Buildup," *New York Times,* April 18, 1982. See also the transcript of President Reagan's news conference of March 31, 1982, in *New York Times,*

April 1, 1982. On March 30, 1983, the president repeated his contention that the Soviets held advantages; see "Reducing the Danger of Nuclear Weapons," *Current Policy,* no. 473, U.S. Department of State, March 31, 1983.

3. See Richard Halloran, "Weinberger Said to Offer Nuclear Superiority Plan to Reagan," *New York Times,* August 14, 1981.

4. Weinberger's plans leaked. See Richard Halloran, "Pentagon Draws up First Strategy for Fighting a Long Nuclear War," *New York Times,* May 30, 1982.

5. Schweitzer was relieved of his job at the National Security Council because of complaints about his remarks. See William Safire's column in the *New York Times,* October 22, 1981. As for Pipes, he decided in 1983 to return to his job at Harvard. For his views, see "The Military and the Soviet State," *Daedelus,* Fall 1980. Jones's remarks before a congressional committee about surviving a nuclear war inspired the title of Robert Scheer's pro-freeze tract, *With Enough Shovels.* Scheer is an old hand at anti-establishment politics. As editor of *Ramparts* magazine in the late 1960s, Scheer edited and wrote the brief foreword to *The Diary of Ché Guevara* (New York: Bantam Books, 1968). In his foreword, Scheer wrote: "We find it fitting that Ché's Diary was made public by his Cuban *compañeros* rather than by those against whom he fought, and we feel privileged to have been involved in its first publication." The book's introduction was by Fidel Castro.

6. The president's accusations about Soviet morality were made in his first presidential news conference. See *Weekly Compilation of Presidential Documents,* vol. 17, no. 5, February 2, 1981, pp. 66–67. On the Soviet Union as "an evil empire," see the *New York Times,* March 9, 1983.

7. Watts's comment may be found in Andy Pasztov, "James Watt Tackles Interior Agency Job with Religious Zeal," *Wall Street Journal,* May 5, 1982.

8. *Weekly Compilation of Presidential Documents,* vol. 18, no. 19, May 17, 1982, p. 602.

9. See "President Says Foes of U.S. Have Duped Arms Freeze Group," *New York Times,* October 5, 1982; the transcript of the president's news conference of November 11, 1982, in the *New York Times,* November 12, 1982; and Leslie Maitland, "Sources Are Cited for Charge of Soviet Tie to Arms Freeze," *New York Times,* November 13, 1982.

10. See Judith Miller, "U.S. Nuclear Protests Found to Be Affected Very Little by Soviet," *New York Times,* December 10, 1982.

11. Judith Miller, "President Says Freeze Proponents May Unwittingly Aid the Russians," *New York Times,* December 11, 1982.

12. Ibid.

13. Ibid.

14. Personal communication from Senator Jackson.

15. See Charles A. Appleby, "Nuclear Strategy at the Crossroads," *SAIS Review,* Winter 1981, p. 79.

16. See the discussion in Colin S. Gray, *Nuclear Strategy and Strategic Planning* (Philadelphia: Foreign Policy Research Institute, 1984), pp. 67-85.

17. Alexander M. Haig, Jr., "Judging SALT II," *Strategic Review,* Winter 1980, p. 13.

18. Ibid.

19. Ibid.

20. Ibid., p. 14.

21. See *Weekly Compilation of Presidential Documents,* vol. 18, no. 19, May 17, 1982, p. 603; Eugene V. Rostow, "Nuclear Arms Control and the Future of U.S.-Soviet Relations," *Current Policy,* no. 245, U.S. Department of State, September 10, 1982, pp. 3-4; and Richard Perle's remarks in U.S. Senate, *Department of Defense Authorization for Appropriations for Fiscal Year 1983, Hearings Before the Committee on Armed Services,* 97th Cong., 2nd sess., 1982. part 7, "Strategic and Theater Nuclear Forces," pp. 4993-94.

22. See John F. Lehman, Jr., and Seymour Weiss, *Beyond the SALT II Failure* (New York: Praeger, 1981), chaps. 3, 9, 11.

23. The Perle-Gelb exchange took place on "Meet the Press," April 17, 1983. (Emphasis added.)

24. See Colin S. Gray, "Nuclear Strategy: The Case for a Theory of Victory," *International Security,* Summer 1979; and Adam M. Garfinkle, "The Politics of Space Defense," *Orbis,* Summer 1984, pp. 26-41.

25. "Negotiation from Strength: An Interview with Eugene Rostow," *Fletcher Forum,* Summer 1983, p. 231. See also Carnes Lord, "The ABM Question," *Commentary,* May 1980. Lord later joined the Reagan Administration.

26. See John D. Steinbruner, "Nuclear Decapitation," *Foreign Policy*, Winter 1981–82.

27. One exception is Richard Ned Lebow's "Misconceptions in American Strategic Assessment," *Political Science Quarterly*, Summer 1982. Also see Michael Howard, "The Forgotten Dimension of Strategy," *Foreign Affairs*, Summer 1979.

28. "Which Comes First, Arms Control or Security?" *New York Times*, March 21, 1982.

29. "Negotiation from Strength," p. 238. See also Fred Charles Iklé, "Strategic Principles of the Reagan Administration," *Strategic Review*, Fall 1983, pp. 14–15; and Paul Wolfowitz, "Preserving Nuclear Peace," *Naval War College Review*, March/April 1983, pp. 69–80. A shorter version of this piece appeared originally as "Preserving Nuclear Peace in the 1980s," *Current Policy*, no. 406, U.S. Department of State, June 22, 1982.

30. See Adam M. Garfinkle, "SALT and International Stability: An American View," *Disarmament*, May 1981, pp. 30–31.

31. Ibid., pp. 29–30.

32. See Adam M. Garfinkle, *"Finlandization": A Map to a Metaphor* (Philadelphia: Foreign Policy Research Institute, 1978).

33. Colin S. Gray, "Strategic Nuclear Forces: The Reagan Story," *International Security Review*, Winter 1981–82, p. 446.

34. "Which Comes First."

35. Leslie Gelb, "Nuclear Bargaining," *New York Times Magazine*, June 27, 1982, p. 23.

36. See, for example, Daniel Patrick Moynihan, "Reagan MX Plan Commits U.S. to First-Strike Policy," *Long Island Newsday*, July 26, 1983. Moynihan also presents this argument in a chapter in his short book, *Loyalties* (New York: Harcourt, Brace, Jovanovich, 1984).

37. "An Interview with Eugene Rostow," *National Defense*, April 1982, p. 69.

38. Alexander M. Haig, "Arms Control for the 1980s: An American Policy," *Current Policy*, no. 22, U.S. Department of State, July 14, 1981, p. 2.

39. "Negotiation from Strength," p. 230.

180

40. Ibid., p. 229. See also James L. Buckley, State Department Counselor. "Freezing Chances for Peace," *Current Policy*, no. 428, U.S. Department of State, October 27, 1982, pp. 2-3.

41. "Which Comes First."

42. Richard N. Perle, "Clearing the Air on Arms Control Negotiations," *Defense/83*, May 1983, p. 25. This general perspective is also voiced by Richard Burt, "Implications of a Nuclear Freeze," *Current Policy*, no. 470, U.S. Department of State, March 9, 1983, and by R. James Woolsey, "Defense and Arms Control," *The New Republic*, March 3, 1982, pp. 22-23.

43. Kehler is quoted in "How to Avert an Atomic War," *U.S. News and World Report*, December 5, 1983, p. 32.

44. Alexander Cockburn, "Beat the Devil," *The Nation*, March 3, 1984, p. 246.

45. Perle's foes at the *Washington Post* tried to reduce his influence first by accusing him of conflicts of interest—a kind of morals charge, Washington-style—and then by accusing him, in essence, of insubordination to Deputy Secretary of Defense Paul Thayer, who was a sort of super-manager at the Pentagon. But Perle demonstrated easily that he had done nothing wrong, and it was Thayer who resigned amid questions about his own integrity.

46. Testimony of Richard Perle, assistant secretary of defense for international security policy, before the Special Panel on Arms Control and Disarmament, Subcommittee on Procurement and Military Nuclear Systems, House Armed Services Committee, July 12, 1983, p. 1.

47. Ibid., p. 2.

48. See "President and a Student Indirectly Debate Arms," *New York Times*, June 17, 1983.

49. *Foreign Affairs*, Spring 1982, pp. 753-68.

50. See Bernard D. Nossiter, "Soviet Forswears Using A-Arms First," *New York Times*, June 16, 1982.

51. Serge Schmemann, "Soviet Police Bar Disarmament Meeting," *New York Times*, June 14, 1982.

52. See Judith Miller, "U.S. Is Cool to Declaration by Soviet on Use of A-Bomb," *New York Times,* June 16, 1982.

53. Buckley, "Freezing Chances for Peace," p. 2.

54. Ibid., pp. 3-4.

55. Testimony of Perle, p. 1. See also Richard Perle, "A Freeze Means Thin Ice," *New York Times,* September 7, 1982.

Chapter 6

THE FREEZE COMES TO WASHINGTON

Tickertape ain't spaghetti.

—Fiorello La Guardia

The Conservative Mainstream in Action

The Reagan Administration has been in possession of a cohesive strategic theory, and its view of the freeze movement, though emotional, has been informed by a dispassionate analysis of the problems of arms control. One can argue with particulars of this theory or analysis, but it is not illogical, overtly irresponsible, or merely an obfuscating dissimulation, as many freeze advocates have contended.

Nevertheless, the Reagan Administration has had a good deal of trouble transforming its analysis into coherent policy. During the first stage of the freeze phenomenon, which lasted from its inception in 1981 through its introduction to the Congress through Senators Kennedy and Hatfield in March 1982 and the first freeze debate that summer, the Reagan Administration opposed the freeze without notable success.[1] Indeed, its approach was too combative to have been anything but mildly counter-productive. By the beginning of June 1982 public opinion data revealed that more than 72 per cent of the public supported a nuclear freeze so long as it did not materially benefit the Soviet Union.[2]

In its opposition to the freeze, the administration had some help from both inside and outside the government, but in the latter domain it could not compete with the size and sophistication of the freeze movement. Inside the Senate, the administration was aided by a resolution designed to counter the Kennedy-Hatfield resolution offered by Senators Henry M. Jackson and John Warner. (See Appendix D.) The Jackson-Warner resolution out-polled the freeze in the Senate, for which President Reagan was thankful.[3] He was not as thankful to Senator Jackson for openly

183

disputing his contention that the Soviet Union had achieved nuclear superiority.[4] Outside government, the administration's position was supported by think tanks like the Heritage Foundation,
the National Strategy Information Center, and the Hoover Institution, by other groups like Midge Decter's Committee for the
Free World, the Coalition for a Democratic Majority, Social
Democrats USA and, most surprising, by Andrei Sakharov![5] Despite the growth and popularity of the freeze, the 97th Congress
voted down a freeze resolution on August 5, 1982 by a count of
204 to 202.[6] (See Appendix E for the text.)

In this early stage, the freeze movement was still growing
fast numerically and broadening its base politically and institutionally. As the nation approached the November 1982 midterm
elections, the freeze movement was caught up in the partisan
whirlwind. Many Democrats tried to seize the issue for partisan
purposes, but in the end few races were decided by the freeze
issue.[7] As for freeze and "peace with jobs" resolutions that passed
nearly everywhere, save in Arizona and a few isolated congressional districts their meaning was uncertain. Many were phrased
in "have you stopped beating your wife" language, crafted to
imply that those who dared to oppose the resolutions actually
enjoyed the prospect of nuclear carnage.[8]

The second phase of the freeze involved its integration into
the formal political process and its merging into congressional
politics as a whole. This phase dates roughly from December 1982
to the passage of the freeze resolution in amended form in May
1983. In this period, the freeze movement as a whole reached a
sort of middle-aged maturity. It was less strident and less certain
of itself than it was in its 1982 adolescence, and certainly less
infantile in that it was less guilty of grandiose expectations and
less inclined to deny reality than it had been in 1981. It was in
this second phase that the freeze movement confronted an avalanche of other issues: the MX, the "build-down," the Adelman
nomination, and especially the Scowcroft Commission report.

The Dense Pack Debacle

The Scowcroft Commission was assembled in January 1983
after the Reagan Administration, notably Caspar Weinberger's
Department of Defense, had bungled itself into a thorough mess

over the MX missile. Under direction from the White House, the Department of Defense had labored long to find a basing mode for the MX missile that was both militarily rational and politically possible. On November 22, 1982, President Reagan urged adoption of the "Dense Pack," or closely spaced basing, plan.[9] Dense Pack would have concentrated the deployment of 100 MX missiles, each with ten warheads, within ten to twelve square miles, so that the survival of a large number of them would be ensured by the "fratricide" of incoming warheads. Fratricide is the term for the hypothetical phenomenon wherein one nuclear detonation disrupts its immediate successors to the extent that an attacker cannot be assured of a successful military mission. The administration was also said to have considered protecting the narrow corridor through which Soviet warheads would have to come with endoatmospheric ballistic missile defense.[19]

There was no lack of irony in the Reagan Administration's having offered Dense Pack to close the "window of vulnerability"—a phrase coined during the SALT II debate to refer to the Soviet Union's hypothetical ability to destroy nearly all U.S. land-based forces in a first strike and still have enough forces in reserve either to deter or answer effectively a U.S. retaliation. The MX missile was originally designed to combine a counterforce capability with some degree of mobility, but Dense Pack would have made the MX just another static blockbuster. It is also ironic that Dense Pack would not have been nearly as intrusive environmentally as the multiple protective shelter (MPS) plan of the Carter Administration, which was far more sensitive to environmental issues than the Reagan Administration.

Most ironic of all, an administration that rode into office on a wave of pro-defense sentiment, buoyed by the Iranian hostage crisis and Soviet aggression in Afghanistan, frittered away through irresolution and internal squabbles the strong consensus that might have enabled it to close the so-called window of vulnerability. First, as a result of some ill-considered remarks,[11] the political capital that had been expended to assure congressional consent to the MPS system was squandered before either the president or the secretary of defense had in mind a reasonable alternative. Second, the Defense Department was so slow in developing alternatives that it was forced finally in October to suggest the interim basing of forty MX missiles in unprotected fixed silos. When this interim scheme evoked numerous objections, the administration promised to superharden the silos while it searched for a final solution.[12] Then, a short time later, the administration reversed itself on the interim basing plan, deciding that it was not cost-effective to superharden fixed silos for the MX.[13]

This irresolution provoked the criticism of many who were otherwise inclined to support the administration, including William R. Van Cleave, who was a member of President Reagan's post-election transition team, and members of the Committee on the Present Danger, whose former executive director, Eugene V. Rostow, became the head of the Arms Control and Disarmament Agency.[14] The administration also encountered unexpected problems with Congress. One of its most stalwart congressional allies, Republican Senator John Tower of Texas, Chairman of the Senate Armed Services Committee, had earlier joined in an effort to block funds for the MX in order to force the administration to reach a decision on a basing mode—an issue that the administration itself had deliberately portrayed as being of immediate and vital concern to national security.[15] It was this congressional pressure that was the most proximate origin of Dense Pack.

Within days, even hours, after the Dense Pack scheme had been unveiled, it was assailed by expert criticism, by Congress, and by the media. Attacks from those who opposed the missile altogether were expected, but the avalanche of criticism that cascaded from defense analysts outside (and, in *sotto voce,* inside) the government was a rude awakening.[16] Dense Pack soon earned the epithet "Dunce Pack" as manifold flaws in the system were revealed.[17] The president decided to rename the MX "Peacekeeper," after a gun that his new national security adviser, Judge William P. Clark, kept in his office, but it was no use. He was accused of Orwellian antics and the Congress rejected Dense Pack in a huff of contempt.[18] The Reagan Administration found itself with few options and headed straight into a political disaster of its own making not only with the Congress but also with the conservative wing of the Republican party. To rescue itself, the administration sought to broaden the burden of indecision with yet another delay for the MX. It assembled a prestigious panel of experts to examine not only the problem of basing the MX—not *whether* to base the

MX—but the entire strategic modernization program as it affected land-based systems. The Scowcroft Commission, named after its chairman Brent Scowcroft, former national security adviser to President Gerald Ford, was given six weeks to do the job.

While the Reagan Administration sought to use the Scowcroft Commission to show how fair-minded and open to objective study it was, and to demonstrate that it could even work with Democrats and recently fired secretaries of state,[19] the real reason for the commission slipped from the lips of a White House staffer when he said: "Our duty now is to minimize further damage to the President."[20] As part of the general effort to walk softly with Congress, the administration indicated that some substantial cuts in defense outlays for fiscal year 1983 might be acceptable to the president.[21] This claim was greeted with both hope and suspicion. The president also gave prominent media play to his desire to make progress on arms control.[22]

Double, Double Toil and Trouble

The Reagan Administration's general campaign to appease Congress by appearing reasonable and flexible was soon spoiled by the evident disarray between the Arms Control and Disarmament Agency (ACDA), the White House, and U.S. negotiators in Geneva. On January 12, 1983 ACDA Director Eugene V. Rostow was ousted from the administration in part for arguing and acting on behalf of the "walk in the woods" negotiating proposal for the INF talks generated by Paul Nitze and his Soviet counterpart Yuli Kvitsinsky in September.[23] Details of this formula appeared in the press, as did Rostow's expression of support for the deal after his ouster. To most congressional observers, the "walk in the woods" formula had the makings of an honorable compromise, but the administration stood by its rejection of the entire notion and in doing so missed a chance to pin the rap on the Soviets, who also rejected the idea and reportedly disciplined Ambassador Kvitsinsky for exceeding his authority. With Rostow's firing, Nitze evidently had thoughts of resigning. Instead, he managed to persuade the White House to give him a bit more flexibility to explore room for agreement.[24]

It is hard to know exactly what the reasons were for Rostow's dismissal. His aggressive approach to bureaucratic, turf politics undoubtedly annoyed the Reagan White House; indeed, all strong advocacy outside 1600 Pennsylvania Avenue seemed to have this effect, as Alexander Haig discovered soon after the inauguration. Rostow, for example, pushed hard for the formal confirmation of his acting deputy, Robert Grey, which had been held up by Senator Jesse Helms, who thought Grey was an appeaser. Instead of backing Rostow, however, the White House withdrew Grey's name from consideration.[25] Rostow's detractors also accused him of having tried to force his way into issues—like the Middle East—that were outside his authority. Rostow seems also to have run afoul of strong forces in the Defense Department who opposed serious bargaining over intermediate-range nuclear forces until *after* the NATO deployments had begun.[26] This view had been overruled in mid-1981, when the decision was made to issue a public proposal for the INF negotiations. But the proposal itself, the so-called zero proposal of November 18, 1981, was a radical one and seemed, at least to freeze advocates if not to others inside the government, to bear the imprint of those who knew beforehand that it would be summarily rejected. Just as Nitze, with Rostow's support, tried to broaden the possibilities of the INF negotiations, Rostow was dumped. Lingering in the background too was the resentment, not from the Defense Department but from other more political quarters, against both Rostow and Nitze for their both being Democrats. Though both Rostow and Nitze were properly considered "hawks" by most, their broad experience in government and their maturity pushed them toward the Pragmatic Center in the sense that they both saw practical utility in arms control and understood that compromise was essential for agreement. This inevitably aroused the zeal of those further to the right.

The Reagan Administration soon compounded its difficulties by proposing that Kenneth Adelman take Rostow's job—evidently at the urging of Judge William Clark.[27] Adelman had little background for the ACDA job and critics of the administration leaped on his nomination to illustrate their case that the Reagan Administration was not "serious" about arms control.[28] In Adelman's first set of confirmation hearings he fared poorly, leading even some Republicans in the Senate to question his credentials.

Indeed, the Republican-dominated Senate Foreign Relations Committee declined to endorse Adelman in a 9 to 8 vote.[29] In the end, Adelman was confirmed by the Senate on April 14, but only after surviving another attack, which accused him of conspiring with Edward Rowny, the administration's START negotiator, to "cleanse" the START negotiating team and the Arms Control and Disarmament Agency itself of the ideologically suspect.[30]

On top of this, despite earlier hints that the administration might compromise on the fiscal year 1984 defense budget, President Reagan stumped hard in February and March for the full amount even as popular support for his defense policy eroded.[31] As part of this effort, the administration updated and released its *Soviet Military Power* pamphlet, a *j'accuse*-style summary of Soviet capabilities so obviously designed for popular consumption that its effectiveness was marginal at best, and perhaps counterproductive.

It is difficult to say whether Adelman's confirmation was worth the trouble it caused. Throughout 1983 the Reagan Administration and the Congress had their hands full with each other on a multitude of defense-related issues. The crises were many and thoroughly intertwined politically. The president had asked in January for record increases in defense spending that even many hawks agreed were excessive in light of general economic and fiscal conditions. On top of this basic disagreement, a volatile combination of personalities was added. Senators pressed Defense Secretary Weinberger to prioritize defense needs, and Weinberger refused to do so, claiming that everything requested was necessary in equal measure.[32] At least one senator was convinced that Weinberger's behavior was not a tactical ploy in the budget bargaining that is endemic to relations between the White House and Congress, as was widely believed, but rather a reflection of his general ignorance of defense issues. Other comments were even less kind. On top of this, the president's "Star Wars" speech of March 23, whatever its intrinsic merit or lack thereof, was seen by many observers as an awkwardly implemented and poorly conceived attempt to save the defense budget and the MX by redefining the terms of debate.[33] It did not help the president with the Congress, as James Baker and Ed Meese reportedly had warned. This was reportedly yet another of Judge Clark's exploits that ended poorly.[34]

Another issue concerned arms control negotiations, both INF and START. The feeling in Congress was that the administration was moving too slowly in these negotiations and its motives were suspect. The administration contended that progress was being made, but it persuaded few disposed to doubt.[35] By April the issues seemed to collapse on each other. Democrats in the House and Senate, and even a few Republicans, tied their support for the MX and the budget request as a whole to signs of increased "flexibility" and "seriousness" in the administration's attitude to arms control. Meanwhile, the Scowcroft Commission was known to be readying a report that, while it supported building 100 MX missiles, emphasized the dangers of MIRV'd systems and suggested building larger numbers of small, single-warheaded missiles.[36] This new emphasis not only allowed but mandated a major change in the administration's original START proposal of May 7, 1982, which had emphasized reductions in launchers but now needed to emphasize reductions of warheads and/or throw-weight.[37] At the same time, in late March the president changed the U.S. INF position from its earlier zero proposal to one that proposed equality of warheads rather than missiles and that involved a U.S. offer to reduce its planned deployments if Moscow would limit its own forces.[38]

As if this were not enough, still two more complications arose. In mid-March, as signs of change in the U.S. START proposal were becoming apparent, Senators William S. Cohen and Sam Nunn, together with Congressmen Albert Gore, Jr., (Dem., Tennessee) and Norman Dicks (Dem., Washington), urged the administration to alter its new START position to include the "build-down" concept, wherein two or more old warheads would be retired for each new warhead deployed.[39] The congressmen implied strongly that this was *their* measure of the administration's "seriousness" and that they might withhold their support for the MX and the budget request if the president declined serious consideration of the proposal. Since these four gentlemen had both the reputation and associates to hurt the administration, this too was forced onto the president's lap.[40]

The second matter concerned accumulating evidence that the

Soviet Union had violated the terms of the SALT II treaty and the 1972 ABM treaty as well.[41] This evidence presented a number of problems, some stemming from the administration's ambiguous attitude toward SALT II and some from ambiguities in the treaty itself.[42] But the real problems were political. If the administration made a public case against the Soviets, it would be accused of cynical manipulation of a sensitive issue in order to influence Congress and public opinion on the fiscal year 1984 budget, the freeze resolution before the House of Representatives and the Senate, the future of the MX missile, and the administration's go-slow approach to the two sets of U.S.-Soviet negotiations in Geneva.[43] If the administration made no formal accusations in public, but rather took the complaint to the Standing Consultative Committee (SCC) set up in 1972 to handle such issues, it could only anticipate a repeat performance of dozens of doleful past experiences, namely; (1) the United States notes a Soviet violation, they deny it or invent a U.S. violation to "trade off"; (2) the United States offers evidence, the Soviets claim it is inconclusive or fabricated; (3) the United States insists the Soviets reverse the violation, the Soviets deny the violation; (4) the United States insists on its perspective, the Soviets insist on theirs; (5) the United States eventually sees the futility of the exercise and, in the end, nothing happens. This is what Ambassador Nitze referred to in 1979 when he admitted in Senate testimony that there were no unresolved issues before the SCC, but only because "they were resolved by accepting what was done in violation."[44] The administration elected not to push its accusations in public, only to air them briefly. But it did more than merely rely on the SCC. Higher-level representations by the United States to the Soviet Union in April requesting a rapid reply produced instead further violations in May.[45]

The Reagan Administration was clearly in a nasty dilemma. It wished to negotiate with the Soviet Union, but to do so armed with a hefty budget, an MX missile on line, and congressional backing for the entire package. The president stated his view plainly: "Unless we modernize our land-based missile systems, the Soviet Union will have no real reason to negotiate meaningful reductions," and a freeze, in particular, "would pull the rug out from under our negotiators. . . . After all, why should the Soviets negotiate if they've already achieved a freeze in a position of advantage to them?"[46] The President was also concerned about the proclivity of the Soviets to cheat on obligations if they thought they could get away with it, and understood the need to confront violations rather than smooth-talk them away as had been the practice of previous administrations. Yet the cost of showing resolve to the Soviets over their treaty violations might be the MX, without which there was little hope of meaningful progress in START. The MX became a bargaining chip in the most perverse fashion, not a bargaining chip working for the administration in U.S.-Soviet negotiations, but a bargaining chip working against it in administration-congressional negotiations.[47] While the freeze movement did not create this double bind, it did contribute to its acuteness.

The Scowcroft Commission to the Rescue

It was in this political context that the Scowcroft Commission issued its report on April 11, 1983. The report had both predictable and surprising aspects. The most predictable was its affirmation of the MX missile; considering its origins, it could hardly have done anything else. What was surprising about the report was that by *seeming* to play down the "window of vulnerability" issue about which the Reagan Administration had made so much in 1982, and by advancing a general argument against MIRV'd land-based systems, the report undercut both the credibility of the administration and the strictly *military* rationale for the MX. Critics of the administration, the MX, and the Scowcroft commission as savior of the former and midwife of the latter were quick to seize on these surprises.

The commission report did say that "to deter . . . surprise attacks we can reasonably rely both on our other strategic forces and on the range of operational uncertainties that the Soviets would have to consider in planning such aggression" and added: "Whereas it is highly desirable that a component of the strategic forces be survivable when it is viewed separately, it makes a major contribution to deterrence even if its survivability depends in substantial measure on the existence of one of the other components of the force."[48] This sounds much like the tenet of minimum deterrence theory which states that so long as any single leg of the triad is capable of inflicting heavy damage in a retaliatory second strike, none of the forces is in practice (as opposed to "in theory") vulnerable. Some liberal commentaries on the Scowcroft report that *accept* the Scowcroft package give the impression that through these statements alone the commission had repudiated the principles of PD-59, the view of Soviet strategic culture that undergirded it, and the counterforce capabilities needed to implement it. *The New Republic,* for example, commended the report for its candor, and added that this candor:

should be satisfying to certain critics of the administration's strategic thinking as it should be embarrassing to the Administration. Some of the Administration's most fundamental strategic axioms—which the President has put to good political use, in the form of such slogans as "the window of vulnerability"—do not survive the Scowcroft Commission's scrutiny. . . . The vulnerability of America's land-based forces, in other words, is not the vulnerability of America. Or, to put it differently, we, without a first-strike force, are deterring them, and they, with a first-strike force, are deterred.[49]

Feeling vindicated in its basic views, the senior editors of the *The New Republic* were gracious enough to buy the MX if it meant, ultimately, the demise of MIRV and progress in arms control. Even David Holloway, generally a careful scholar, stated erroneously that the commission "implied that the vulnerability of land-based ICBMs *did not really matter* if the Triad's other elements—submarines and bombers—could survive and retaliate.[50]

If one reads what the Scowcroft Commission report actually had to say on this matter however, one gets a rather different view:

Effective deterrence of any Soviet temptation to threaten or launch a massive conventional or a limited nuclear war thus requires us to have a comparable ability to destroy Soviet military targets, hardened and otherwise. . . . A one-sided strategic condition in which the Soviet Union could effectively destroy the whole range of strategic targets in the United States, but we could not effectively destroy a similar range of targets in the Soviet Union, would be extremely unstable over the long run. Such a situation could tempt the Soviets, in a crisis, to feel they could successfully threaten or even undertake conventional or limited nuclear aggression in the hope that the United States would lack a fully effective response. A one-sided condition of this sort would clearly not serve the cause of peace. . . . Consequently our strategic forces must be modernized, as necessary, to enhance to an adequate degree their overall survivability and to enable them to engage effectively the targets that Soviet leaders most value.[51]

And again, near its final conclusion, the report advises:

The serious imbalance between the Soviet's massive ability to destroy hardened land-based military targets with their ballistic missile force and our lack of such a capability must be redressed promptly. Our ability to assure our allies that we have the capability and will to stand with them, with whatever forces are necessary, if the alliance is threatened by massive conventional, chemical or biological, or limited nuclear attack is in question as long as this imbalance exists. Even before the Soviet leaders, in a grave crisis, considered using the first tank regiment or the first SS-20 missile against NATO, they must be required to face what war would mean to them. In order to augment what we would hope would be an inherent sense of conservatism and caution on their part, we must have a credible capability for controlled, prompt, limited attack on hard targets ourselves. . . . Consequently, in the interest of the alliance as a whole, we cannot safely permit a situation to continue wherein the Soviets have the capability promptly to destroy a range of hardened military targets and we do not.[52]

Now this is exactly what the "window of vulnerability" meant in its original context, and precisely how Henry Kissinger, Alexander Haig, Paul Nitze and others used the phrase during the SALT II hearings of 1979. If it was simplified into mindlessness in the 1980 campaign and thereafter, that is another matter. While the Scowcroft Commission report did not use the phrase "window of vulnerability," it clearly held that a vulnerability of some significance continued to exist and continued to plague Western security, whatever one preferred to call it.

Liberal and Left-Liberal critics who did not buy the Scowcroft compromise—and this includes the overwhelming majority of freeze supporters—looked at the report very differently. McGeorge Bundy likewise noted that the report "destroys one of the principal myths on which Mr. Reagan campaigned in 1980— the myth of the 'window of vulnerability,' " which, says Bundy, is now "slammed shut on the fearful fingers of the Committee on the Present Danger."[53] But Bundy recognized, at least, that the report called for U.S. weapons that could strike at hard targets, even though he muddied distinctions and skirted entirely the commission's reasons. He wrote that the main reason for the report's recommendation concerning the MX was that its authors "want these first-strike weapons because the Soviet Union has them," as if the entire logic behind the report could be reduced to that of an eight-year-old who only wants what he wants in order to keep up with his equally immature peers. He also wrote: "Because the Russians do have weapons that can strike first at hard targets, the commission concludes that we must have them, too. When you disentangle all the Report's complex language, that is all there is, and the commissioners neglect to tell us that we have plenty of weapons already that can strike hard targets second."[54] Here Bundy cites bombers, as if a B-52 had the same operational characteristics as a modern ballistic system. Bundy, and freeze supporters generally, opposed the report as a whole, opposed the idea of building smaller, single warhead counterforce-capable missiles—dubbed Midgetman—as well as the MX, and urged the Congress to choose carefully from among its recommendations.

The truth was that the Scowcroft Commission's justification for the MX on *military* grounds was weak, and it took a considerable risk by juxtaposing its support for deploying the MX and its well-articulated anti-MIRV philosophy in the same document. The only convincing justification for the MX, as seen by the commission, the president, and congressional leaders who were a party to the deliberations was the "bargaining chip" argument. Indeed, the emphasis on this point in the report, and after its publication by administration spokesmen, left the impression that if the Soviet Union did not help the United States kill the MX by agreeing to compromise in START, then the United States would be forced to deploy the MX against its better judgment. The report put it this way: "It is illusory to believe that we could obtain a satisfactory agreement with the Soviets limiting ICBM deployments if we unilaterally terminate the only new ICBM program that could lead to deployment in this decade."[55] In other words, only by threatening to build the MX could the United States hope to obviate the need for doing so. And similarly, with respect to the INF talks, the United States must threaten to deploy cruise and Pershing II missiles, and actually do so, in order to force a negotiated reduction in Soviet systems wherein their continued or permanent deployment, ideally, would be made unnecessary.

There is nothing logically wrong with this general concept, because to redress a military disadvantage one can either build up one's own forces or convince the adversary to reduce his. No military system is *absolutely* necessary, but only of *relative* value seen against the forces of the other side. But while the general concept is valid, its validity is vitiated in practice when threatened deployments lack firm military rationales. Putting the MX in unprotected silos is one example of this; deploying cruise missiles on land in Western Europe, where they are more vulnerable to pre-emption, rather than at sea is another. Both these problems illustrate the dangers of letting the military balance erode, because in playing catch-up there is less margin for error and less bargaining leverage simultaneously. They also illustrate the dangers of allowing too wide a gulf to open up between the political and military aspects of defense decisions. Land-basing for cruise and Pershing II missiles in Western Europe may have a justifiable *political* rationale, but the potentially unsettling military consequences of deployment on land may in the end exceed any political benefits. As to the MX, the political problems associated with some of the better basing modes have pushed the United States into settling for a vulnerable system whose real effects on stability are unknown and could be pernicious. This has encouraged many critics to assert that there *are* no relatively invulnerable land-basing modes for MX, when in fact there are.[56] The problems, again, are less technical than political.

The Freeze Debate: Round Two

After the Scowcroft report, the Reagan Administration had about forty-five days to convince Congress to buy the package. Unfortunately for the administration, these forty-five days coincided with what promised to be the final denouement of the freeze debate in the House, which had been plodding along for months. The administration feared a coattail effect, that a vote on the freeze would come so close that it would influence the more important vote on the MX. If this turned out to be the case, the "mere symbolism" of the freeze resolution would prove to be something more substantive than anticipated by either side. This was ironic, for this danger was made possible by administration allies and by the administration itself, which had managed to delay the freeze resolution and amend it into an intellectual cobweb beyond all expectation. It came as a rude shock to some members of the administration when they realized that this tactical triumph might precipitate a strategic route. Indeed, as Thomas Hobbes once put it, Hell is seeing the truth too late.

The second round of debate on the nuclear freeze in the House was a curious affair. During the first debate in the summer of 1982, politicians took turns venting their spleens on the dangers of nuclear war or, alternatively, on the wrong-headedness of taking refuge in simplistic, escapist remedies for complex problems. People got very angry at each other, emotions ran high, and policy analysis at any level became scarce as the debate divaricated into contending metaphorical abstractions. If there was a center position in the first debate, it was drowned out by the din of dithyrambic offerings resounding through the chamber, some of which made their way into tailor-made congressional hearings documents.[57] Moreover, the first freeze debate took place in something more of an arms control vacuum. START had not yet begun, INF had not yet become the urgent issue it was to become in 1983, and "build-down," Midgetman, and the Scowcroft Commission were catch phrases not yet known. No one knew or cared who Kenneth Adelman was, and the MX missile was so obscured in a sea of administration indecision that most politicians would not have been able to locate it as an issue even if they had wanted to.

The second debate was born into a different intellectual and political environment. The passing of so many events in the nine-month interval between July 1982 and April 1983—including the election of the 98th Congress, one more inclined toward the freeze than the 97th—had a modestly edifying effect on the second freeze debate. The tactical argument for the freeze, that it would prod the Reagan Administration toward arms control, had nearly run its course. The impact had been registered—for better or for worse, depending on one's viewpoint—and the virginal magic of first effect had faded away. Moreover, the ebb and flow of debate

197

over MX, Midgetman, build-down, START, INF, and the like had the effect of educating—or reminding—some congressmen, journalists, and others as to the complexities of the issues involved, and this cast the freeze campaign and the freeze proposal in a completely new light. This was reflected in the fact that the freeze resolution itself had been reworded in the direction of ambiguity and moderation when it was reintroduced for floor debate in March 1983. (See Appendix F for text.)

In response to serious queries about the effects of a freeze on the strategic balance, on arms control prospects, and on U.S.-Soviet relations, the pro-freeze experts, by now increasingly members of the Left-Liberal Establishment, tried to refine and explain the freeze to both skeptics and sympathetic but honest others. As this process continued, three effects were noticeable. First, old supporters of the freeze in the House either could not answer the serious questions or answered them in a cascade of mutually exclusive assertions. Second, as a result, the considerable political differences between the original creators of the freeze on the Professional Left and its adherents in the Left-Liberal Establishment were sharpened, and whatever smathering of unity the movement ever had as a wall-to-wall coalition dissipated greatly. Third, as the complexities of arms control intruded on the fantasy world of the freeze in its most pristine, quixotic version, and as the minions of truth increasingly found themselves at one another's throats, the emotional fervor of the freeze's supporters drained away. The difference in the emotional temperament of the first debate compared to the second was like the difference in tone between the Great Crusades as they set off from Europe and the Great Crusades as they returned to Europe nervously pushing booty before the swords of Saladin.

Many congressional supporters of the freeze simply grew tired of the thing. Since it was clear that the president would not sign a freeze resolution as a "joint resolution" of Congress, and would not have to veto it either because the Senate surely would bury it, the entire affair acquired a certain hollowness. As the debate droned on through delay after delay, some supporters were reduced to arguing in essence, "Look, this is only a symbol, so why not just let us have it?" Expressing his astonishment that anyone would argue over the issue, freeze supporter Leon E. Panetta (Dem., California) pleaded with his colleagues: "Whether you are a hawk or dove or something in between, you can interpret anything you want in this resolution. When you go back home," as Mr. Panetta wanted so desperately to do, "you can say anything you want about this resolution."[58]

A good example of how diffuse and confusing the freeze had become emerged during the debate in a *New York Times* column by Tom Wicker, a supporter of the freeze. In March, Wicker took President Reagan to task for not understanding properly the text of the freeze resolution. Wicker wrote that "when and if" the president reads the resolution, he will see that it "does *not* call for an immediate, unconditional stop-in-your-tracks freeze of American and Soviet nuclear forces, achieved by some magical stroke from on high."[59] Rather, said Wicker, "the resolution establishes several objectives that Congress calls upon Mr. Reagan to seek in transformed Soviet-American nuclear arms negotiations. The most significant of these objectives is as follows." Wicker then quotes the resolution itself: "Deciding *when and how* to achieve a mutual, verifiable freeze on testing, production and further deployment of nuclear warheads, missiles and other delivery systems." Thus, according to Wicker, reductions in START and INF could still be compatible with a freeze because the resolution does not specify at which levels the freeze is to take place. Similarly, Wicker noted that the terms of the joint resolution also "would not preclude deployment of Pershing IIs as part of an overall freeze agreement," nor would it necessarily preclude "some new weapons deployments on either side . . . as long as the overall limits of the freeze were observed." In a reference to the build-down proposal, later offered as an amendment to the freeze by Congressman Elliott H. Levitas (Dem., Georgia) and defeated, Wicker added that a new single-warhead missile might be substituted, for example, for one or two multiple-warhead missiles as part of a freeze.[60] In a fit of frustration, the congressional floor leader of the freeze, the late Clement Zablocki, was even more assertive. "Nothing will be frozen until the Freeze is signed, approved and ratified," he said. "Any item both sides do not agree to freeze is not frozen. Any item that cannot be verified is not frozen." Moreover, "No element of the Reagan defense program is stopped by the resolution."[61]

All this was a far cry from what the freeze movement originally had in mind, so it is no surprise that there was widespread disenchantment on the Left with what had become of the freeze. Nevertheless, those in the movement who had been charged with shepherding the resolution through Congress tried to seem unperturbed at moving ever closer to the lowest, least meaningful common denominator of definition of what the freeze really meant. Randall Kehler, still head of the freeze's St. Louis clearinghouse, denied that Zablocki's "clarifications" significantly diluted the freeze proposal. "We've all worked on these definitions. These refinements mean that the freeze is no longer just a word or a symbol." Kehler referred to the postponement of the vote that took place in March because of confusion over what the resolution actually would and would not permit as "a blessing in disguise": "It forced us all to do our homework. You're seeing the results of that today."[62]

Kehler's sudden enthusiasm for moderation, education, and compromise was odd. In February, at the freeze's annual convention in St. Louis, some 600 delegates voted on a resolution to make an antinuclear testing drive bilateral and a U.S. cessation contingent on a Soviet response. The resolution was resoundingly defeated. The convention urged the freeze movement to concentrate on forcing Congress to cut off funds for all weapons testing and merely to "call on" the Soviet Union to do the same.[63] Randall Forsberg averred that President Reagan should agree to comply with the movement's demands. "He would not only win re-election," she said, "he would go down as the greatest President of the 20th Century." But in an outburst of the sour grapes of wrath, Forsberg added: "President Reagan is not smart enough to know that."[64] As to Kehler, when he was asked if he continued to reject as flawed the entire strategy of nuclear deterrence, he answered without hesitation:

Certainly. First, it assumes that we won't have any accidents, that these weapons can just be sitting around and some mad general on either side won't push a button or some computer won't make an error. Second, it assumes that we can somehow keep tinkering with these devices, improving them, making them more "usable," and not somehow increase the danger of their being used.

But the most fundamental flaw is moral and ethical: Our security as a nation should not be based on the threat to annihilate millions of men, women and children who have done nothing to us in any way but whose government happens to be our enemy.[65]

This last point is surprising coming from Kehler for it is exactly the same argument and uses language similar to that advanced by opponents of countervalue targeting postures. Kehler obviously opposes counter*force* targeting, but here we see that he evidently opposed counter*value* targeting as well. Put simply, he *opposes targeting altogether*—hence his rejection of the very concept of deterrence. Kehler does not accept the need even for a minimum deterrence posture; he cannot accept any justification for any nuclear weapons whatsoever. If this is indeed what Kehler believes, then the source of his supportive attitude toward Zablocki's "clarifications" and his gratitude for having been forced to do his homework must be something other than what first catches the eye. As one pro-freeze activist put it, the movement claimed victory in May 1983 because claiming victory sounded like a better idea than admitting defeat.

Despite Kehler's efforts—perhaps sincere, perhaps not—to paint the diffusion of the freeze as a good thing as opposed to an inevitable tactical compromise, those in opposition to the freeze resolution also claimed victory.[66] After a certain point in the consideration of dozens of amendments, logic met a familar fate as an "us against them" mentality seized the House. Words did not mean what they said any more; all motives were suspect. Thus, an attempt to tack the build-down onto the freeze—ultimately defeated—was seen by freeze supporters as political sabotage. Edward Markey said of the build-down: "This proposal is tantamount to letting us trade two cross-bows for one artillery piece. It's only an attempt to soft-sell an arms buildup."[67] (One wonders what Markey's attitude might have been had President Reagan not expressed an interest in the notion.) Similarly, an amendment proposing an emphasis on reductions was also defeated. Supporters of the freeze suspected a ruse. Thomas Downey put it this way: " 'Reductions' do not mean reductions. Reductions mean more weapons." Even a resolution introduced by Congressman James G. Martin (Rep., North Carolina) calling for "essential equivalence" between U.S. and Soviet arsenals as the result of a freeze—a desideratum that few would gainsay under more normal conditions and already law according to the Jackson amendment to the SALT I agreements of 1972—was defeated mainly because Martin was known to oppose the resolution.[68]

The Reagan Administration played its part too in all this, although it was not clear to what effect. The president termed the nuclear freeze both dangerous and divisive and ridiculed the "peace hype" of the "so-called peace movement," likening their naiveté to that of Neville Chamberlain.[69] The president's efforts at arm-twisting some twenty-five congressmen had ambiguous results. A few were won over, most were not. Frank McCloskey (Dem., Indiana), on the other hand, called the session—especially Secretary Weinberger's part in it—"mildly bizarre," adding that it "somewhat revitalized my support for the freeze."[70]

One vignette in the debate, captured for posterity by a *Washington Post* reporter, summed up the scene quite well. Les Aspin, taking a break from the proceedings to talk to journalists, was complaining: "We're losing votes. People are getting fed up. They can't see the differences between the bill and the amendments," when he was interrupted by Congressman Markey. Markey "emerged from the chamber looking frazzled" and addressed Aspin, "Can you get back in here? We need someone to explain the difference between a Blackjack and a Backfire bomber."[71] The frustration of most congressmen, it seems, was matched only by their aversion to relevant details.

The divarigations of the House debate elicited predictable comment. The Professional Left lamented the unsurpation of the revolution by the congressional bourgeoisie, while the ideologues of the Far Right failed to see much difference between this freeze resolution and any other, or between the likes of the WRL's David McReynolds on the one hand and Les Aspin on the other. The Left-Liberal Establishment, in support of the freeze for less ambitious reasons, and the Conservative Mainstream, epitomized by the Reagan Administration, both stood ready to declare a victory as the dust cleared.[72] Democratic presidential aspirants Walter Mondale, John Glenn, and later Gary Hart seized on the diffusion of the freeze to support it *and* aspects of U.S. strategic modernization simultaneously, clearly the safest course in the early running.[73]

Only in the Pragmatic Center, it seems, was there much taking stock of what was happening. Aspin summarized the situation in practical terms. "This year," he said, "a majority of the Congress has decided that the administration needs public and Congressional prodding to get serious in Geneva. The question for some Congressmen now is whether the freeze is the appropriate vehicle for that pressure."[74] Much of the Pragmatic Center thought not. A prevailing opinion was that the whole freeze episode was a diversion from the main event. Harold Brown put it in his usual measured language: "Strategic parity is a band, not a point, and though our position in that band is relatively worse off with respect to the Soviet Union than it was 10 years ago, we remain in that band." To stay in that band, argued Brown, we need both specific and realistic arms control negotiations *and* new strategic programs to buttress them. "The freeze proposal is not likely to help accomplish any of our major goals of enhancing stability," said Brown, and is likely to detract from more practical positive steps.[75] Elizabeth Drew, a frequent contributor to the *New Yorker,* observed that "the more one thinks about it, the more freeze negotiations sound like arms reductions negotiations without the reductions."[76] She accused politicans of pandering to the freeze movement and ducking the hard questions. "A declaration that one is four-square in favor of a nuclear freeze is a guaranteed applause line, but that's about it. It doesn't answer the hard questions about arms control, questions that the candidates know exist."[77]

The most biting criticisms of the freeze came from somewhat unexpected quarters: the editorial pages of the *New York Times* and the *Washington Post,* both firmly in the Pragmatic Center— at least on this issue. The *Post* took the resolution to task for the "special attention" it accorded "destabilizing weapons," noting that this language "goes to a major and central defect of a freeze— that it would block new programs designed to take Soviet and American nuclear forces off a hair trigger, to create more 'stability.' "[78] The *Post* pointed out, as had the Harvard Study Group, that some new weapons can be stabilizing. The *Post* had a problem with the freeze movement's answers to questions about what would and would not be permissible in a freeze, what would or would not be destabilizing. "To the extent that they have addressed it," said the *Post,* "freeze advocates tend to say that each new system should be judged on its own merits. But, "the *Post* went on to say in a flash of editorial temper, "it is not easy to find new systems in which they see merit. The letter of the movement honors mutual negotiated cuts. But its spirit is patently unilaterist: no more nukes." The *Post* concluded, "A freeze would undercut not only Mr. Reagan's negotiating program, but also the freeze's own."[79]

The *Times* also captured the spirit of the Pragmatic Center when it said that "the freeze idea, once a useful prod to an administration lukewarm toward arms control, has become a catchall to exploit fear and discontent."[80] The *Times* reiterated the flaws of a freeze and observed that despite months of advocacy, "the proposals of the freeze movement have barely evolved past the original, simplistic formula of 'stop now.' . . . Where is the program to match the piety?"[81]

In the end, the springtime ordeal of the nuclear freeze came to naught. On April 28, opponents of the resolution blocked a vote for the fifth time.[82] Looking back to January, proponents and opponents alike could only marvel at how enormously wrong House Speaker Tip O'Neill had been when he predicted that the resolution would pass in a day by fifty votes.[83] The resolution finally did pass in May, by a vote of 278 to 149, only to be buried without ceremony by the Senate a few weeks later. (See Appendix F.) But the passage of the freeze did not put an end to the battle between staunch freeze supporters in the Congress and the White House; it merely moved to other, already familiar grounds—the MX and the defense budget.

A few days after the passage of the freeze, the same House of Representatives appropriated funds for the MX, leading freeze movement zealots to despair and to charge perfidy. SANE, in a press release the day after the MX vote, charged: "The American people have been betrayed today by politicians who claim to support a nuclear weapons freeze, but who have repudiated that idea by voting for the most deadly, destabilizing nuclear weapon system ever devised."[84] But according to the wording of the resolution, there *was* no contradiction between the freeze vote and the MX vote; there was no plainer illustration of this than the depths to which freeze tacticians had sunk to win approval for the resolution.[85] Section 6 of the freeze resolution stated: "Until such time as the final instrument embodying [the freeze] has been fully ratified by both the Soviet Union and the United States, nothing in this joint resolution should be construed to prevent whatever modernization and deployment of U.S. weapons may be required to retain the credibility of the U.S. nuclear deterrent." The evolving compromise between the administration and the Congress proved fragile because no comparable, stable compromise had been reached within either the freeze movement or the Democratic party. Democrats who supported the freeze vigorously opposed the MX and the Scowcroft Commission package, insisted that the president's protestations of "seriousness" and "flexibility" were plain lies, and did not give up trying to stop the MX.

During the July 4 recess the more radical side of the freeze movement did its best to wreck the compromise. Congressman Tony Coelho (Dem., California) told one journalist that new lobbying efforts made the prospects for a turnaround on the MX on the House floor "excellent." Thomas Downey (Dem., New York), who led the anti-MX campaign in the House, noted with alacrity that the ninety congressmen who voted both for the freeze and for the MX "had a lot of explaining to do when they were home. We're going to make a fight of it." Downey also had words for Les Aspin, who spent his holiday worrying aloud that the Democratic presidential candidates were being perceived as "bordering on unilateral disarmers." Downey averred that "Aspin and company have become irrelevant. The issue has passed them by."[86] Senator Gary Hart attempted to help the anti-MX forces by providing extra time through an unusual Senate filibuster.

But on July 26 the Congress voted for compromise and the MX in an authorization bill. A little over a month later, the shooting down of a Korean Air Lines jet by the Soviet Union on September 1 punched the wind out of anti-defense forces in the Congress long enough for President Reagan to gain approval for most of his fiscal year 1984 military budget requests—including the final fiscal year 1984 appropriation for the MX on November 3. In the end, all the huffing and puffing of the freeze movement could not match the blush of reality that a few MiG fighters were able to insert in the debate. Aspin and company had not become quite as irrelevant as Downey had thought, nor was the Reagan Administration as vulnerable on the "peace issue" as Coelho and his associates had hoped. The Pragmatic Center had helped pass both the freeze resolution and the MX. The curious thing was that most of its members had little real fondness for either one.

The second freeze debate had the general effect of bringing the Reagan Administration and Congress closer together. The vehicle for this was the indefatigable workers of the Pragmatic Center and the continuing utility of the Scowcroft Commission. While weary congressmen were jabbing at one another in the House debate, Les Aspin quietly urged the administration to charge the Scowcroft Commission with finding a way to integrate the "build-down" concept into the U.S. START proposal. In the end, this is precisely what happened, though the president reportedly had to overrule General Rowny to do it.[87] Although perhaps timed to affect votes on the MX and the defense budget due later in October, the new administration START position was really far more important insofar as the real prospects for arms control were concerned than the fate of the freeze movement. The road that the administration had traveled in arms control by the end of 1983 was not so much *because* of the freeze movement as in spite of it.

NOTES

1. See, for example, Bernard Gwertzman, "State Dept. Calls Arms Freeze Plan 'Dangerous' to U.S.," *New York Times,* March 12, 1981; and Don Oberdorfer, "Reagan: Arms Freeze 'Isn't Good Enough'," *Washington Post,* March 17, 1982.

2. See Judith Miller, "Poll Shows Nuclear Freeze Backed If Soviet Doesn't Gain," *New York Times,* May 30, 1982. This support was remarkably stable. See the public opinion data in *National Journal,* July 30, 1983, p. 1617.

3. Judith Miller, "Fifty-eight Senators Back Alternative Plan on Nuclear

Arms," *New York Times,* March 31, 1982. One observer, noting the similarity of the language of the two resolutions, suggested that they be merged, thus really missing the partisan gist of the whole episode. See Brewster C. Denney, "Two Camps, One Freeze," *New York Times,* July 25, 1982. Some congressmen were very unhappy with the superficiality of the whole business, which Congressman Henry J. Hyde (Rep., Illinois) dubbed "government by bumper-sticker." See Judith Miller, "House Takes up Nuclear Freeze and Rival Plan Reagan Supports," *New York Times,* August 6, 1982.

4. See Judith Miller, "Reagan's View on Lag in Arms Being Disputed," *New York Times,* April 2, 1982; and Adam Clymer, "Two Senators Deny Soviet Arms Lead," *New York Times,* April 5, 1982.

5. See, for example, Jeffrey Barlow, "A Freeze Makes No Sense," Heritage Foundation Executive Memorandum no. 3, July 28, 1982; Jeffrey Barlow, "The Hard Facts the Nuclear Freeze Ignores," Heritage *Backgrounder,* no. 225, November 3, 1982; W. Bruce Weinrod, "The Nuclear Freeze: Myths and Realities," Heritage *Backgrounder,* no. 251, March 3, 1983. Other Heritage publications include "The Flawed Premises Behind a Nuclear Freeze," *National Security Record* (Heritage), April 1982; "Soviet Violations of Arms Agreements," *National Security Record,* May 1982; and Barlow's "Moscow and the Peace Offensive," Heritage *Backgrounder,* no. 184, May 14, 1982. In 1983 the National Strategy Information Center published a pamphlet by Joyce E. Larson and William C. Bodie, *The Intelligent Layperson's Guide to the Nuclear Freeze and Peace Debates.* See also Rita Freedman, executive director of Social Democrats USA, "A Nuclear Freeze Imperils Peace," *New York Times,* June 17, 1982; and Andrei Sakharov, "A Dangerous Remnant," *Christian Science Monitor,* May 24, 1983. See also Sakharov's longer and most eloquent statement, "The Dangers of Thermonuclear War," *Foreign Affairs,* Summer 1983.

6. There were many such close votes in the 97th Congress, and the 98th Congress was more pro-freeze than its predecessor. See the chart "The New House," in *New York Times,* November 4, 1982; and "The National Security Margin in the 97th Congress," *National Security Record,* no. 50, October 1982.

7. See Judith Miller, "Democrats Seize Weapons Freeze as Issue for Fall," *New York Times,* June 20, 1982; and Judith Miller, "Nuclear Freeze Debate Important in Few Races," *New York Times,* October 19, 1982.

8. For example, a "peace with jobs question" resolution in Philadelphia in November 1983 read as follows: "Shall more federal funds be made available for local jobs and programs such as quality education, public transportation, energy efficient housing, and improved health care, by reducing the amount

of our tax dollars spent on nuclear and conventional weapons, and military programs *beyond the defensive needs* of our nation?" (Emphasis added.)

9. This background discussion follows my "Dense Pack: A Critique and an Alternative," *Parameters,* December 1982, pp. 14-16. See Lou Cannon, "Reagan Urges MX 'Dense Pack' in Wyoming," *Washington Post,* November 23, 1982; and Richard Halloran, "Reagan Urges Congress to Weigh MX Missile Plan with Sympathy," *New York Times,* November 23, 1982.

10. Charles Corddry, "Reagan Approves MX Basing," *Baltimore Sun,* May 19, 1982.

11. See, for example, "Environmentalist Action May Slow MX Basing," *Aviation Week and Space Technology,* February 9, 1981, p. 27; and "Fumbling Away MX," *Aviation Week and Space Technology,* December 20, 1982, p. 9.

12. See "Two Weapons Facing Capitol Questions," *New York Times,* November 1, 1981.

13. See Tom Wicker, "A Switch for the MX," *New York Times,* February 19, 1982; Bernard Weinraub, "MX Deadline Raises Host of Questions," *New York Times,* May 16, 1982; and Steven R. Weisman, "Reagan Abandons Plan to Reinforce First Forty MX Silos," *New York Times,* February 12, 1982.

14. See "Is the Reagan Defense Program Adequate?" Committee on the Present Danger, Washington, D.C., March 17, 1982. For his trouble, Van Cleave was deprived of the chairmanship of ACDA's General Commission on Arms Control and Disarmament. See Michael Getler, "Panel Says Ex-member Reagan Fails to Bolster Defense," *Washington Post,* March 18, 1982. It also evoked the wrath of Colin S. Gray, an analyst respected by the administration and otherwise inclined to support it. See Gray's "Strategic Forces: The Reagan Story," *International Security Review,* Winter 1981-82, pp. 439-440.

15. Steven V. Roberts, "Senators Reject Plan for Placing MX Missiles in Silos," *New York Times,* December 3, 1981.

16. In the first category, see, for example, Kosta Tsipis, "An MX 'Dense Pack' Would Need ABMs, Both Periling Security," *New York Times,* December 1, 1982; and Anthony Lewis, "The MX Message," *New York Times,* December 9, 1982. One variety of criticism, aided eagerly by the Soviet Union, was that "dense pack" would violate SALT II. This was, however, just another way to kill the MX, not an expression of concern for the law. See my "SALT and the MX: The U.S. Loses," *Philadelphia Inquirer,* December 11, 1982. As evidence accumulated in early 1984 of unambiguous Soviet

violations of the ABM treaty and SALT II, the Soviets adopted a similar ploy, and the Left-Liberal Establishment, as usual, swallowed the argument. The Kremlin charged that the deployment of cruise and Pershing II missiles in Western Europe violated the noncircumvention clause (Article XII) of the SALT II treaty. See Don Oberdorfer, "New Arms Are Linked to SALT II," *Philadelphia Inquirer,* January 26, 1984. In the second category, even the majority of the Joint Chiefs of Staff expressed their reservations. See Richard Halloran, "Three of Five Joint Chiefs Asked Delay on MX," *New York Times,* December 9, 1982; See also "Dense Pack or 'Dunce Pack'?" *Newsweek,* July 19, 1982, pp. 24–25; and Charles Mohr, " 'Pindown' Tactic Called Peril to Tightly Packed MX Missiles," *New York Times,* July 21, 1982.

17. See my "Dense Pack: A Critique and an Alternative," pp. 16–18.

18. See Richard Halloran, "House, 245-176, Votes Down $988 Million for MX Missile; Setback for Reagan Policy," *New York Times,* December 8, 1982. Some critics could not resist high humor. See the amusing piece by Ira Nerken, "Dense Unpacking," *The New Republic,* December 27, 1982, pp. 10–11.

19. The panel included Alexander M. Haig, former secretary of state: New Jersey senator Nicholas Brady; former Texas governor William C. Clements, who was a deputy secretary of defense under Presidents Nixon and Ford; MIT dean of science John Deutch; former CIA director Richard Helms; John Lyons, the AFL-CIO's man on defense; Vice-Admiral Levering Smith, former director of special projects for the navy; and former undersecretary of the navy R. James Woolsey. The views of two other men were also influential: Henry A. Kissinger, and former Defense Secretary Harold Brown, who at first was on the panel itself. The panel's composition reflected broad political motivation, as did the reported blackballing of Donald Rumsfeld and James Schlesinger by Secretary Weinberger. See Rowland Evans and Robert Novak, "MX: A Direct Hit," *Washington Post,* January 14, 1983.

20. See Evans and Novak, "MX: A Direct Hit"; and Carl Macy, "MXing up Priorities," *New York Times,* January 10, 1983. Macy urged the commission to look not at *how* to base the MX but at *whether* to base the MX and at the full range of arms control and strategic issues. He admitted that such expectations were "pie in the sky."

21. Steven R. Weisman, "Aides Say Reagan May Permit a Cut in Arms Programs," *New York Times,* January 8, 1983.

22. See Bernard Gwertzman, "President Pledges to Make Progress on Arms Control," *New York Times,* January 15, 1983.

23. See Bernard Gwertzman, "Rostow Defends Arms Agreement Disowned by U.S.," *New York Times;* and especially the account by John Newhouse, "A Reporter at Large: Arms and Allies," *New Yorker,* February 28, 1983, pp. 69-75.

24. After avowing "no change" in the zero-option, the following suggestive article appeared: Bernard Gwertzman, "Nitze Suggests U.S. Might Be Flexible in Missile Talks," *New York Times,* January 22, 1983. See also Leslie Gelb, "An Arms Negotiator Determined to Get His Way," *New York Times,* February 2, 1983. It was not, however, Nitze's persuasiveness alone that effected the shift, but also pleas from European allies not to undercut their prospects in impending elections in West Germany and Great Britain.

25. See "Reagan Said to Drop Arms Agency Nominee," *New York Times,* January 11, 1983.

26. In this the Defense Department had a new ally. This period in the mercurial bureaucratic balance of power in the Reagan Administration witnessed the ascendancy of National Security Adviser William P. Clark, who was in alliance with Secretary Weinberger on a broad range of issues. See Strobe Talbott, "Behind Closed Doors," *Time,* December 5, 1983, pp. 18-37.

27. Elizabeth Drew, "A Political Journal," *New Yorker,* May 9, 1983, p. 578.

28. See, for example, Senator Alan Cranston's letter in the *Washington Post,* January 27, 1983, or Philip Geyelin's more gentle analysis, "Kenneth Adelman Missed His Chance," *Washington Post,* February 15, 1983. For more general comments, including those of Senators Jackson and Warner, see Michael Getler, "Administration Reeling Again from Controversies on Personnel," *Washington Post,* March 20, 1983.

29. See David Shribman, "Panel Asks Senate to Block Adelman for Top Arms Post," *New York Times,* February 25, 1983.

30. See Charles Mohr, "Dispute Arises After Report of Purge in Arms Talks Unit," *New York Times,* March 12, 1983.

31. See Juan Williams, "Reagan Steps Up Defense Push," *Washington Post,* March 9, 1983; and Brad Knickerbocker, "Reagan Pulls Out All Stops to Lobby for Defense Buildup," *Christian Science Monitor,* February 23, 1983.

32. In the end, Weinberger's behavior helped the Senate reduce the president's budget—White House staffers admitted as much. See Lou Cannon and David Hoffman, "Weinberger Blamed for Defeat on Buildup," *Washington Post,* April 9, 1983. See also Drew, "A Political Journal," pp. 54-55.

33. See, for example, reportage of the Democratic "rejoinder" to the speech, given by Senator Daniel K. Inouye of Hawaii, in Michael Getler, "Democrats Charge Reagan Distorted Balance of Power," *Washington Post,* March 25, 1983; Stephen Chapman, "Reagan Cries Wolf on Defense," *Chicago Tribune,* March 27, 1983; "Behind Reagan's Star-Wars Strategy," *Newsweek,* April 4, 1983, pp. 29–31; and Drew, "A Political Journal," p. 54.

34. Drew, "A Political Journal," p. 57.

35. Hedrick Smith, "Movement Is Cited on Strategic Arms," *New York Times,* April 7, 1983.

36. See Leslie Gelb, "Panel Considering a Mobile Missile Smaller Than MX," *New York Times,* February 8, 1983; and Hedrick Smith, "Basing of MX in Minutemen Silos Expected as Panel's Interim Plan," *New York Times,* March 23, 1983.

37. "U.S. Studies Shift in Stand at Strategic Arms Talks," *New York Times,* April 30, 1983; and Hedrick Smith, "U.S. Expects MX Report to Lead to a New Arms-Control Strategy," *New York Times,* April 10, 1983. This had been the original position of the Defense Department, and Rostow supported it. Both the Joint Chiefs of Staff and the State Department had opposed couching an agreement in terms of throwweight—although for different reasons. See Michael R. Gordon, "Administration Debates Arms Cuts with Congress as Well as the Soviets," *National Journal,* August 6, 1983, pp. 1624-29.

38. See Bernard Gwertzman, "Reagan Offers Cut in U.S. Missile Plan for West Europe," *New York Times,* March 31, 1983.

39. See William S. Cohen, "A Guaranteed Arms Builddown," *Washington Post,* January 3, 1983; William S. Cohen, "Consensus on Arms," *New York Times,* March 2, 1983; and especially Cohen's diary-like article on the build-down, "The Arms Build-Down Proposal," *Washington Post,* October 9, 1983.

40. The freeze movement for the most part looked down on the build-down idea because it would allow counterforce-oriented modernization, including the MX. See, for example, John Loretz, "Pitfalls of a Nuclear 'Build-Down'," *New York Times,* April 7, 1983; Herbert Scoville, "Build-Down (-Doom?)," *New York Times,* October 11, 1983; and Robert C. Toth, "Missile Build-Down: Idea Simple, Problems Complex," *Los Angeles Times,* October 12, 1983.

41. The *New York Times* reported the potential violations on April 21-23, 1983. See especially Hedrick Smith, "Panel Tells Reagan the Russians Seem to Have Broken Arms Pacts," *New York Times,* April 21, 1983.

42. See Adam M. Garfinkle, "Violating SALT II," *Contemporary Review*, September 1983, pp. 123-27.

43. Senator Alan Cranston made this accusation; see *New York Times*, April 22, 1983.

44. See *The SALT II Treaty, Hearings Before the Senate Foreign Relations Committee*, 96th Cong. 1st sess., July 1979, part 1, quoted in Robert Jastrow, "Why Strategic Superiority Matters," *Commentary*, March 1983, p. 30.

45. Garfinkle, "Violating SALT II," pp. 123-24.

46. The president's remarks can be found, respectively, in Frances X. Clines, "Reagan Endorses Plan to Base MX in Existing Silos," *New York Times*, April 20, 1983; and in "Reducing the Danger of Nuclear Weapons," *Current Policy*, no. 473, U.S. Department of State, March 31, 1983, pp. 4-5.

47. See Michael R. Gordon, "Reagan's Geneva Offer May Determine How He Fares on MX in Washington," *National Journal*, September 17, 1983, pp. 1880-85.

48. See "Excerpts from Report," *New York Times*, April 12, 1983.

49. "The Scowcroft Revolution," *The New Republic*, May 9, 1983, p. 7.

50. David Holloway, "The View from the Kremlin," *Wilson Quarterly*, Winter 1983, p. 107. (Emphasis added.)

51. "Excerpts from Report," *New York Times*, April 12, 1983.

52. Ibid.

53. McGeorge Bundy, "MX Paper: Appealing, but Mostly Appalling," *New York Times*, April 17, 1983. As one of those who brought us the war in Vietnam, Bundy should know quite a bit about myths. See also Tom Wicker, "MIRV and the Window," *New York Times*, April 19, 1983, for a hagiographic view of Bundy. Note also the comments of Senator Cranston, who claimed that instead of a "window of vulnerability" there was now a "window of credibility." At the time, Cranston was building his presidential aspirations around the arms control issue. See Clines, "Reagan Endorses Plan."

54. Bundy, "MX Paper."

55. "Excerpts from Report," *New York Times*, April 12, 1983.

56. See Adam M. Garfinkle, "Dense Pack: A Critique and an Alternative." Even Brent Scowcroft himself said as much; see Steven V. Roberts, "Leader of MX Panel Says Politics Played Key Role in Decision," *New York Times,* April 19, 1983.

57. For some examples, see Ronald V. Dellums, *Defense Sense: The Search for a Rational Military Policy* (Cambridge, Mass.: Ballinger, 1983); a study by Gary Guenther made at the request of Congressman Ted Weiss (Dem., New York), "The Implications of a Nuclear Freeze for the U.S. Economy in the Short Run," Congressional Research Service, Library of Congress, August 3, 1982; and Samuel Stratton, *The Dicey Impact of a "Nuclear Freeze" on the Defense of the Free World, Report Together with Dissenting View of the Procurement and Military Nuclear Subcommittee of the Committee on Armed Services,* U.S. House, 98th Cong., 1st sess., March 11, 1983.

58. Margot Hornblower, "Freeze Debate Founders as House Bickers," *Washington Post,* April 24, 1983.

59. Tom Wicker, "An Evolving 'Freeze'," *New York Times,* March 11, 1983.

60. Ibid.

61. Zablocki is quoted in Judith Miller, "Atom Arms Freeze Gains in House," *New York Times,* April 14, 1983; and Margot Hornblower, "House Backers of Arms Freeze Scolded by Pentagon Official," *Washington Post,* February 18, 1983.

62. Miller, "Atoms Arms Freeze Gains." Michael Barone was of the same opinion; see his "Why the Second Thoughts on the Freeze?" *Washington Post,* April 28, 1983.

63. See Joanne Omang, "Freeze Groups Plan to Move on Congress," *Washington Post,* February 18, 1983; and Charles Krauthammer, "Half a Freeze," *The New Republic,* March 7, 1983, p. 13.

64. Forsberg is quoted in Omang, "Freeze Groups Plan."

65. See Kehler's remarks in "How to Avert an Atomic War," *U.S. News and World Report,* December 5, 1983, p. 32.

66. See Dennis Farney, "Nuclear Freeze Resolution Clears House; Both Sides in Arms Debate Claim Victory," *Wall Street Journal,* May 5, 1983.

67. Miller, "Atom Arms Freeze Gains."

68. Downey is quoted in Hornblower, "Freeze Debate Founders." The "re-

ductions" amendment was offered by Congressman Mark D. Siljander (Rep., Michigan), and it was so innocuous that Congressman Jim Leach (Rep., Iowa), one of the freeze's sponsors and supporters, voted for it. This brought down on him the wrath of the freeze movement. See Mary McGrory, "Peacenik Gloom," *Washington Post,* April 10, 1983, and "Democrats Shepherd Plan on Atomic Freeze Toward House Vote," *New York Times,* April 21, 1983.

69. See Steven R. Weisman, "Reagan Calls Nuclear Freeze Dangerous," *New York Times,* April 1, 1983; and Frances X. Clines, "Reagan Ridicules Arms Protestors for Peace 'Hype'," *New York Times,* August 24, 1983.

70. See "Lobbying Increase on Freeze Proposal Before House Today," *New York Times,* April 3, 1983; and George C. Wilson, "President Calls in Twenty-five Democrats on Nuclear Freeze Resolution," *Washington Post,* April 13, 1983.

71. Hornblower, "Freeze Debate Founders." At this point, Markey still had his eyes on a seat in the U.S. Senate, but this came to naught. As to the details of arms control, Markey once told a group of Democratic congressional aspirants that all they needed to know about arms control was a few phrases: "Don't bother about the complicated details; the issue is hot and its ours." See Martin Peretz, "Cambridge Diarist," *The New Republic,* May 28, 1984, p. 43.

72. See Judith Miller, "In the Heat of House Debate on Nuclear Freeze," *New York Times,* April 23, 1983.

73. See, for example, excerpts from the text of Walter Mondale's speech to the annual convention of the American Newspaper Publishers Association on April 26 in the *New York Times,* April 27, 1983. See also the report by Robert Pear, "Democratic Candidates Disagree over Adequacy of Nuclear Force," *New York Times,* November 6, 1983.

74. Miller, "In the Heat of House Debate."

75. Harold Brown, "A Nuclear Freeze?" *Washington Post,* March 28, 1982.

76. Elizabeth Drew, "Yes! Yes! Yes! I'm for a Freeze," *Chicago Sun-Times,* July 24, 1983.

77. Ibid.

78. "The Freeze Debate," *Washington Post,* March 20, 1983.

79. Ibid.

80. "The Lord and the Freeze," *New York Times,* March 11, 1983.

81. " 'Stop Nukes'; Then What?" *New York Times,* April 19, 1983.

82. "Conservatives in House Block Nuclear Freeze Vote Again," *New York Times,* April 29, 1973.

83. Quoted in Hornblower, "Freeze Debate Founders," April 24, 1983. See also Martin Tolchin, "House to Vote Today on Nuclear Freeze Proposal," *New York Times,* March 16, 1983, for O'Neill's original faux pas.

84. SANE press release dated June 13, 1983.

85. See Alexander Cockburn and James Ridgeway, "Has the Freeze Failed?" *The Village Voice,* June 7, 1983. Cockburn and Ridgeway admitted this point, which is what prompted the question in the title of this article.

86. Quotations are from Mary McGrory, "Freeze Backers Set to Call Congress to Account in Next MX Vote," *Washington Post,* July 14, 1983.

87. Leslie H. Gelb, "Arms Talks: Shift by U.S.," *New York Times,* October 5, 1983. But these reports were false. The truth was that the advocates of the build-down each had a slightly different idea of what it entailed and of how the notion could be incorporated into the U.S. START proposal. It fell to General Rowny to bring the congressional build-down advocates to a unified proposal. Besides, reports of Rowny's opposing the build-down concept flew in the face of U.S. objectives in START, which are thoroughly compatible with a build-down.

Chapter 7

LOOKING BACK, LOOKING AHEAD

It ain't over til it's over.

—Yogi Berra

Freeze PAC '84

The current pulse of political activity in the United States over nuclear weapons, nuclear doctrine and strategy, and arms control seems at first glance to be merely the latest chapter in an old story of episodic public activism in national security affairs. In many ways it is. But if the nuclear freeze movement shares a historical paternity with other antiwar and antimilitary movements in U.S. history, it does so with a special twist. Not only has the strategic environment changed greatly with the onset of the nuclear age, but so has the intellectual one. We live at a time when the ideological parameters of national debate have traversed the bounds of the Constitution and the contending rationalist philosophies of John Locke and Edmund Burke, Thomas Jefferson and Alexander Hamilton. For the original prime movers of the nuclear freeze movement—but not for most of its sympathizers—the relevant terms of reference derive from the vocabularies of Marxist and socialist ideology and avant-guarde leftism, where real meaning reputedly resides in labels such as "military-industrial complex," "liberation theology," "economic democracy," and "nuclearism." At its outer edges, even liberalism in the United States is no longer the province of John Stuart Mill and Montesquieu, but of Karl Marx and Jean-Jacques Rousseau. Its watchwords are no longer liberty, individualism, and limited power, but equality, redistribution, and social reconstruction.[1]

Nevertheless, the nuclear freeze movement has been fueled by the passion of a natural pulsation in the American body politic, and its main concern and central anxiety—prospects for nuclear war or peace—rest within the province of all political viewpoints. But as the freeze entered the realm of the political center, it was buffeted by those who sought to profit from it and molded into

217

the contours of existing political institutions. The freeze has never been the same and most likely it will never be much of an autonomous force again. If the episode has served any useful purpose, its service seems to be at an end. What we have left, like the trash after the parade, is neither very interesting nor very pretty. If the nuclear anxiety that helped catapult the freeze into national prominence in 1981 and 1982 can be so banalized as to form the theme for a prime-time television bomb-opera like ABC's *The Day After,* or a mass-market paperback novel like *Warday,* the freeze is probably on the way to a kind of cultural graveyard, along with the gold standard, hula-hoops, and both Senators Joseph and Eugene McCarthy.[2] How much strength it retains and its rate of political decay are important matters, however, for freeze activists have turned their attention to the 1984 presidential elections and beyond.

The deacons of the freeze movement met in large numbers — over 500 national and regional leaders — in St. Louis on December 2-4, 1983, to plot strategy. The meeting was marred by disagreements about strategy and tactics, the founders of the Professional Left assailing the newcomers of the Left-Liberal Establishment, for the most part. From time to time, the rhetoric from the dais was much further left than those on the floor wished to hear, and a number of votes on tactics occasioned considerable acrimony.[3] Nevertheless, the freeze movement as a whole did emerge from the meeting with a revised strategy, one shaped by the upcoming presidential election. Instead of planning mass marches and general fund-raising campaigns as top priorities, the freeze leadership planned instead to lobby directly for candidates at all levels, including the Senate and the White House. The movement had, in its own language, moved from "public education to political action." According to Bill Curry, executive director of Freeze Voter '84 — the freeze's specially established political action committee (PAC) for the election — "the freeze movement has come of age and understands the realities of the political process. We are not easily fooled by press releases."[4] Curry believes that the shock of a Janus-faced Congress, which passed the freeze one day and voted for the MX the next, taught the movement that unless support for the freeze could be channeled politically it was unlikely to accomplish anything practical. Therefore, Freeze Voter '84 targeted thirty congressmen and ten senators specifically and hoped to become the most powerful organized lobby in the 1984 elections. Curry sought to bring together as many as one million supporters of the freeze who would pound the sidewalks for pro-freeze candidates in what he calls the congressional "build-down," the "trading in of two obsolete Congressmen for one committed to the freeze."[5]

The Freeze and the Democrats

Freeze Voter '84 came upon Democratic congressmen and congressional hopefuls as mixed news, and the party's reaction was also mixed. Some feared Reagan's strength in 1984 and dared not put too much distance between themselves and the president on this issue. Thus, although the Democratic National Committee had effusive praise for the pastoral letter in September, the House Democratic Caucus's "Renewing America's Promise"—a kind of pre-campaign platform—listed in January 1984 three "grave threats" on which to focus: the budget deficits, the decline of investment, and *last of all,* the "accelerating nuclear arms race."[6] Others who felt that their districts strongly would support the freeze and could be motivated to vote for or against a candidate based primarily on this issue welcomed the resources of Freeze Voter '84 with open arms. Pre-election polls by Peter D. Hart Research Associates Inc. on behalf of the Democratic Congressional Campaign Committee indicated that the freeze was perhaps the one issue strong enough to encourage voters to split their tickets in November, those who vote for President Reagan making the effort nevertheless to vote for a pro-freeze congressional candidate.[7] Pro-freeze sentiment also seemed to dovetail closely with the so-called gender gap, another fact of political life that Democrats hoped to exploit in the election.

The effects of the freeze were evident for some time in the Democratic presidential politics of 1984. Senator Alan Cranston based his head-start campaign on the "peace issue" and sought Freeze Voter '84's endorsement. But, although he attended the December meeting in St. Louis, he was unable to sway the movement, which preferred a Democrat with a better chance to beat President Reagan—at that time, Walter Mondale, whose political fortunes subsequently fell, only to rise again some months later. Nevertheless, Cranston's early success in using the freeze politically, most notably in the Wisconsin straw poll of June 1983, forced most other contenders to announce support for the freeze, at least in some form.[8] Luckily for Mondale, Glenn, and Hart, the House debate over the freeze had so obfuscated its actual content that the Democratic hopefuls, like Congress itself, could support both the freeze and elements of the Reagan Administration's strategic modernization program at the same time.[9]

The strong influence of freeze supporters in the Democratic party was also a function of two other factors, one structural and one by happenstance. The structural factor was that for many years party professionals and amateur activists among the Democrats have been much further left than the rank and file. (This is one reason why AFL-CIO support for Democratic presidential candidates has eroded over the past twenty years.) This means that in order to win the party's nomination, a candidate must speak one way, but to win the election, he must speak another way. The happenstance was the unexpected absence of Senator Henry M. Jackson, who passed away in September 1983 of a heart attack. Jackson was the bastion of the party's center and had his own considerable national constituency. His passing threw the balance of the party on foreign and defense issues decidedly to the left.[10] No one could fill the role that Senator Jackson played. Other influential Democrats with views similar to Jackson's discredited themselves in party eyes by going to work for a Republican administration (Rostow, Nitze, Perle, Kirkpatrick, and others), and those who remained, like Senator Nunn and Senator Moynihan, lacked either the clout or the nerve. As Morton Kondracke reported after the Dartmouth College Democratic debate of January 1984:

If the consensus of Democratic foreign policy intellectuals no longer is as isolationist and pacifist as it was prior to the bitter experiences of the Carter Administration in Iran, Nicaragua, and Afghanistan, younger Democrats in Congress seem as isolationist as ever. As one Mondale adviser put it, "their foreign policy is based on guilt. It's corrupt, in fact. If something's hard or ambiguous, their advice is, 'Don't do it. Don't get involved in any struggle that might get our skirts dirty.' That puts a lot of pressure on Mondale." For Mondale to suggest that Grenada somehow was comparable to Afghanistan or Poland—the Grenadians happen to be free now, the Afghans are not—suggests that Mondale has been affected by his party's moral confusion.[11]

Along with Congressmen Aspin, Gore, and others, Kondracke—also a Democrat—rightly feared that the public, "which counts strength as much as peace among its goals, will sense that the Democrats have learned nothing from the Carter years and again choose Reagan."[12] With even more direct reference both to Senator Jackson's death and the nuclear freeze, a liberal Democratic senator was reported to have confided privately, "Without Jackson we campaign for the Presidency on a platform from which we cannot govern."[13] Thus it was that the freeze was destined to become part of the Democratic program in 1984 in far less equivocal language than it had been at the party's mini-convention in Philadelphia in 1982.[14]

Whatever its original intentions—noble, disingenuous, or both—the freeze movement has sharpened the expression of national disagreements over strategic issues and helped make them hostage to narrow partisan goals. In the current political environment, this has rendered a truly unified national policy more difficult to construct and maintain. For those members of the Professional Left who originally saw the freeze as a way to save the world from nuclear peril, the track record of the freeze movement thus far has on balance probably been counterproductive. If indeed we are no closer to arms agreements with the Soviet Union, it is not only or primarily because the United States has been unrealistic about necessary compromises or "unserious" about arms control. It is rather because the U.S. freeze movement—like the peace movement in Western Europe—tempted the Soviet leadership to think that by playing to the gallery it could help create restraints on U.S. strategic modernization programs without having to promise reciprocal restraints on its own programs. But for those who saw the freeze primarily as a way to generate political trouble and, potentially, political defeat for the Reagan Administration and its constituency, the record of the last few years must be at least mildly encouraging. One thing is for certain: the inherent open-endedness and high stakes of the strategic debate are such that no administration can be wholly passive or boldly innovative in this area without touching off a cascade of political risks. Those risks tend to rise, it seems, in rough proportion to an administration's tactical ineptitude.

The Freeze in Perspective

One of the most striking aspects of U.S. political culture is the openness of the debate in which military strategy is shaped in peacetime. There are few societies in which the advice and expertise of the professional military figure so little in this realm of public policy and in which such a wide variety of social and political forces figure so much. The historical roots of this tradition are clear. The American Revolution was molded by its opposition to centralized and arbitrary authority and by the colonies' unpleasant experience with occupying British armies. The determination of the Founding Fathers that there should be no standing army in peacetime was as strong as their insistence on the separation of governmental powers and on the decentralized federal character of the state.

It is much more difficult to explain how this openness survived two centuries of American history, with its half-dozen wars and even the transition into the nuclear age, virtually unscathed. One might have expected the pressures of crisis and war to bend the novel organization of national security in the New World toward the sturdier and more practicable methods of the Old World. The United States has had its share of military heroes, of course, and some of them even have become president. But strong constitutional traditions, the relative absence of mortal threats to U.S. sovereignty and security, and the dominance of political and economic over narrower military interests in the continental expansion of the nation—all combined to safeguard the apolitical character of the military and civilian political control of military planning in peacetime. The same factors also helped institutionalize the freedom to dissent. The "revolt" of New England against the War of 1812 and the Mexican War, the draft riots of the 1860s, and widespread opposition to U.S. involvement in both world wars composed a major part of the political environment in their respective eras and clearly influenced the role of the United States in these conflicts.

While the openness of the national security debate persists and even grows, the general strategic environment has changed significantly in the nuclear age. The United States is no longer protected from the entanglements of global politics by vast expanses of ocean; its population can be devastated without its armed forces being defeated. The sharp dividing line between peace and war has vanished in the nuclear age. National mobilization no longer follows the transition from peace to war; instead, a high level of specialized technical and resource mobilization has become a constant feature of keeping the peace. Moreover, the technological sophistication and awesome destructive power of modern weapons have put all but the simplest and most gruesome military operations beyond the comprehension of most people. The capacity of citizens to remain well informed about the basic issues has been diminished even as their exposure to images and opinions about them has grown.

Finally, strategy in the nuclear age has been detached from direct human experience. In the past, military preparation generally followed from the lessons and perceptions of recently fought wars. But military strategy in the nuclear age rests more on theoretical abstraction than on personal knowledge. For this reason alone, nuclear strategy has become a logically open-ended enterprise, and the paradoxes of the nuclear age go unsolved because in the absence of the direct experience that we pray we will never have, they are unsolvable. That is why neither this study nor any other honest study can come to authoritative conclusions about which of the the five main strategic theories described above is best or the most accurate reflection of strategic reality. Besides, the relationship between this "reality" and human theories about it is more complex than first meets the eye. As in most other social situations, we are not discovering reality through our theorizing about it; we are in large part *creating* that reality. How we imagine nuclear reality influences our planning for deterrence and war, and this planning in turn shapes how deterrence works—or does not work—and how a nuclear war would be fought if deterrence fails. Social life in general is recursive; that is, it freezes into itself the conceptions we hold of it. Through its material consequences, history reflects back to posterity the mélange of judgments, assumptions, prejudices, pathologies, and ideals that human beings bring to its making.[15]

The central paradox of the nuclear age stands before us sphinx-like: the stability of deterrence is dependent on two conditions—the unacceptable enormity of risk and the undeniable possibility of military use—that push policy in opposite directions. One impulse counsels us to maximize the potential enormity of destruction in the hope of making the prospect of nuclear weapons usage maximally remote—indeed, to remove the prospect altogether from the vicissitudes of international politics. The other impulse drives us to rationalize and control the military utility of nuclear weapons both in order to deter war in the midst of political struggle and to give ourselves a second chance should deterrence ever fail. Pragmatic strategists try to marry these impulses to give us both kinds of deterrence at once, but since these impulses pull in opposite directions, the parson at this wedding must be ambiguity itself.

Still, ambiguous solutions to problems shrouded in uncertainty are much to be preferred to those that are clearcut and wrong. The vexatious truth is that no nuclear strategy is riskless, neither a strategy that follows one face of the nuclear Janus or the other to its logical extreme, nor one that would try endlessly to square the circle. In the last analysis, we are working with a volatile ratio where the magnitude of the risks we run is inversely proportional to how often we are willing to run them. We should choose the mix of risk we prefer knowing full well that our choices are not reflections of a reality-in-being so much as they are, together with choices that others make, the source of a reality-in-the-making.

The spirit of the nuclear freeze movement, as well as that of its most vociferous detractors, is to deny the open-endedness of the nuclear dilemma, and to insist that the basic realities before us are obvious to anyone who cares to look. Its spirit easily accepts the ultimate and final separability of deterrence from politics because, just as it seeks an end to strategic ambiguity and change, it seeks an end to politics-as-usual. The nuclear freeze movement bespeaks of a rush to closure, driven by intense emotion, in circumstances that deny that closure. To those dedicated to a nuclear freeze as well as to all opposed to it who engage in illusions of certainty, let us recall Nietzsche's warning: "Convictions are more dangerous enemies of truth than lies."

NOTES

1. See Robert Nisbet, *Prejudices: A Philosophical Dictionary* (Cambridge, Mass.: Harvard University Press, 1982), p. 21.

2. For a similar observation on *The Day After,* see Paul Attanasio, "Big Bang, Little Box," *The New Republic,* December 5, 1983, pp. 13-14.

3. Personal communication from James Bell, who was at the St. Louis conclave as an observer.

4. Curry is quoted in Richard E. Cohen, "The Big Freeze," *National Journal,* December 10, 1983, p. 2583. See also David M. Rubin, "Can the Peace Groups Make a President?" *Harpers,* February 1984, pp. 16, 18-20.

5. Quoted in Cohen, "The Big Freeze," p. 2583.

6. See Phil Gailey, "Democrats Urge Steps to Prevent Nuclear Warfare," *New York Times,* September 21, 1983; Steven V. Roberts, "Group in House Stresses Three Issues," *New York Times,* January 8, 1984; and Cohen, "The Big Freeze," p. 2583.

7. Cohen, "The Big Freeze," p. 2583.

8. See the letters under the heading "Cranston, the Freeze, and the Straw Poll," *Washington Post,* June 19, 1983.

9. See Mondale's address to the Association of American Newspaper Publishers, *New York Times,* April 27, 1983.

10. This is ably discussed in Leslie Gelb, "The Democrats and Foreign Policy," *New York Times Magazine,* December 18, 1983. See also Charles Krauthammer, "What Happened to the Center?" *Time,* December 19, 1983, and Leon Wieseltier, "Pitfalls of the Peace Issue," *Washington Post,* May 27, 1984, p. C-5.

11. Morton Kondracke, "The Candidates Cross-examined," *The New Republic,* February 6, 1984, p. 13.

12. Ibid.

13. Quoted in Michael Novak, "In Memoriam: Henry M. Jackson," *Commentary,* January 1984, p. 49.

14. See "Democratic Party Goals and Principles, Draft Workshop Statements," Issues Workshops, Philadelphia, June 25-27, 1982, pp. 9-10.

15. See Peter Berger and Thomas Luckmann, *The Social Construction of Reality* (Garden City, N.Y.: Anchor Press/Doubleday, 1966), and Erving Goffman, *Frame Analysis* (New York: Harper and Row, 1974).

APPENDIX A

"Call to Halt the Nuclear Arms Race": Proposal for a Mutual U.S.-Soviet Nuclear Weapon Freeze

To improve national and international security, the United States and the Soviet Union should stop the nuclear arms race. Specifically, they should adopt a mutual freeze on the testing, production and deployment of nuclear weapons and of missiles and new aircraft designed primarily to deliver nuclear weapons. This is an essential, verifiable first step toward lessening the risk of nuclear war and reducing the nuclear arsenals.

The horror of a nuclear holocaust is universally acknowledged. Today, the United States and the Soviet Union possess 50,000 nuclear weapons. In half an hour, a fraction of these weapons can destroy all cities in the northern hemisphere. Yet over the next decade, the USA and USSR plan to build over 20,000 more nuclear warheads, along with a new generation of nuclear missiles and aircraft.

The weapon programs of the next decade, if not stopped, will pull the nuclear tripwire tighter. Counterforce and other "nuclear warfighting" systems will improve the ability of the USA and USSR to attack the opponent's nuclear forces and other military targets. This will increase the pressure on both sides to use their nuclear weapons in a crisis, rather than risk losing them in a first strike.

Such developments will increase hairtrigger readiness for a massive nuclear exchange at a time when economic difficulties, political dissension, revolution and competition for energy supplies may be rising worldwide. At the same time, more countries may acquire nuclear weapons. Unless we change this combination of trends, the danger of nuclear war will be greater in the late 1980s and 1990s than ever before.

Rather than permit this dangerous future to evolve, the United States and the Soviet Union should stop the nuclear arms race.

A freeze on nuclear missiles and aircraft can be verified by existing national means. A total freeze can be verified more easily than the complex SALT I and II agreements. The freeze on warhead production could be verified by the Safeguards of the International Atomic Energy Agency. Stopping the production of nuclear weapons and weapon-grade material and applying the Safeguards to US and Soviet nuclear programs would increase the incentive of other countries to adhere to the Nonproliferation Treaty, renouncing acquisition of their own nuclear weapons, and to accept the same Safeguards.

A freeze would hold constant the existing nuclear parity between the United States and the Soviet Union. By precluding production of counterforce weaponry on either side, it would eliminate excuses for further arming on both sides. Later, following the immediate adoption of the freeze, its terms should be negotiated into the more durable form of a treaty.

A nuclear-weapon freeze, accompanied by government-aided conversion of nuclear industries, would save at least $100 billion each in US and Soviet military spending (at today's prices) in 1981-1990. This would reduce inflation. The savings could be applied to balance the budget, reduce taxes, improve services, subsidize renewable energy, or increase aid to poverty-stricken third world regions. By shifting personnel to more labor-intensive civilian jobs, a nuclear-weapon freeze would also raise employment.

Stopping the US–Soviet nuclear arms race is the single most useful step that can be taken now to reduce the likelihood of nuclear war and to prevent the spread of nuclear weapons to more countries. This step is a necessary prelude to creating international conditions in which:

- further steps can be taken toward a stable, peaceful international order;
- the threat of a first use of nuclear weaponry can be ended;
- the freeze can be extended to other nations; and
- the nuclear arsenals on all sides can be drastically reduced or eliminated, making the world truly safe from nuclear destruction.

228

APPENDIX B

The American Security Council's Peace Through Strength Resolution

Whereas the Soviet Union has exploited U.S. peace initiatives to build up its strategic and conventional warfare capabilities;

Whereas this has given the Soviet Union the means to support increasingly bolder worldwide aggression;

Whereas there is basis for concern that the Soviets may next use these forces in Pakistan, Iran, and Yugoslavia;

Whereas the Soviet Union has demonstrated an unwillingness to live by international law;

Whereas the United States is the one world power that can stop Soviet expansionism: Now, therefore be it

Resolved by (Name of State Legislature, County Commission, Town Council, or Organization) that the United States adopt a National Strategy of Peace Through Strength, the general principles of which would be—

(1) to inspire, focus and unite the national will and determination to achieve this goal of peace and freedom,

(2) to achieve overall military and technological superiority over the Soviet Union,

(3) to create a strategic defense and a civil defense which would protect U.S. citizens against nuclear war at least as well as the Soviets defend their citizens,

(4) to accept no arms control agreement which in any way jeopardizes the security of the United States or its allies, or locks the U.S. into a position of military inferiority,

(5) to reestablish effective security and intelligence capabilities,

(6) to pursue positive non-military means to roll back the growth of Communism,

(7) to help our allies and other non-Communist countries defend themselves against Communist aggression,

(8) to maintain a strong economy and protect our overseas sources of energy and other vital raw materials.

Whereas it will take the combined efforts of many State Legislatures, County Commissions, Town Councils, and Organizations to achieve the adoption of a National Strategy of Peace Through Strength, now therefore be it

Resolved by (Name of State Legislature, County Commission, Town Council, or Organization), that it will join The Coalition for Peace Through Strength to work with other State Legislatures, County Commissions, Town Councils, or Organizations for the adoption of a National Strategy of Peace Through Strength. However, (Name of State Legislature, County Commission, Town Council, or Organization) reserves to itself the right to make its own decisions as to how the principles shall be applied on individual issues.

APPENDIX C

Kennedy/Hatfield Resolution, Joint Resolution on Nuclear Weapons Freeze and Reductions (S.J. Res 163), March 10, 1982

Whereas the greatest challenge facing the earth is to prevent the occurrence of nuclear war by accident or design;

Whereas the nuclear arms race is dangerously increasing the risk of a holocaust that would be humanity's final war; and

Whereas a freeze followed by reductions in nuclear warheads, missiles, and other delivery systems is needed to halt the nuclear arms race and to reduce the risk of nuclear war;

Resolved by the Senate and the House of Representatives of the United States of America in Congress assembled,

(1) As an immediate strategic arms control objective, the United States and the Soviet Union should:

(a) pursue a complete halt to the nuclear arms race;

(b) decide when and how to achieve a mutual and verifiable freeze on the testing, production, and further deployment of nuclear warheads, missiles, and other delivery systems; and

(c) give special attention to destabilizing weapons whose deployment would make such a freeze more difficult to achieve.

(2) Proceeding from this freeze, the United States and the

230

Soviet Union should pursue major, mutual and verifiable reductions in nuclear warheads, missiles, and other delivery systems, through annual percentages or equally effective means, in a manner that enhances stability.

APPENDIX D

Jackson/Warner Resolution (S.J. Res. 177), March 30, 1982

Whereas, a nuclear war would kill or injure millions and millions of people and threaten the survival of the human race;

Whereas, there can be no assurance that a nuclear war, once initiated, would remain limited in scope;

Whereas, there exists the ever-present risk that nuclear weapons might be employed through accident or miscalculation;

Whereas, the American people, who are a people of peace, maintain nuclear armaments only in the defense of freedom and yearn for world conditions in which they could do far more to lift the burdens of human privation and despair;

Whereas, the current nuclear force imbalance is destabilizing and could increase the likelihood of nuclear war;

Whereas, sizeable and verifiable mutual reductions of Soviet and United States nuclear forces to an equal and far-lower level would enhance stability and the maintenance of peace; and

Whereas, President Reagan, on November 18, 1981, stated that the United States "will seek to negotiate substantial reductions in nuclear arms which would result in levels that are equal and verifiable";

Resolved by the Senate and House of Representatives of the United States of America in Congress assembled, That

(1) The United States should propose to the Soviet Union a long-term, mutual and verifiable nuclear forces freeze at equal and sharply reduced levels of forces;

(2) The United States should propose to the Soviet Union practical measures to reduce the danger of nuclear war through accident or miscalculation and to prevent the use of nuclear weapons by third parties, including terrorists;

(3) The United States should challenge the Soviet Union to join in the historic effort to channel the genius of our two peoples away from the amassing of nuclear armaments and to focus the energy and resources of both nations on attacking the ancient enemies of mankind—poverty, hunger and disease; and

(4) The United States should continue to press month after month, year after year, to achieve balanced, stabilizing arms reductions, looking, in time, to the elimination of all nuclear weapons from the world's arsenals.

APPENDIX E

The First Freeze Resolution in the House of Representatives (H.J. Res. 521), Defeated 204-202 on August 5, 1982

Whereas the greatest challenge facing the Earth is to prevent the occurrence of nuclear war by accident or design;

Whereas the increasing stockpiles of nuclear weapons and nuclear delivery systems by both the United States and the Soviet Union have not strengthened international peace and security but in fact enhance the prospect for mutual destruction;

Whereas on May 9, 1982, President Reagan announced that he had written to Soviet President Brezhnev to propose negotiations to achieve an agreement that significantly reduces the number of nuclear weapons, enhances stability, and opens the way to even more far-reaching steps in the future;

Whereas the SALT II agreement mandates the prompt reduction of Soviet strategic forces by two hundred and fifty-four deployable strategic nuclear delivery vehicles; imposes significant restrictions on Soviet multiple-warhead deployable intercontinental ballistic missiles, and on warheads for these missiles, in terms of numbers and throw-weight; prohibits equipment for rapid reload of intercontinental ballistic missile silos; and in these and other verifiable respects improves the ability of the United States strategic forces to carry out their deterrent mission;

Whereas the United States and the Soviet Union have observed the SALT II agreement since its signing;

Whereas adequate verification of compliance has always been an indispensable part of any international arms control agreement; and

Whereas a mutual and verifiable freeze followed by reductions in nuclear weapons and nuclear delivery systems would greatly reduce the risk of nuclear war: Now, therefore, be it

Resolved by the Senate and House of Representatives of the United States of America in Congress assembled, That the United States and the Soviet Union should immediately begin the strategic arms reduction talks (START) and those talks should have the following objectives:

(1) Pursuing a complete halt to the nuclear arms race.

(2) Deciding when and how to achieve a mutual verifiable freeze on the testing, production, and further deployment of nuclear warheads, missiles, and other delivery systems.

(3) Giving special attention to destabilizing weapons whose deployment would make such a freeze more difficult to achieve.

(4) Proceeding from this mutual and verifiable freeze, pursuing substantial, equitable, and verifiable reductions through numerical ceilings, annual percentages, or any other equally effective and verifiable means of strengthening strategic stability.

(5) Preserving present limitations and controls on current nuclear weapons and nuclear delivery systems.

(6) Incorporating ongoing negotiations in Geneva on land-based intermediate-range nuclear missiles into the START negotiations.

In those negotiations, the United States shall make every effort to reach a common position with our North Atlantic Treaty Organization allies on any element of an agreement which would be inconsistent with existing United States commitments to those allies.

Sec. 2. The United States shall promptly approve the SALT II agreement provided adequate verification capabilities are maintained.

MR. ZABLOCKI. Mr. Chairman, I offer an amendment.

The Clerk read as follows:

Amendment offered by MR. ZABLOCKI: Page 4, strike out lines 19 through 21 and insert in lieu thereof the following:

Sec. 2. The United States shall continue to adhere to the SALT II agreement so long as the Soviet Union adheres to that agreement and so long as it is in the national security interests of the United States to continue to adhere to that agreement.

APPENDIX F

Joint Resolution Calling for a Mutual and Verifiable Freeze on and Reductions in Nuclear Weapons (H.J. Res. 13), May 4, 1983

NOTE
Underlined text was added by amendments on the House floor.

Whereas the greatest challenge facing the Earth is to prevent the occurrence of nuclear war by accident or design;

Whereas the United States and the Soviet Union have signed the Joint Statement of Agreed Principles for Disarmament Negotiations, known as the McCloy-Zorin Agreement, enumerating general principles for future negotiations for international peace and security;

Whereas the increasing stockpiles of nuclear weapons and nuclear delivery systems by both the United States and the Soviet Union have not strengthened international peace and security but in fact enhance the prospect for mutual destruction;

Whereas adequate verification of compliance has always been an indispensable part of any international arms control agreement; and

Whereas a mutual and verifiable freeze and reductions in nuclear weapons and nuclear delivery systems would greatly reduce the risk of nuclear war: Now, therefore, be it

Resolved by the Senate and House of Representatives of the United States of America in Congress assembled, That, consistent with the maintenance of essential equivalence in overall nuclear capabilities at present and in the future, the Strategic Arms Reduction Talks (START) between the United States and Soviet Union should have the following objectives:

(1) Pursuing the objective of negotiating an immediate, mutual, and verifiable freeze, then pursuing the objective of negotiating immediate, mutual, and verifiable reductions in nuclear weapons.

(2) Deciding when and how to achieve a mutual verifiable freeze on testing, production, and further deployment of nuclear warheads, missiles, and other delivery systems and systems which would threaten the viability of sea-based nuclear deterrent forces, and to include all air defense systems designed to stop nuclear bombers. Submarines are not delivery systems as used herein.

(3) Consistent with pursuing the objective of negotiating an immediate, mutual, and verifiable freeze, giving special attention to destabilizing weapons, especially those which give either nation capabilities which confer upon it even the hypothetical advantages of a first strike.

(4) Providing for cooperative measures of verification, including provisions for onsite inspection, as appropriate, to complement National Technical Means of Verification and to ensure compliance.

(5) Proceeding from this mutual and verifiable freeze, pursuing substantial, equitable, and verifiable reductions through numerical ceilings, annual percentages, or any other equally effective and verifiable means of strengthening strategic stability, with such reductions to be achieved within a reasonable, specified period of time as determined by the negotiations.

(6) Preserving present limitations and controls on nuclear weapons and nuclear delivery systems.

(7) Incorporating ongoing negotiations in Geneva on intermediate-range nuclear systems into the START negotiations. Discussing the impact of developing comprehensive defensive systems consistent with all provisions of the Treaty on the Limitation of Anti-Ballistic Missile Systems.

(8) Nothing in this resolution shall be construed by United States negotiators to mandate any agreement that would jeopardize our ability to preserve freedom.

In those negotiations, the United States shall make every effort to reach a common position with our North Atlantic Treaty Organization allies on any element of an agreement which would be inconsistent with existing United States commitments to those allies.

Sec. 2. In the absence of a bilateral agreement embodying the objectives set forth in this joint resolution, nothing in this resolution is intended to prevent the United States from carrying out its responsibilities under the December 1979 North Atlantic Treaty Organization decision regarding intermediate range nuclear forces.

Sec. 3. (a) Consistent with pursuing the overriding objective of negotiating an immediate, mutual, and verifiable freeze, nothing in this resolution shall be construed to prevent the United States from taking advantage of concurrent and complementary arms control proposals.

(b) Nothing in this resolution shall be construed to supercede the treatymaking powers of the President under the Constitution.

Sec. 4. This resolution does not endorse any type of unilateral disarmament on the part of the United States.

Sec. 5. Consistent with pursuing the overriding objective of negotiating an immediate, mutual, and verifiable freeze, nothing in this resolution should be construed to prevent measures necessary for the maintenance of and credibility of the United States nuclear deterrent.

Sec. 6. Until such time as the final instrument embodying the objectives set forth in section 1 has been fully ratified by both the Soviet Union and the United States, nothing in this joint resolution shall be construed to prevent whatever modernization and deployment of United States weapons may be required to maintain the credibility of the United States nuclear deterrent.

Sec. 7. The Congress proposes that the House Committee on Foreign Affairs and the Senate Committee on Foreign Relations study measures relating to reductions pursuant to the first section, and relating to concurrent and complementary arms control proposals pursuant to section 2, especially those aimed at progressive reductions in the number of destabilizing weapons through a mutual "build-down" or other verifiable processes.

Sec. 8. Any freeze agreement negotiated pursuant to this resolution should not prevent the United States from taking such measures with respect to our strategic systems as are necessary to protect the lives of the United States personnel operating those systems.

Sec. 9. For purposes of this resolution, a nuclear delivery vehicle is a device whose primary or exclusive mission requires it to carry a nuclear weapon into territory of or occupied by hostile forces.

Sec. 10. A freeze agreement in accordance with this resolution will not preclude the one-for-one replacement of nuclear weapons and nuclear delivery vehicles in order to preserve the credibility of the United States nuclear deterrence, provided the new weapon or delivery vehicle is the same type as the old.

Sec. 11. Nothing in this joint resolution shall be construed—

(1) to prevent, during any negotiations pursuant to this resolution, or

(2) to require that, in any negotiations pursuant to this resolution, the United States agree to a provision which would prevent, such modernization and depolyment of United States new or improved dual capable delivery systems as the United States may determine is required to maintain the capability of the United States defense posture.

Sec. 12. Consistent with Public Law 88-186, as amended, no action shall be taken under this Act that will obligate the United States to disarm or to reduce or to limit the Armed Forces or armaments of the United States, except pursuant to the treaty-making power of the President under the Constitution or unless authorized by further affirmative legislation by the Congress of the United States.

Sec. 13. Consistent with the provisions of Public Law 92-448, as amended, negotiations undertaken pursuant to this Act shall provide for the maintenance of a vigorous research, development, and safety-related improvements program to assure that the United States would not be limited to levels of nuclear deterrent forces inferior to the force levels of the Soviet Union. Further, such negotiations should recognize the difficulty of maintaining essential equivalence and a stable balance in nuclear deterrent capabilities in a period of rapidly developing technology, and that any future arms control agreements should promote a stable international balance and enhance the survivability of United States nuclear deterrent forces.

Sec. 14. In all negotiations pursuant to this resolution, the United States shall make every effort to ensure that any agreement reached shall provide for full compliance by all parties with preexisting international treaties, obligations, and commitments.

Sec. 15. Any item both sides do not agree to freeze would not be frozen.

Sec. 16. The President shall take all necessary steps to ensure that any agreement embodying the objectives set forth in this joint resolution can be adequately verifed, including pursuing the objective of providing for cooperative measures of verification (including provisions for onsite inspection as appropriate) to complement National Technical Means of Verification and to ensure compliance.

Sec. 17. Nothing in this joint resolution shall be construed to prevent safety-related improvements in strategic bombers.

INDEX

A

A. J. Muste Memorial Institute, 12
abortion, 23, 39n
Abzug, Bella, 14
Accuracy in Media (AIM) Report, 62
action–reaction cycle, 95, 99, 101-02
active measures, 62
Adams, Ruth, 117
Adelman, Kenneth, 188-89, 197;
 ACDA nomination of, 184
AFL-CIO, 63, 209n, 220
Afghanistan, 65, 78, 100, 113, 176,
 185, 220-21
Aldridge, Robert, 119n
Allende, Salvador Gossens, 3
All-Volunteer Force, 106
American Federation of Teachers, 31
American Federation of Scientists, 94,
 117n
American Friends Service Committee
 (AFSC), 1, 5-10, 13, 21, 23, 35-36n,
 37n, 77-78, 80-81, 85
American Life Lobby, 59
American Medical Association
 (AMA), 16
American Nazi Party, 45
American Security Council (ASC), 65,
 66, 68; Peace Through Strength
 Resolution, 229-30
anarchists, 16-19, 38n, 72n
anti-ballistic missiles (ABM), 129, 130,
 133, 166-67
Anti-Ballistic Missile (ABM) Treaty,
 129-30, 166-67, 191, 208-09n, 235
antisatellite (ASAT) weapons, 144
antisubmarine warfare (ASW), 144
apocalypse, 27, 54, 177
Apocalypse Now, 11
Arafat, Yasir, 3, 6
Archives Project, 43n
Arkin, William M., 35n

armageddon, 28, 54, 148
arms control, 78, 95, 97, 101, 147, 169,
 171, 213, 217; and Les Aspin, 147;
 Conservative Mainstream and, 169-
 71; Council for a Livable World
 (CLW) and, 100; Democratic Party
 and, 148; Harvard Study Group and,
 142-43; Kennedy/Hatfield Resolution and, 183; Edward T. Markey
 and, 103; negotiations, 97, 165, 168;
 Pragmatic Center and, 141, 166,
 203-04, 206, 209n; Professional Left
 and, 4, 8, 64, 66, 81, 93; Reagan Administration and, 78-79, 82, 103-04,
 155, 157-58, 173-74, 183, 187-88;
 SALT II and, 83, 101-02; Scowcroft
 Commission and, 193, 197; Soviet
 Union and, 61, 66, 133-34, 157-58,
 168, 176
Arms Control Association, 83, 94, 103
Arms Control and Disarmament
 Agency (ACDA), 92, 117, 160, 167,
 175, 181n, 186-89, 208n
Arms Control Today, 93
arms race, 102, 106, 107, 141, 223; and
 Conservative Mainstream, 170;
 Ground Zero on, 92; Left-Liberal
 Establishment on, 124; Pragmatic
 Center on, 125, 141; Professional
 Left on, 93; Reagan Administration
 on, 176-77; Soviet Union and, 135
The Arms Race Hurts Our Economy, 107
Armstrong, James, 91
Aron, Raymond, 32
Asians, immigration of, 50
Aspin, Les, 83, 104, 147, 155, 201,
 203, 205, 206, 220
assured destruction, 126-28, 164
The Atlantic Monthly, 142
Atomic Cafe, 43n
Augustine, 46-47

239

241

counterforce targeting, 129, 226-27; *Call to Halt the Nuclear Arms Race,* 227-28; complete, 144; equity, 163-65; defined, 94-95; and finite (minimum) deterrence, 95-97; Randall Forsberg on, 111; imbalance in, 171; Randall Kehler on, 201; Left-Liberal Establishment on, 94, 98-99, 101; Limited, 131, 136; and Midgetman, 195; and MX, 185, 211n; and parity, 138-39, 163-64; Pragmatic Center on, 161, 165-66; and pre-emption, 151n; Scowcroft Commission on, 193; and second-strike, 140; and James Schlesinger, 137; and Soviet Union, 133-35; and U.S. strategic thinking, 130-31

Countervalue targeting: and assured deterrence, 161; and Conservative Mainstream, 136; and deterrence, 140; Randall Kehler on, 201; Left-Liberal Establishment on, 94; and mutual assured destruction (MAD), 166; and retaliation, 151n

countervailing strategy, 137-38, 161, 163, 165-66

Cox, Arthur Macy, 150n

Cranston, Alan, 212, 219

Craver, Mathews, Smith and Company, 86

Creative Initiatives, 43n

crises escalation, 131

Crisp, Mary, 91

cruise missiles, 79, 111, 172, 195, 209n

Crumley, James, 91

C.S. Fund, 85

Cuban Revolution, 146

Curry, Bill, 218-19

D

damage limitation, 127, 132-33, 139, 166

Dartmouth College Democratic Debate, 220-21

Daughtry, Herbert, 87-88

The Day After, 18, 218

decapitation, 168

Decter, Midge, 180

deep cuts, 79, 82

defense budget, 79, 107, 110, 119n

detruncation, 168

Defense Monitor, 93, 108

Dellinger, David, 14

Dellums, Ronald, 14, 62, 98, 119n

Democratic National Committee, House Caucus of, 219

Democratic Congressional Campaign Committee, 219

Democratic Congressman, 63, 82; back freeze and SALT II, 90; and Freeze Voter '84, 219; and Left-Liberal Establishment, 155; and support for freeze, 205; Democratic Party, 219-21; and AFL-CIO, 220; and arms control, 190; and 1980 elections, 83; and 1982 elections, 184; freeze movement's fear of being co-opted by, 84; and Freeze Voter '84, 219; and Georgia Mafia, 159; internal struggles, 148; and Henry M. Jackson, 217; Ku Klux Klan (KKK) influence in, 49; and margin of safety, 156; and Paul Nitze, 197; and 1984 presidential candidates, 202, 219; and Eugene V. Rostow, 188

Dense Pack, 184-86, 208n

Denton, Jeremiah, 62

Department of Defense, 79-80, 91-92, 129, 159, 184-85, 188, 211n

Department of State, 5, 21, 62, 78-80, 92, 159, 175, 211n

Department of the Treasury, 160

Derian, Patricia, 74n

detente, 61

Deterrence: and arms control, 104; and assured destruction, 128; Harold Brown, 138; and build-down, 109; and Carter Administration, 125; and Conservative Mainstream, 160, 162, 168; and extended deterrence, 96, 124; Far Right on, 159-60; and first strike, 193; and Ford Administration, 125; Freeze Resolution on, 232; Harvard Study Group on, 144; Randall Kehler on, 200; Left-Liberal Establishment on, 82, 84, 94; minimum (finite), 94-97, 110, 118n, 123-25, 192, 201; and mutual assured destruction, 135-36, 138; and nuclear strategy, 223-24; Pragmatic Center on, 161; Professional Left on, 4; James Schlesinger on, 137; sea-based, 130, 230; and Soviet Union, 131, 133, 164, 170, 172, 176; and U.S. strategic modernization, 205

Deutch, John, 209n

The Diary of Ché Guevara, 178

Dicks, Norman, 190

Direct Cinema, 43n

disarmament, 3, 5, 8, 63, 87, 88, 93, 142

Disarmament Times, 93

Dolan, Terry, 56

Donner, Frank, 15-16, 63-64

Donovan, Ray, 160

Doty, Paul, 117n, 142

Downey, Thomas, 98, 201, 205-06

Drell, Sidney, 117n

Drew, Elizabeth, 203

Dr. Stranglove, 25

Duff, Peggy, 14

Dunce Pack, 186

Dymally, Mervyn, 99

E

economic democracy, 217

ecotastrophe, 17

Educators for Social Responsibility, 32, 42n

Edwards, James, 160

Edwards, Lee, 59

Eight Minutes to Midnight, 43n

Einstein, Albert, 12

Eisenhower, Dwight D., 90

El Salvador, 3, 11, 12, 37n, 88

Environmental Action, 17, 91

environmentalism, 17

Equal Rights Amendment (ERA), 56

escalation dominance, 131

Europe: defense of, 66, 114, 134; and extended deterrence, 96, 100, 124; independent nuclear forces in, 96; Intermediate-range Nuclear Forces in, 170; missile deployments in, 79, 112-13, 172, 196, 209n; peace movement in, 15, 221; president's political position in, 80; and Soviet Union, 79, 174-75 exterminism, 108

F

Faisal, King of Saudi Arabia, 54

Falwell, Jerry, 49, 54, 59, 70n, 105

Falk, Richard, 4, 5, 28, 107

Federal Bureau of Investigation (FBI), 2, 57, 63, 158, 174

Federal Reserve Board, 50

Federation of American Scientists (FAS), 91

Feld, Bernard, 91

Fellowship of Reconciliation (FOR), 1, 7, 8, 13, 35-36n, 77, 81, 85

The Final Epidemic, 31, 68

Finlandization, 170

First Amendment, 105

first strike: and counterforce, 136-37; and MX, 100, 139; and nuclearism, 5; preparations for, 96; Scowcroft Report on, 190; and Soviet Union, 129-30, 132, 136-37, 140, 185

Fisher, John M., 65-66

fixed silos, 186

flexible response, 127, 135

Florio, James, 104

Ford Administration, 125, 160, 209n

Ford Foundation, 85

Ford, Gerald R., 59, 187

Foreign Affairs, 175

Foreign Policy Association, 137

Forsberg, Randall: in Berlin, 112; biography, 6-7, 35n; on counterforce, 138-39; early activities, 81; ideology,

243

110-12; and New York City rally, 87; on Ronald Reagan, 200; receives grant, 85

Fortress America, 59

Fourteenth World Methodist Council, 91

Fourth International, 13

France, 68, 132

Frank, Jerome, 4, 25

fratricide, 185

Frederick-Joliot Curie Gold Medal for Peace, 6

Free Silver Movement, 49

freeze resolution, 184

Freeze Voter '84, 218-19

Friends of the Earth, 17, 91

Friends World Committee, 21

Frye, Alton, 108

Fulbright, William, 92, 129, 130

Greek Orthodox Diocese of North and South America, 91

Green, Gil, 15

Greenpeace, 17, 88, 91

Greens, 71n, 62

Grenada, 62, 220

Grey, Robert, 188

ground-launched cruise missiles (GLCMs), 113, 172

Ground Zero, 42n, 82

Gromyko, Andrei, 175

Gross, Ariela, 175

The Guardian, 2

Gund Foundation, 85

Hickey, James A., 22
High Frontier, 60, 69
High Times, 18
Hill, Joe, 17
Hilton, Gregg, 59
Hiroshima, 26
Hobbes, Thomas, 30, 56, 197
Hoffman, Stanley, 142
holistic medicine, 16
Hollenbeck, Harold, 103
Holloway, David, 193
Holm, Celeste, 91
Hoopes, Townsend, 92
Hoover Institution, 184
House Committee on Foreign Affairs, 236
House Interior Committee, 157
How Realistic is the Nuclear Freeze Proposal?, 66
Human Events, 59, 62, 69-70
human liberation, 16, 18-19
Humphrey, Hubert H., 159
Hunthausan, Raymond, 22
Huntington, Samuel P., 142

I

Iahonos, Archbishop, 91
intercontinental ballistic missile (ICBM): and Anti-Ballistic Missile (ABM) Treaty, 133; and counterforce, 138, 164; and MX, 170, 193; production of, 128; silos, 232; with single warhead, 141; Soviet ICBMs, 130, 133-34, 136, 138, 164, 195; vulnerability of, 112, 132, 134
If You Love This Planet, 68
India, 114
Industrial Workers of the World (IWW), 17
Information Digest, 62
Inquiry, 69-70
Institute for Defense and Disarmament Studies, 6
Institute for Policy Studies (IPS), 1, 3, 10, 62-63, 69-70

Institute for World Order, 42n, 43n
Institute of American Relations, 65
Intermediate-range Nuclear Forces (INF): and Conservative Mainstream, 170; and first freeze debate, 197; and first freeze resolution, 233; and joint freeze resolution, 236; and negotiating agenda, 111; and Reagan Administration, 173; and Eugene Rostow, 177; and Scowcroft Commission, 148, 195; and second freeze debate, 198-99; and "walk in the woods," 187; and zero proposal, 188, 190
Internal Revenue Service (IRS), 177
International Atomic Energy Agency, 228
International Communism, 65
International Physicians for the Prevention of Nuclear War (IPPNW), 31
In These Times, 1
Iran, 220, 229; hostage crisis in, 185; revolution in, 57, 77
Irvine, Reed, 62
Isolationism, 59, 69-70, 220
Israel, 3, 54

J

Jackson Amendment, 202
Jackson, Henry M., 115n, 159, 183, 220-21
Jackson, Jesse, 62
Jackson/Warner Resolution, 183, 231
James, A. Pendleton, 160
James, William, 77
Jeffords, James, 99
Jefferson, Thomas, 217
Jesuits, 49
Jews, 22, 24, 50
Jobs with Peace, 42n
John Birch Society, 62
John, Mary, MIRV and MARV, 43n
John Paul II, 23
Johnson Administration, 123, 142

Johnson, Lyndon B., 128
Joint Chiefs of Staff, 211n
Jones, Gail Slocum, 91
Jones, T. K., 157, 178n
Jordan, Hamilton, 158
José Martí Farabundo Front, 3

K

Kaldor, Mary, 113
Kay, Alan F., 108, 116n
Kehler, Randall, 7, 81, 85, 87, 173, 200-01
Kennan, George, 82, 92, 110, 143, 175
Kennedy Administration, 123, 127, 142, 146
Kennedy, Edward, 85, 90, 107, 124, 183
Kennedy/Hatfield Resolution, 90-91, 93, 183, 230
Kennedy School of Government (Harvard University), 142
Keys, Donald, 10
KGB, 6, 15, 45, 54, 62-63, 74, 158
Kierkegaard, Sören, 87
Kincade, William H., 103
King, Coretta Scott, 91
King, Jr., Martin Luther, 12, 37n, 62
Kingsley, Ben, 11
Kirkpatrick, Jeane, 160, 220
Kissinger, Henry A.: on deterrence, 135; and Far Right, 53; and New Right, 59, 125, 149; on SALT I, 27; on SALT II, 137; and Scowcroft Commission, 209n; on the evolution of U.S. strategic doctrine, 127; on window of vulnerability, 194
Kistiakowsky, George, 117n
Klare, Michael, 70
Know-Nothing Party, 49
Kondracke, Morton, 32, 220-21
Kopkind, Andrew, 146
Korean Air Lines, 205
Korean War, 126-27
Kremlin, 60, 136, 175, 209n
Kropotkin, Peter, 17

Kubrick, Stanley, 25
Ku Klux Klan, 45, 49-50, 71n
Kvitsinsky, Yuli, 187

L

Labor-Anarchists, 17
LaGuardia, Fiorello, 183
Laird, Melvin, 129
La Rocque, Gene, 76n
Larson, Reed, 59
The Last Slide Show, 43n
The Late Great Planet Earth, 48
Latin America, 22, 54
launch-on-warning, 96, 125, 171
launch-under-attack, 96, 125
Lawyers Alliance for Nuclear Arms Control, 94
Leach, Jim, 214n
The Lean Years, 3
Lear, Norman, 105
Lebanon, 126
Leeds, Steve, 7
Legvold, Robert, 131
Leninism, 3, 55, 94, 146
Leninist theory of imperialism, 3
Lens, Sidney, 6, 14
Levitas, Elliott, H., 199
Lewis, Kevin, 41n
liberation theology, 22
Libya, 114
Lifton, Robert Jay, 4, 25, 28
Libertarian Party, 50, 69-70
limited nuclear options, 136-37, 150n
limited nuclear war, 79, 99, 138
Lindsey, Hal, 48
Linebaugh, David, 118n
linkage, 140, 168
Living with Nuclear Weapons, 142-44
Locke, John, 218
Lodge, Henry Cabot, 92
Lofton, John, 61
Long, Huey, 50
Lowry, Joseph, 91
Ludd, Ned, 20
Lutheran Church of America, 91
Lyons, John, 209n

M

Machiavelli, Nicólo, 23
Mach, Ernst, xiii
Mack, John E., 32
Macy, Carl, 209n
Madison Avenue, 19
Manhattan Project, 90
Manoff, Robert Karl, 26-27
margin of safety, 156, 177n
Markey, Edward T., 90, 100, 102, 106, 107, 138, 201-02, 214n
Martin, James G., 201-02
Marx, Karl, 47, 213
Marxism, 2, 16, 17, 46, 51, 87, 217
Marxism-Leninism, 1, 60
Massachusetts Institute of Technology (MIT), 6, 83, 90, 209n
massive retaliation, 126, 137
MacArthur Foundation, 85
McCarthy, Eugene, 218
McCarthy, Joseph, 45, 218
McCarthyism, 15, 62
McCloskey, Frank, 202
McCloskey, Paul, 3
McCloy-Zorin Agreement, 234
McCornack, Reuven, 159
McDonald, John, 48, 54
McDonald, Larry, 62
McHenry, Donald, 74n, 92
McNamara, Robert S.: and Harold Brown, 166; and Mutual Assured Destruction (MAD), 96, 126-28, 135; on no first use, 110, 175; and nuclear strategy, 127; support of freeze, 109
McReynolds, David, 14, 88, 202
Meacham, Stewart, 6
Meese, Ed, 160, 190
Melman, Seymour, 10, 34n, 36n, 107
Mencken, Henry Louis, 123
Menninger, Karl, 91
Mexican War, 218
Michigan International Council, 43n
Middle East, 188
Midgetman, 195, 197-98

militarism, 16
military-industrial-complex, 3, 7, 93, 217
multiple independent reentry vehicle (MIRV) ICBMs: and anti-ballistic missiles, 130; and freeze, 144; and MX, 193, and non-MIRV'd ICBMs, 141; Scowcroft Commission on, 190, 192, 195; and Soviet Union, 111, 136
Mill, John Stuart, 217
military economy, 9, 36n
military superiority, 65-66
Minh, Ho Chi, 3
Minuteman (ICBM), 45, 125, 163, 171
Mobilization for Survival (MFS), 1, 8, 14, 15, 37n, 63, 85-88
Model Peace Through Strength Resolution, 68, 229-230
Modern Times, 20
Moffett, Toby, 25
Molander, Earl, 81
Molander, Roger, 81
Mondale, Walter F., 159, 202, 219-21
Montesquieu, 217
Moral Majority, 49, 59, 89, 105
Morgenthau, Hans, 177n
Mormon church, 48
Morrison, Philip, 90
Moscow, 53, 62, 64, 78, 80, 115, 134, 164, 171, 190
Mother Jones, 1
Mott, Charles Stewart, 63, 85
Movement for a New Society, 18, 38n
Moynihan, Daniel Patrick, 83, 180n, 220
Multiple Protective Shelter (MPS) Plan, 185
Musil, Robert K., 145-46
Muste, A. J., 12-14
Mutual Assured Destruction (MAD): and ABM treaty, 133; and ballistic missile defense (BMD), 167; conception of, 96, 128; and Conservative Mainstream, 160, 162, 166; and countervalue targeting, 161; and

247

Left-Liberal Establishment, 200; in Nixon Administration, 129; and Pragmatic Center, 125, 146, 162; and James Schlesinger, 136-37; and Soviet Union, 130, 135

MX Missile: and arms control, 193; basing of, 171, 186-87, 196, 209n; and build-down, 211n; compromise on, 149; and Congress, 204-05, 218; costs of, 106; Council for a Livable World on, 100; and counterforce, 100, 182; and first strike, 139-40; and freeze movement, 184, 197-98, 204; Albert Gore, Jr. on, 148; Left-Liberal Establishment on, 98; named Peacekeeper, 185; and Pragmatic Center, 134, 206; and Reagan Administration, 79, 185-86, 189, 201, 196; and SALT II, 208n; SANE on, 8; and James Schlesinger, 137; and Scowcroft Commission, 147, 187, 190, 192, 195; and Soviet Union, 170, 191-92, 195; and START, 111

N

The Nation, 1, 15, 146
National Audubon Society, 91
National Conference of Black Mayors, 92
National Council of Churches, 91
National Council of La Raza, 91
National Education Association (NEA), 30, 32, 42n, 62, 91
National Organization for Women, 91
National Review, 63
National Rifle Association, 56
National Right to Work Committee, 59
National Security Council, 82, 129, 142, 157, 178n
national security state, 4, 93, 146
National Strategy Information Center, 184
National Strategy of Peace Through Strength, 229

national technical means of verification (NTM), 235, 238
Neidle, Alan, 118n
Nelson, Gaylord, 92
Network to Educate for World Security, 42n
neutron bomb, 68, 113
New Deal, 58
New Jerusalem, 47-48
New Jewish Agenda, 24
A New Majority, 56
Newman, Paul, 91, 108
new imperialism, 10
new national security policy (UCS), 99
The New Republic, 82, 115, 193
New York rally, 86-89, 90
New Yorker, 89, 203
New York Times, 82, 93, 199, 203, 204
Nicaragua, 3, 37n, 216
Nietzsche, Friedrich, 1, 225
Nisbet, Robert, 5, 29
Nitze, Paul, 160, 187-88, 194, 201, 210n, 220
Nixon Administration, 123, 125, 129, 134, 160, 209n
Nixon, Richard M., 56, 59, 129, 149n
no first use, 110, 175
No Frames, No Boundaries, 43n
Nonproliferation Treaty (1967), 97, 113, 228
North Atlantic Treaty Organization (NATO): and American Security Council, 66, 68; conventional forces in, 113; effects of freeze on, 170; Far Right on, 54, 68; and first freeze resolution, 233; flexible response in, 135; and joint freeze resolution, 234; Libertarians on, 69; military spending in, 9; missile deployment in, 112, 172, 188; and SALT II, 83; and Soviet Union, 194; and theater nuclear negotiations prospect, 65, 113
Notre Dame University, 91
November 12 Coalition, 37n
nuclear forces (French, British, Chinese), 112

nuclear holocaust, 18
nuclear moratorium, 5
nuclear priesthood, 24-25, 27, 40-41n
Nuclear Times, 1
Nuclear War and the Second Coming of Christ, 54
Nuclear War: What's In It For You?, 82
Nuclear Weapons Freeze Campaign, 100
Nuclear Weapons Freeze Campaign Fact Sheet Number 1, 26, 101–03
nuclearism, 4, 5, 25-26, 108, 217
Nunn, Sam, 190, 200
Nye, Jr., Joseph S., 142, 145

O

O'Neill, Thomas P. (Tip), 204
Oswald, Lee Harvey, 62
overkill, 94, 111, 145

P

pacifism, 9, 13-14, 22
Packard Manse Media Project, 43n
Pakistan, 113, 229
Palestine, 48
Palestine Liberation Organization (PLO), 3, 24
Palme, Olof, 3
Palmerston, Lord, 106
Panama Canal, 55
Panetta, Leon E., 104, 198-99
parity: and assured destruction, 110; Harold Brown on, 203; central strategic, 136, 169; Far Right on, 60; and Randall Forsberg on, 110; and freeze movement, 169-70, 228; Left-Liberal Establishment, 99; and margin of safety, 177n; Reagan Administration on, 156; and SALT, 128; Soviet Union, 128, 135, 138, 169-70
pastoral letter, 22-23, 39n, 85
Pauling, Linus, 14, 91
Paul Revere Club, 71n
Pax Britannica, 69

Pax Christi, 20-23, 85
Peace Pac, 100, 118n
Peace Through Strength Resolution (ASC), 229-30
Pease, Donald, 98
Peck, Sidney, 15
Pentagon, 3, 70, 91, 127, 155, 157, 188
Pentagon capitalism, 10, 93
Pentagon Capitalism: The Political Economy of War, 10
People for the American Way, 105
Percy, Charles, 3
Perle, Richard: on arms control, 115n, 173-74; on arms race, 176; member of Democratic Party, 220; in Reagan Administration, 150, 172-74; on SALT II, 165; and *Washington Post,* 181n
Pershing II: deployment of, 172; first strike capabilities of, 98, 100; Randall Forsberg on, 112; and joint freeze resolution, 199; opposition to deployment, 79; and Scowcroft Commission, 193; and Soviet Union, 209n
Peter D. Hart Research Associates, Inc., 15
Peterson, Russell, 91
Philadelphia yearly meeting, 77
Phillips, Howard, 56
Physicians for Social Responsibility, 28, 31-32, 42n, 43n, 94, 115
Pickett, Eugene, 91
Piel, Gerard, 117n
Pinochet, Augusto, 3
Pipes, Richard, 157, 178n
Podesta, Anthony, 105
Poland, 22, 100, 113, 220
Polaris submarines, 143
polling data, 115n
population-hostage relationship, 132
premillenarianism, 28, 48, 89
Presidential Commission on Strategic Forces (see Scowcroft Commission)
Presidential Directive 59 (PD-59), 126, 137, 140, 144, 161, 193

SANE: education fund, 145; as freeze support group, 81; and Mobilization for Survival, 63; on MX, 204; and Professional Left, 1, 14-15; and Reagan Administration, 81; mass mail solicitation of, 8-12, 107
Sarandon, Susan, 14
Save America Gun Club, 71n
Scheer, Robert, 178n
Schell, Jonathan, 4, 5, 25, 28-9, 89-90, 146
Schlafly, Phyllis, 56, 59
Schlesinger, James, 82, 135-37, 209n
Schmidt, Helmut, 79
Schneider, Claudine, 101
Schumacher, E. F., 38n
Schweiker, Richard, 160
Schweitzer, Robert 157, 178n
Scientific American, 41n, 110, 113
Scott, Lawrence, 9
Scott, Robert, 175
Scoville, Herbert, 117n, 119n
Scowcroft, Brent, 125, 187
Scowcroft Commission, 144, 147, 184, 187, 190, 192, 195-97, 205, 206
second strike, 139-40, 195
Security and Peace in the Nuclear Age, 67
Seeger, Pete, 14
Seidita, Nick, 84, 86, 90
selective freeze, 82
Senate Armed Services Committee, 186
Senate Foreign Relations Committee, 129, 189, 231
Senate Judiciary Committee, 62
Sepulveda Unitarian-Universalist Society, 84
Shanker, Albert, 31
shared liability, 133
Sheen, Martin, 11-12, 14
Shockley, William, 30
Shultz, George, 125
Sieberling, John, 99
Sierra Club, 17
Sigal, Leon, 82
Siljander, Mark D., 214n

Sisters of the Blessed Sacrament, 91
single integrated operating plan (SIOP), 136
Sixty (60) Minutes, 40n
Smeal, Eleanor, 91
Smith, Gerard, 110, 175
Smith, Levering, 209n
Smith, Martin Cruz, 74n
Smith, William French, 160
Social Darwinism, 47, 51
Social Democrats USA, 55, 184
Social Security, 106
Society, 76n
Sojourners, 24
Soldiers in Revolt, 10
Solidarity, 22
Southern Christian Leadership Conference, 91
Soviet General Staff, 119n
Soviet Military Power, 186
Soviet strategic culture, 126, 132, 139, 193
Soviet Union: antisatellite (ASAT) capability of 144; and arms control, 80, 134, 154, 173-74, 217, 225; and arms race, 228-29; attitude toward assured destruction, 128; and build-down, 62; in *Call to Halt the Nuclear Arms Race,* 227-28; nuclear capabilities of, 127; and Carter Administration, 163; civil defense program of, 168; Conservative Mainstream on, 163-64, 169-70; counterforce capabilities of, 78, 98, 112, 130, 135, 138, 165; and countervailing strategy, 137-38; and Dense Pack, 185; desire for freeze, 174-75; and deterrence, 130-34; and Europe, 79; and Far Left, 60; and Far Right, 53, 58, 60-62, 65-66, 157; in first freeze resolution, 232-34; and first-strike on, 99-101, 140, 163, 195; Randall Forsberg on, 110-11; freeze convention calls upon, 200-01; in freeze resolution, 205; and *High Frontier,* 167; and INF negotiations, 190-96; Jackson/

251

Warner Resolution on, 231-32; in joint resolution, 234-35; and Left-Liberal Establishment, 6, 81-82, 96, 98, 110, 198; military build-up of, 164; and Mutual Assured Destruction (MAD), 128-29; and MX, 170-71; and NATO, 68; New Right on, 63-64; nuclear superiority of, 184; in Peace through Strength Resolution, 229; Richard Perle on, 173-74; and Pragmatic Center, 130-34; and Professional Left, 93; and Reagan Administration, 78-80, 140, 156, 158, 191, 199; relations with U.S., 169, 198-99; Eugene Rostow on, 172; and SALT II, 83, 166, 191, 232; James Schlesinger on, 135-39; Scowcroft Commission on, 194-95; and *Soviet Military Power,* 189; and Strategic Arms Reductions Talks, 134, 235; strategic culture of, 139, 193; strategic forces of, 232; strategic parity with, 203; third strike on, 163; Third World intervention of, 113, 146; treaty violations of, 61-62, 65-66, 157, 176; Richard Viguerie on, 65-66; "walk in the woods," 187; war fighting view of, 96; and World Peace Council, 159

space defense, 68

Spanish syndicalists, 17

The Spike, 73n

Spock, Benjamin, 1, 14, 86

Sputnik, 126

SS-4, 112

S-5, 112

SS-17, 139

SS-18, 100, 133, 139

SS-19, 139

SS-20, 112, 194

Stability: arms race, 143; crises, 143, 145; deterrence, 143

Stahlman, Rhonda, 59

Standing Consultative Committee, 191

Stark, Fortney, 25

statism, 19

Star Wars speech, 189

Stevens, Wallace, 123

Stewart Mott Enterprises, 85

Stockman, David, 160

St. Louis Nuclear Freeze Clearinghouse, 85, 98, 100, 102, 107, 160, 200, 218

Stockholm International Peace Research Institute (SIPRI) 5, 35n

Stop ERA, 59

Strategic Arms Limitation Talks (SALT) I, 103, 129, 134, 136, 137, 202, 227

SALT II: arms control, 101; and *Call to Halt the Nuclear Arms Race,* 227; defeat of, 7; Fact Sheet Number 1 on, 103; Far Right attitude toward, 65; First Freeze resolution and, 232-34; Leslie Gelb on, 165-66, 171; and Johnson, Lyndon, 128; Left-Liberal Establishment on, 81-83; mutual counterforce postures and, 137; Pragmatic Center and, 165, ratification of, 81-83; Reagan Administration on, 79, 185; revival of, 90; James Schlesinger and, 137; Soviet Union and, 134, 191, 208n, Caspar Weinberger on, 114; and window of vulnerability, 191n, 194

SALT III, 81

Strategic Arms Reduction Talks (START): Kenneth Adelman on, 186; and build-down, 148, 190, 206; and Congress, 232, 235; Fact Sheet Number 1 on, 102; first freeze debate and, 194; and MX, 191, 195; and original freeze proposal, 111; Reagan Administration and, 148, 158, 164, 172-73, 190; Edward Rowny on, 189; Scowcroft Commission on, 148, 206; second freeze debate and, 198-99; Soviet Union and, 134, 195

strategic forces budget, 109-11

Streep, Meryl, 91

Stubbs, Gilbert S., 66
Student-Teacher Organization to Prevent Nuclear War (STOP Nuclear War), 42n
Subcommittee on Security and Terrorism, 62
submarine-launched ballistic missile (SLBM), 111, 130
sufficiency, 129
supply-side economics, 109
Sutton, Antony C., 71n
SWAPO, 3
Synagogue Council of America, 40n, 91
syndicalism, 17

T

Taylor, Priscilla E., 42n
Teller, Edward, 68
Thayer, Paul, 181n
Third World, 1, 2, 4, 60, 69, 87-88, 146
Third World and Progressive People's Coalition, 87
Third-World-Within, 87
third strike, 164
Thompson, E. P., 3, 4, 107
Thought, 39n
Thurber, James, 45
Tower, John, 186
Townes, Charles H., 117n
triad, 78, 126, 128, 193
Trident II, 100, 111, 134, 148
Trident submarine, 98, 100
Trilateral Commission, 3, 4, 107
Trimtab Factor, 108
trimtab rudder, 108
Turgeon, Lynn, 36n
Twain, Mark, 145

U

unilateral disarmament, 22, 97, 100, 108
Union of American Hebrew Congregations, 91

Union of Concerned Scientists (UCS), 31, 94, 99-100, 102, 118
Unitarian Church, 85
Unitarian-Universalist Association, 91
United Nations, 15, 53, 175
United Nations Second Special Session on Disarmament, 86, 175
United Presbyterian Church USA, 91
United States Committee Against Nuclear War (USCANW), 100, 102, 104, 106, 139
United States Congress: build-down, 215; and Democratic party, 220; on Dense Pack, 186; election of, 194; INF and, 187; freeze debate of 98, 101, 220; freeze resolution and, 198-200, 214; first freeze resolution and, 227-28; Jackson/Warner Resolution and, 231; joint resolution and, 235; Kennedy/Hatfield Resolution and, 183, 230-31; MX and, 171, 219; Pragmatic Center and, 146; Reagan Administration and, 148, 155, 173, 177, 183, 186-87, 189, 196, 201, 203-06; Scowcroft Commission and, 148, 195-98; second freeze debate in, 206; START and, 190; liberal congressmen, 90; lobbying, 105
United States Peace Council, 1, 14-15
United States Senate: and Adelman confirmation, 189; and build-down, 190; and first freeze resolution, 148, 233; freeze lobby in, 218; and Jackson/Warner Resolution, 183, 231; Joint Resolution before, 198, Kennedy/Hatfield Resolution and, 90, 183, 230; Caspar Weinberger and, 210
United States strategic targeting doctrine, 126
University of Wisconsin, 15

V

Van Cleave, William R., 186, 208n
Vatican, 21-22

victory denial posture, 161–62
victory seeking posture, 162
Vietnam, 11–12, 47, 55–56, 86, 104, 127, 212n
Viguerie, Richard A., 51–52, 55–57, 59, 65, 125
The Village Voice, 1, 70, 89

W

Wald, George, 14, 91
"walk in the woods," 187
Wall Street, 19
War Day, 214
War of 1812, 222
war fighting strategy, 132, 166, 170
War Without Winners, 43n
Warner, John, 183
Warnke, Paul, 74n, 92, 100, 119n
War Resister's League (WRL), 1, 7, 8, 11–14, 63, 80, 81, 113, 202
Washington Legal Foundation, 65
Washington Post, 82, 93, 181n, 202, 203–04
Washington Times, 61
Waskow, Arthur, 24, 40n
Watson, Thomas, 92
Watt, James, 157, 160
Weinberger, Caspar, 157, 184, 189, 201, 209–20n
Weisner, Jerome, 91, 117
Weiss, Ted 14
welfare, 51–52, 106
Wertheimer, Fred, 25
West Germany, 58, 79, 210n
West Watch, 75n
Weyrich, Paul, 56, 59
White House, 136, 140, 160, 185, 187–88, 203, 210, 218
Wicker, Tom, 199
Wilderness Society, 91

Willens, Harold, 86, 107–09, 117n
window of credibility, 212n
window of vulnerability, 78, 185, 192–93, 211n
Winpisinger, William, 119n
Wisconsin straw poll (June 1983), 220
Women's International League for Peace and Freedom (WILPF), 1, 8, 81, 85
Women's Strike for Peace, 1
Women's Survival Corps, 71
Wonder, Stevie, 91
Woodward, Joanne, 108
Woolsey, R. James, 209n
World Council of Churches (WCC), 21, 23–24, 62
World Council for Curriculum and Instruction, 42n
World Peace Council (WPC), 6, 14–15, 62–63, 159
Wurtzerger, Walter, 91

Y

Yarmolinsky, Adam, 91
Yergin, Daniel, 34n
YMCA, 92
Young, Andrew, 91
Young, Robert, 30
Youth Against War and Fascism, 1

Z

Zablocki, Clement, 98, 196–98, 234
Zahm-Hurwitz Productions, 43n
Zamora, Ruben, 88
zero option, 210n
Zimmerman, Bill, 86
Zill, Anne, 63
Zionism, 54

254